Jewish Quarter of Safed

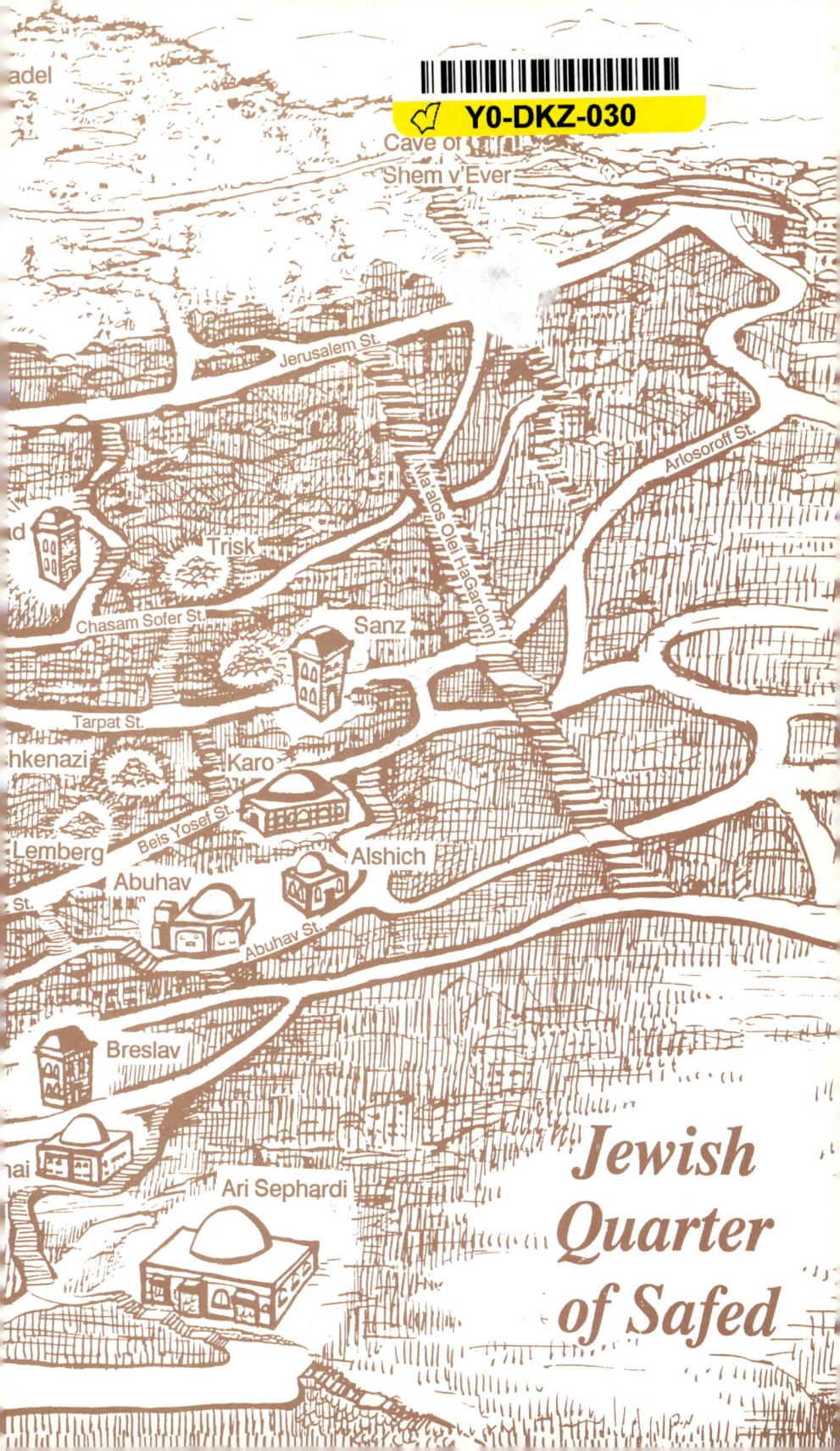

SAFED
The Mystical City

Dovid Rossoff

Sha'ar Books

Jerusalem

First Published 1991

ISBN 0-87306-566-2

Copyright © 1991 by Dovid Rossoff

All rights reversed

No part of this publication, including photographs and graphics,
may be translated, reproduced, stored in a retrieval system or transmitted,
in any form by any means, electronic, mechanical, photocopying,
recording or otherwise, without the prior permission
in writing from the copyright holder.

> Violation of this prohibition constitute a nullification
> of the sale, i.e. stealing!

Edited by Fruma Spielberg

Graphics by Moshe Palmer

Photo credits: The author took all the photos except the old
photographs. Daniel Eidensohn: pp. 154, 210, 233

Published by: *Sha'ar Books*
3109 Bedford Ave.   P.O.Box 5437
Brooklyn, N.Y.11210   Jerusaelm

Distributed by:
Philipp Feldheim Inc.
200 Airport Executive Park
Spring Valley, N.Y. 10977

Printed in Israel

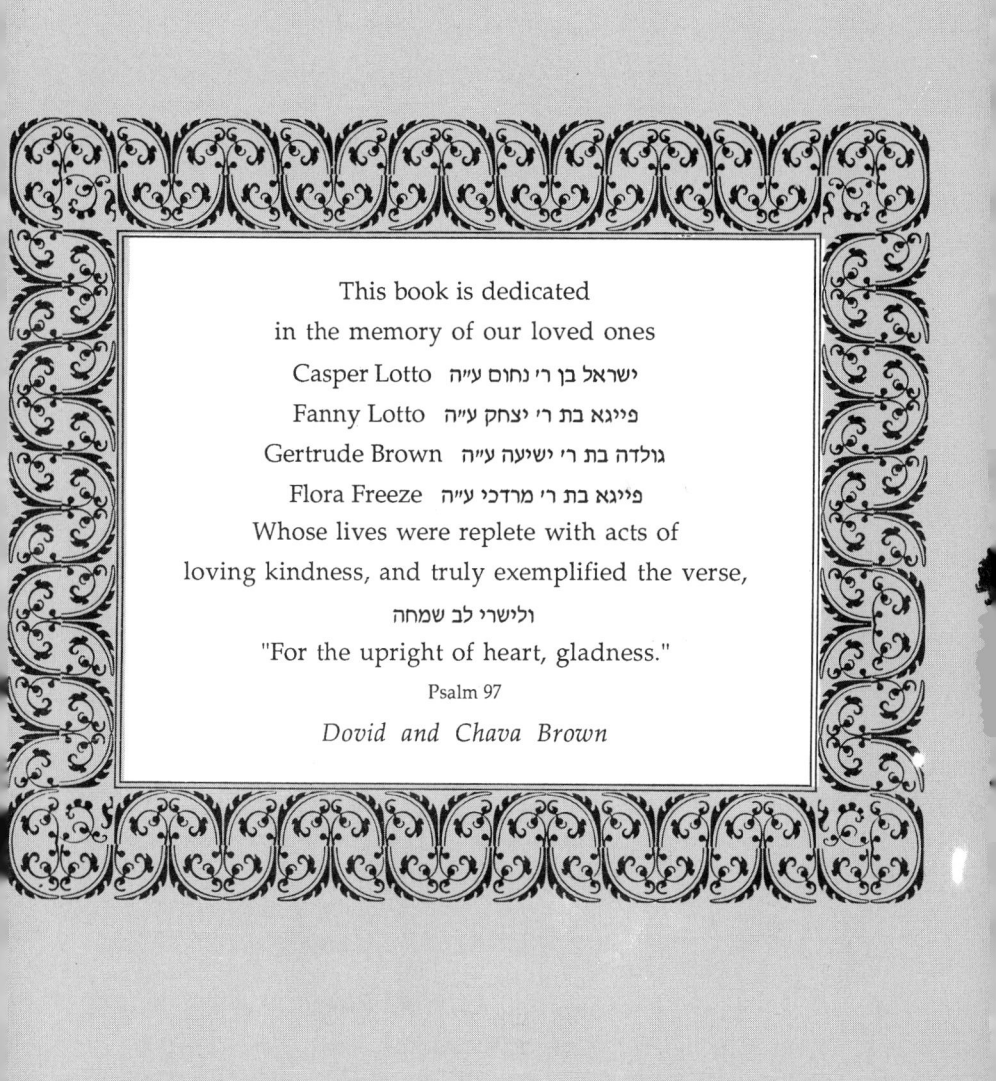

This book is dedicated
in the memory of our loved ones
Casper Lotto   ישראל בן ר' נחום ע"ה
Fanny Lotto   פייגא בת ר' יצחק ע"ה
Gertrude Brown   גולדה בת ר' ישיעה ע"ה
Flora Freeze   פייגא בת ר' מרדכי ע"ה
Whose lives were replete with acts of
loving kindness, and truly exemplified the verse,
ולישרי לב שמחה
"For the upright of heart, gladness."
Psalm 97

Dovid and Chava Brown

CONTENTS

Timeline   **11**

1 ARRIVING IN SAFED   **15**
The Magic of Safed/ Taking Stock/ Filling in the Pieces/ Getting Acquainted

2 SAFED VERSES JERUSALEM   **19**
The Race to Damascus/ One Crown for Two Cities/ Charged with Usurping the Crown/ Advice from the Chasam Sofer/ A Controversy for "The Sake of Heaven"/ R' Yaakov Berav/ Background for Reintroducing Ordination/ *Semicha* is Revived in Safed/ A Question of Timing

3 THE MOUNTAINTOP CITY   **37**
Early History Shrouded in Mystery/ Revival of Torah in Safed/ Ottoman Influence/ Safed Flourishes

4 THE GOLDEN ERA   **49**
A Heavenly Voice/ A Call for Excellence/ Maggid Speaks to R' Yosef/ Unifying the Codes/ In *Eretz Yisrael*/ R' Moshe Alshich/ Other Disciples/ *Shulchan Aruch*/ The Fortress of Safed/ The Power of the Rabbinic Court/ Protecting Repentant Marranos/ A Match for R' Yosef's Son/ Happy Parents

5 THE MYSTICS OF SAFED   **69**
The Light of R' Moshe Cordovero/ Pillars of Fire/ The Ari Comes to Safed/ Ramak's System of

Kabbalah/ The Perfection of Man/ Meditation/ The Author of *Reshis Chachmah*/ *Gerushin:* Self-imposed Exile/ R' Shlomo Alkabetz/ The World of Kabbalah

6 ARIZAL AND HIS DISCIPLES   83

R' Chayim Vital finds a Master/ The News Spreads/ Radbaz Reprimands R' Luria/ Ramak Comes in a Dream/ The Arizal Turns Away Great *Tzaddikim*/ But There are Greater Men than Me/ The Well of Miriam/ Why he Never Wrote/ The Arizal Honors a Youngester/ The Arizal's Method of Teaching/ The Goal/ Shabbos in Jerusalem!/ Power to Bring Everyone Back in Repentance/ Death of the Lion/ Piecing the Broken Vessel Together/ Burning Embers/ The Arizal's House and Synagogue/ The Arizal *Mikve*/ Light of *Mashiach*

7 INFLUX OF CHASSIDIM   115

A Change in the Ruling Power/ Decline of Safed/ A New Generation of Kabbalists/ Refugees from the *Churbah*/ First Half of Eighteenth Century/ First *Aliyah* of Chassidim/ First Earthquake: 1759/ 1764: Second *Aliyah* of Chassidim/ The Great Influx of 1777/ A Ship of Ships/ Realities of Safed/ First Year/ The True Measure of Things

8 INFLUX OF PERUSHIM   137

The Vilna Gaon's Vision/ *Aliyah:* 1808-1809/ Why Safed?/ Settling into Safed/ The Oldest of Problems/ Plague of 1814/ Chayim Parchi Protects his People/ Reign of Terror/ A Harsh Reminder/ A Breathing Spell/ First Jewish Farm Settlement/ In Search of the Lost Tribes/ Druze Massacre of Safed/ *Pe'as HaShulchan*/ The Perushim Withdraw from Safed/ The Final Blow

9 THE TERRIBLE EARTHQUAKE   157
A Long Winter's Night/ The Reality of Daybreak/ A Miracle in the Night/ R' Avraham Dov of Abritish/ R' Shemuel Heller his Disciple/ First Anniversary of Earthquake/ Massacre of 1838/ To Abandon Safed or Not?/ Sir Montefiore's Historic Visit/ Death of a *Tzaddik*

10 REBIRTH OF SAFED   173
Reconstruction of Synagogues/ Safed Comes Back to Life/ Rebuilding Ashkenazi Ari Synagogue/ The Women Gallery/ Jewish Farm Settlements/ R' Heller's *Esrog* Plantation/ The Sephardi Influence/ *Midrash Shemuel*/ R' Heller's Successor/ Revival of *Chassidus*/ Cave of *Shem v'Ever*/ Doorway to the Future

11 TWENTIETH CENTURY SAFED   191
Ridbaz/ *Chacham* Elfandari/ Deeds of a *Tzaddik*/ *Sabba Kedisha*/ First World War/ *Babba Sali* Vanquishes Demons/ Lean Years/ A Change in State/ A Dormant Seed Takes Root/ Growing... Through Loving-Kindness/ Growing... Through Torah/ Vision of the Future

12 ABODE OF THE LIVING: 213
A GUIDE TO THE TOMBS OF THE *TZADDIKIM*
Laws and Customs/ In the Shadow of the *Tzaddik:* A Guide to the Grave Sites/ Prayers/ Rabbi Pinchas ben Yair

13 FAREWELL, OH SAFED   225
Once Upon a Time/ Until Next Time

14 MERON 229

Rabbi Shimon bar Yochai/ Rashbi and His Companions/ The Book of Splendor/ Between Safed and Meron/ The Rashbi's Departure/ The Cave of Rashbi/ The Courtyards of Meron/ Rashbi's Yeshiva/ Approaching Meron/ Studying the Zohar at Meron/ Miracles at Meron/ *Lag b'Omer:* In *Halacha*/ *Hilulah d'Rashbi*/ The *Tzaddik's Yartzeit*/ A Day of Joy/ Initiation into Boyhood/ Rabbi Yochanan HaSandler/ A Day of Soul Searching/ Beware of the Rashbi's Honor/ Hillel and Shammai/ The Light which Never Wanes

Acknowledgements	**258**
Glossary	**259**
Bibliography	**262**
Index	**265**

Timeline

16th Century
 1500 R' Sarogossi, Rav of Safed
 1525 Turkish conquest of *Eretz Yisrael*, era of peace
 1538 Reintroduction of *semicha*
 1555 R' Yosef Karo completes *Shulchan Aruch*
 1568 *Beis Din* protects repentant Marranos
 1570 Arizal moves to Safed
       R' Moshe Cordovero dies
 1572 Arizal dies
 1575 R' Yosef Karo dies

17th Century
 1628 Shelah HaKodesh sojourns in Safed
 1695 R'Avraham Galante, Rav of Safed

18th Century
 1720 Fugitives of *Churbah* form Ashkenazi group
 1740 First group of Chassidim
       R' Eliezer Rokeach
 1759 First Earthquake
 1777 Influx of Chassidim, led by R' Menachem Mendel of Vitebst

19th Century
 1808-1809 Influx of Perushim, led by R' Yisrael of Shaklov
 1814 Plague

SAFED: THE MYSTICAL CITY

1818 Chayim Parchi assassinated
1830 Egyptain Pasha conquers *Eretz Yisrael*
1834 Druze massacre of Safed
1837 Second Earthquake
1838 Druze massacre of Safed
1839 Sir Moses Montefiore visits Safed
1840 R' Avraham Dov of Avritish dies
  Eretz Yisrael returns to Turkish rule
1830-1872 R' Shemuel Heller, Rav of Safed
1870s Revival of Chassidic community

20th Century
1905 Ridbaz opens yeshiva
1910-1925 *Chacham* Elfandari
1916 Typhus epidemic
1948-1988 R' Simcha Kaplan, Rav of Safed

SAFED
The Mystical City

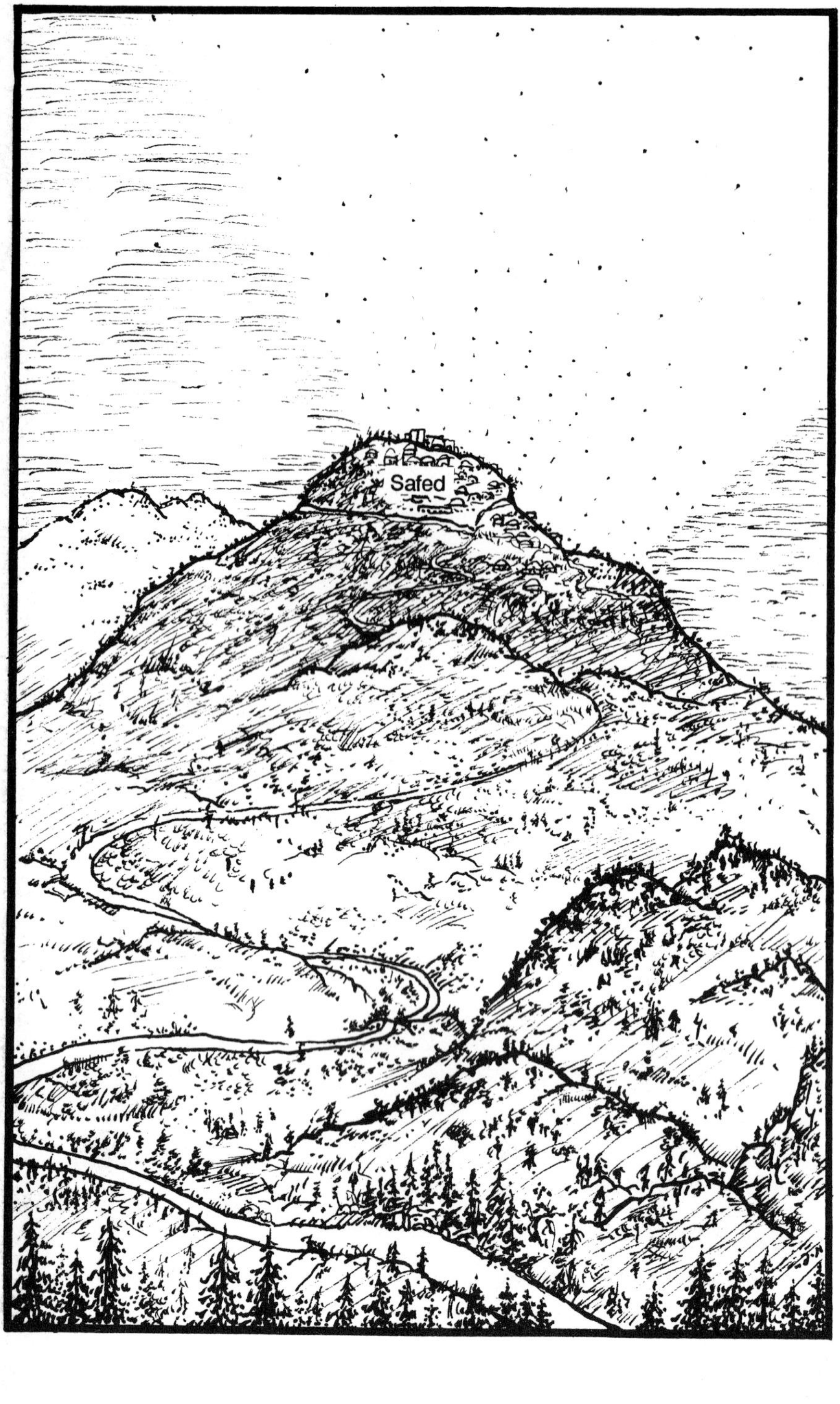
Safed

1
Arriving in Safed

Walking along the curving mountain road into Safed, you feel exhilarated, uplifted by the bracing, clear air. Looking around you are astonished by the apparent newness of this ancient city. Although you've never been here before, it feels somehow familiar.

The Magic of Safed

Safed's magic lies in her mystery. Something in her oldness and eccentricity dazzles your imagination and sparks your curiosity, yet just what it may be is hard to pinpoint. On the one hand, the old Jewish Quarter beckons you to explore its cobblestone lanes and gaze into its ancient synagogues. On the other, the Galilee with its long mountain ranges and lush valleys gives you a sense of spiritual freedom which you've rarely experienced.

Taking Stock

Slowly, you start to take stock. You've heard of the Arizal *mikve* down by the cemetery. How long has it been there? Did the Arizal really use it? And what made the Arizal so great that three shuls in the same small city are named after him?

People have told you of an earthquake which destroyed the original city. When did that happen? During the lifetime of the Arizal? Earlier? Later? This is said to be a mystical city; did any miracles occur during the tragedy? Who rebuilt the synagogues which stand today?

The more you reflect on the dynamic history of Safed, the more you realize that, like a jigsaw puzzle, many pieces must be fitted in to form a clear picture.

Filling in the Pieces

The purpose of this book is to help you fill in those missing pieces and draw a vivid picture of the history of Safed. We'll be concentrating on her spiritual history – the *tzaddikim* who lived and walked on the very lanes you are walking today. The Torah studies of these *tzaddikim*, their selflessness, and their devotion to propagating Torah for generations to come, set off ethereal sparks which we still feel today. Therefore, we will be looking at Safed's history as a living chronicle, weaving together varying facets of their lives and deeds.

Getting Acquainted: How to Make the Most of This Book

Whether or not you are planning a visit to Safed, you will want to make a spiritual and intellectual connection with it. Safed, more than most other places, has a panoramic history which is guaranteed to stir you to the depths of your soul.

To appreciate the richness of history of this noble city, first study the maps carefully. Aim at knowing Safed as well as you know your home town. Our map of the ancient cemetery is the first of its kind, and the one of the Jewish Quarter is designed to help you ramble freely through its maze of narrow lanes as well as to find the old shuls and synagogues with ease.

Next, get an overview of Safed's history by studying the contents and timeline. This orientation is well worth the extra time. As you begin your journey, this book will be a living guide that will deepen and increase your appreciation of Safed.

We often feel pressured to hurry up and know everything while 'standing on one foot.' However, this is not usually the best means of fully appreciating something as unique as the annals of Safed. This book is not an ordinary guidebook, with facts and figures thrown at you from all sides. Instead, we will proceed with a step by step, in-depth chronicle of all the essential phases of the magical history of Safed. Thus, step by step, we can begin to unravel her mystery, and be privileged to experience some of her holy sparks.

* * *

One of the great medieval topographers of Israel, R' Ishtori Haparchi, made a vivid allegory which is well worth bearing in mind while wandering around Safed. "Searching for the location of different historical sites in *Eretz Yisrael*," he wrote, "was more precious to me than an astronomer's scanning the sky to map the stars.... Each of the stellar bodies is constantly circling around us, and most people know nothing about them. And even among astronomers, only a few are capable of discerning the motion of one constellation from the other.

"How aptly this describes the task of locating places in Israel! People are in movement, much like the stellar bodies, without knowing the unique histories of these very special places."

My conclusion is his. "I humbly come forward to present to my fellow Jews what I have found in my searches. My findings do not stem from a greater depth of knowledge than others; rather, I have simply spent more time investigating this subject than they have and feel duty bound to share the fruits of my research with the public."

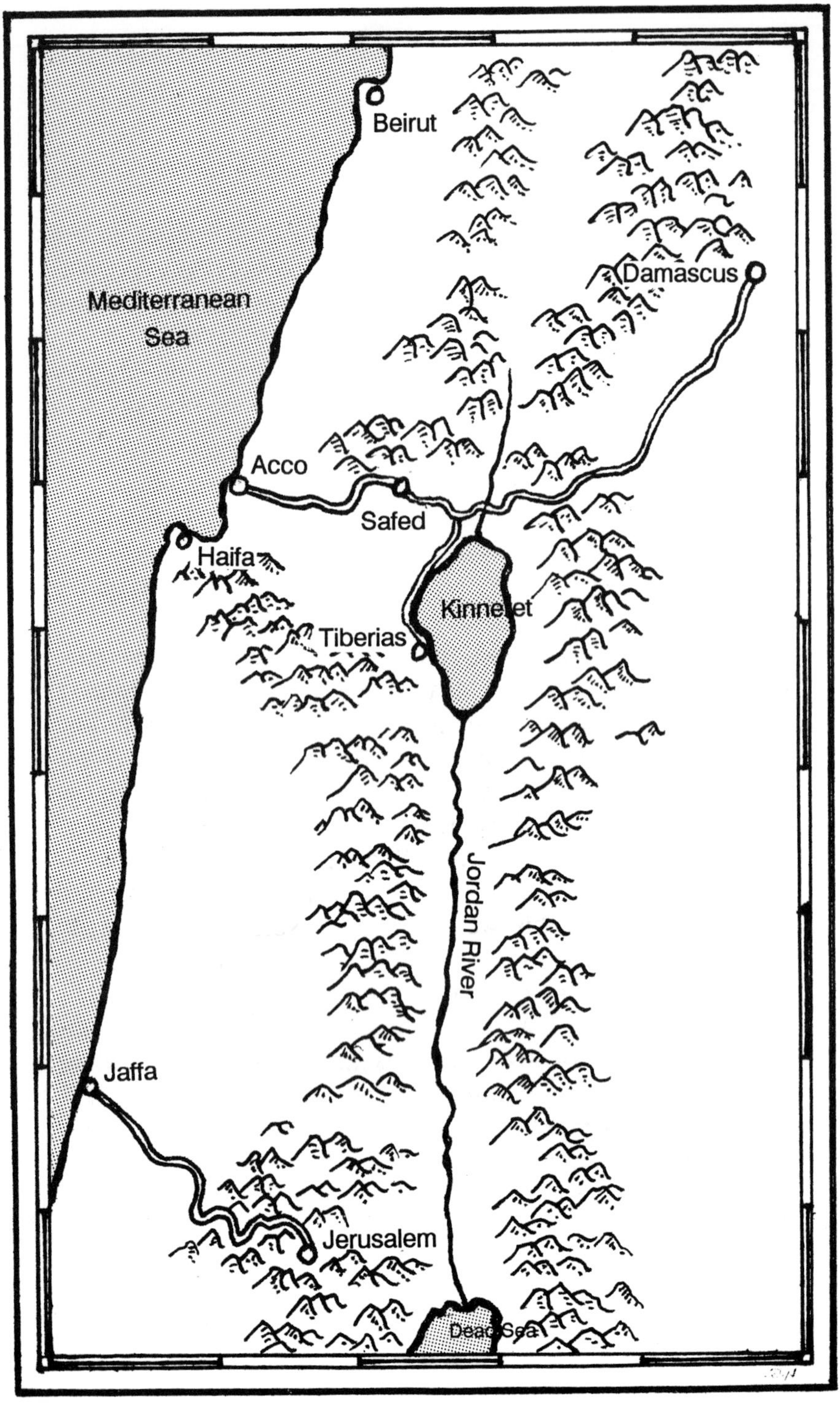
Beirut
Damascus
Mediterranean Sea
Acco
Safed
Haifa
Kinneret
Tiberias
Jordan River
Jaffa
Jerusalem
Dead Sea

2
Safed Verses Jerusalem

The allure of Safed can be most sharply felt in comparison with Jerusalem. Safed's stature, great in and of itself, takes on a new and deeper meaning in association with the City of Cities. The more we begin to explore the fascination of Safed herself, the more we will discover her sublime, inextricably entwined relationship with Jerusalem.

At first glance, however, we find a puzzling kind of tug-of-war between the two cities that lasted hundreds of years. To help us understand this, we'll begin our exploration by traveling back in time and peering over the shoulder of a famous pilgrim on his historic trip to Israel at the beginning of the 17th century.

In the autumn of 1622, word reached Israel that one of the most eminent Torah authorities of the generation, Rabbi Yeshaya Horowitz of Prague, the author of *Shnei Luchos HaBris,* was approaching by caravan from Syria. This news aroused great excitement in all the Jewish communities, particularly Safed and Jerusalem.

Were such a renowned sage to settle in their community, each reasoned, not only would it add great prestige to their city, but all the inhabitants would be inspired to become even more meticulous in their observance of the commandments. Shuls would vibrate with fervent prayer, and the oil lanterns would burn late into the night as men studied Torah. If only he would settle among them, he would be the uniting force between the Sephardim and the Ashkenazim, and, if need be, he could act as mediator between the Jewish community and the ruling Turkish authorities.

The Race to Damascus

Secret delegations were sent to Damascus by the communities of Safed and Jerusalem, each charged with the mission of inviting R' Horowitz to become the Chief Rabbi of their city. First to arrive was the delegation from Safed.

"A two-man delegation from Safed came to me while I was in Damascus," wrote R' Horowitz. "They greeted me and implored me to settle among them. In the name of the city counsellors, they offered me the position of Chief Rabbi.

" 'Am I not on my way to Safed?' I answered them evasively, not wanting to show them my secret desire to settle in Jerusalem. 'Upon my arrival we will discuss the matter fully.' "[1]

The following day R' Horowitz set out from Damascus. On the way, he was met by the emissary from Jerusalem, a respected rabbi of European background. This rabbi presented R' Horowitz with an official letter signed by all the rabbis of Jerusalem earnestly requesting him to accept the post of Chief Rabbi of the Holy City. They also granted him special privileges. The letter ended with a petition that their respected emissary be granted permission to accompany him on the rest of his journey to Israel. R' Horowitz agreed.

For generations the Jews of Safed and Jerusalem had vied for newcomers to the Land. During the previous hundred years, most immigrants had opted for Safed. The reason was clear. Many of the greatest scholars and *tzaddikim* of all times had enlightened this Galilean city with their Torah and righteous ways. This, in turn, galvanized other Jews to follow in their footsteps. Even now, in 1622, when these great *tzaddikim* of olden times were long since gone from this world, their yeshivos were alive with the Torah being learned by earnest students, and their tombs had became focal points for wellsprings of prayer which soared to the heavens.

The Jews of the Holy City felt slighted. Jealousy and tension grew and began to estrange the two communities. Therefore, the rabbis of Jerusalem had particularly requested that their emissary be allowed to accompany their prospective Chief Rabbi. Since R' Horowitz would stop first in Safed on his way to Jerusalem, they were suspicious that the Jews of Safed might interfere and attempt to persuade him to settle there.

As the caravan grew closer to Safed, R' Horowitz considered the respective merits of the two offers. The burning embers of the great Torah luminaries who had earlier flourished in Safed still blazed after half a century. Rabbi Yosef Karo, author of the *Shulchan Aruch*, and two great Kabbalists, R' Moshe Cordovero and R' Yitzchak Luria, were three of the greatest sages ever to live in the same place at one time – in Safed. Their saintliness and Torah learning had imbued the very stones of Safed with an indelible glow.

However, Jerusalem was the site where the Holy Temple had stood. "Even in its destruction," wrote R' Horowitz, "Jerusalem is the joy of all the Land. Although Safed's total population was the greater of the two, the number of Ashkenazi citizens of Jerusalem was double that of Safed. Another important consideration was that a greater number of Torah scholars lived in the Holy City. From a purely material standpoint, too, Jerusalem seemed the best choice. Her inhabitants were well protected from invaders by an encircling wall, built seventy-five years earlier by the Turks, while Safed was open and more vulnerable to attack. Finally, there was the not negligible fact that basic commodities were more readily accessible in Jerusalem than in Safed.[2]

As R' Horowitz weighed the pros and cons of each city, his choice became clear. Jerusalem was still the towering city of great antiquity, where kings and prophets had lived, and where the Sanhedrin had convened in the Chamber of Hewn Stone on the Temple Mount.

"I accept your offer," he declared to the emissary from Jerusalem. "May the Almighty give me life and good health so that I may guide the Jerusalem community according to Torah Law. As a loyal shepherd, may I be granted the strength not to stand as a silent witness to the transgressions which undoubtedly caused so much destruction in the past. My goal will be to establish and intensify the inherent truth of Torah in each and every aspect of life in the city."

One Crown for Two Cities

To better understand the 'pros and cons' which faced R' Horowitz, let us investigate some of the background material, and measure for ourselves on the scales of truth.

There is only one city in the world which is known as the Holy City: Jerusalem. There is only one Temple, and that is in Jerusalem. There is only one gateway to heaven (Gen. 28:17); that, too, is in Jerusalem. It is unimaginable that any other city would challenge that claim and attempt to seize the crown which so clearly befits the Holy City.

Safed, however, did dare to claim the crown, and for a jubilee era — from around 1530 to 1580 — she dominated all Torah dissemination. Like a brazen shepherd boy snatching the crown from the head of a royal prince, Safed flaunted her 'feigned' glory before all, even Jerusalem.

But is the prestige and enchantment of Safed real or is it fictitious?

Safed's claim to royalty is revealed in the writings of one of our great mystics, R' Avraham Azulai, the author of *Chesed l'Avraham*, who lived in Israel at the turn of the seventeenth century. He recorded a hidden tradition concerning Safed.[3]

"Safed," he writes, "has no equal in any other city in Israel. This city was predestined from time immemorial as the most propitious spot to plumb the depths of Torah wisdom, for there is no place in *Eretz Yisrael* where the air is purer and more refined than in Safed."

The *Zohar* states that at the time of the resurrection, the dead will arise and assemble in Safed. There the *Mashiach* will reveal himself to the world, and together they will march to Jerusalem.[4]

Thus, both mountaintop cities laid claim, as it were, to the crown of being the most populated Jewish city in Israel. Each sought new immigrants, especially such esteemed rabbis as R' Yeshaya Horowitz. Each jealously guarded its treasure chests of holy books – so hard to acquire in those days – and Torah scrolls. And each sought to build new shuls and houses for its growing population.

Since medieval times, the crown was claimed, relinquished, and reclaimed by the two cities. In the 12th century, for instance, Safed had an enormous population.[5] Throughout the sixteenth century, the crown rested on Safed. That was the golden era of Torah, when both the revealed and mystical aspects of Torah shone forth. Later, the crown was returned to Jerusalem, and then moved back to Safed at the beginning of the 19th century, afterwards shifting once again to the Holy City.

Charged with Usurping the Crown

Not everyone agreed with R' Azulai's declaration of Safed's claim to royalty. The most outspoken opponent was R' Moshe Sofer, known as the Chasam Sofer.

"Without question," wrote the Chasam Sofer, "both Safed and Jerusalem are holy places and always will be. Jerusalem, however, is holier than any place in Israel. When R' Azulai wrote that Safed is unequalled by any city in *Eretz Yisrael,* he obviously intended to exclude Jerusalem.[6]

"Some people," he explained, "mistakenly say that the greatness of Jerusalem endured only while the Temple stood, and that now Safed wears the crown. This is simply not true.[7]

"Therefore, it is unthinkable to say that Safed is loftier than Jerusalem, or that its air is purer."

R' Sofer, the leading rabbi during the first half of the nineteenth century, elaborated and substantiated his thoughts by bringing evidence from the written Torah. When Jacob had his prophetic dream of the ladder reaching up to heaven, he awoke and said, "How awesome is this place... This is the gateway to heaven" (Gen. 28:17). The place he referred to was Jerusalem, and above it was – and is – the sole gateway to heaven. That gateway has never moved. Safed certainly can not claim to be a second gateway to heaven.

R' Sofer cited an interesting Scriptural distinction between Jerusalem and the rest of *Eretz Yisrael*. Scripture describes Israel as "the Land which the Lord your God cares for: the eyes of the Lord are always upon it" (Deut. 11:12). The verse only mentions God's 'eyes' when describing His influence in all of Israel. When speaking about Jerusalem, however, the Torah mentions both God's 'eyes and heart,' "My eyes and heart shall be there perpetually" (II Chron. 7:16). What is the allegorical difference between God's 'eyes' alone, and His 'eyes and heart,' since both verses indicate that God takes special pride and personal supervision of *Eretz Yisrael* and the Holy City?

The Chasam Sofer explains that 'the eyes of God' is an allusion to the heavenly court of seventy judges, known as the 'wings of the *Shechina*,' which is a less personal supervision of Israel than the 'eyes and heart of God,' which is an expression of the Almighty's Divine Providence, which is much more direct and personal. Thus, he concludes, Jerusalem reigns alone and the crown cannot be shared with any other city.

Safed Versus Jerusalem

R' Moshe Sofer, known as the Chasam Sofer

R' Sofer's beliefs were heartfelt. Thus, in the beginning of 1838, when the horrifying news of the terrible earthquake which had claimed thousands of lives in Safed first reached Europe, R' Sofer touchingly eulogized the victims in the following way:

"Although all things come from God," he said before a crowded assembly in the Pressburg synagogue, "we can perhaps say that the spiritual cause of the earthquake may have stemmed from the resentment Jerusalem felt at being abandoned by her people. For nearly a hundred years, most newcomers to Israel have gone directly to Safed or Tiberias.

SAFED: THE MYSTICAL CITY

Jerusalem was completely forgotten. How can one neglect the city upon which God has placed His name? Even today, it is praiseworthy to go to Jerusalem on the three festivals....

"Just as we are lamenting and weeping over this catastrophe in the Galilee," concluded R' Sofer, "so may we one day be worthy to rejoice over the ingathering of our people within her true borders, and participate in the rebuilding of Zion and *Yerushalayim*."[8]

Advice from the Chasam Sofer

When R' Amram, a disciple of the Chasam Sofer, was about to set forth from Pressburg for Israel in the 1830's, R' Sofer implored him to settle in Jerusalem, that most sacred of cities, and pointed out that the Ramban had done just that in the thirteenth century. R' Sofer made his request because Safed was then the main Torah center in Israel, with both disciples of the Vilna Gaon and a strong Chassidic community, making it very attractive to a newcomer to Israel. The young scholar, however, agreed.

R' Amram sailed across the Mediterranean Sea towards the Port of Jaffa, planning to continue from there directly to Jerusalem. The ship, however, was blown off course by strong gale winds, and was fortunate to anchor at the northern port of Acco. Once there, R' Amram found a caravan traveling to Safed in the Upper Galilee. Upon arriving and establishing living quarters, R' Amram wrote a letter to his mentor requesting advice as to whether he should move on to Jerusalem as planned, or remain in Safed.

R' Sofer well understood his disciple's predicament. R' Amram, happily settled in Safed, had disobeyed his mentor (albeit initially through circumstances beyond his control) and felt duty bound to ask to be released from any implicit promise he may have made in Pressburg. By his letter he sought to appease the Chasam Sofer. R' Sofer, not wanting to force his disciple to move and suffer hardships, and yet still holding firmly to his beliefs regarding the City of Cities, sent a deliberately vague reply, leaving the final decision up to R' Amram. Naturally, he chose to remain in Safed.[9]

A Controversy for "The Sake of Heaven"

To better understand the intense friction between the two communities, we must go back to 16th century Safed and probe into one of the most amazing halachic decisions ever decreed. In 1538, the sages of Safed voted to re-introduce *semicha*, genuine rabbinical ordination. This immediately sparked a controversy with the rabbis of Jerusalem. The resultant dispute reverberates even today.

Today, the term *'semicha'* is applied loosely to any student of Jewish law who passes a series of tests, thus receiving a document entitling him to the titular status of rabbi. This status entitles him to officiate at certain functions and make decisions in certain areas of Jewish law. Even without such a document, an acknowledged scholar may do all of these things. Even today the presiding members of a court of Jewish law, are permitted to rule only in certain carefully defined areas, such as divorce cases and monetary disputes. Thus, *semicha* today is a credential with very specific limitations.

To fully grasp the breadth and depth of the striking 1538 Safed decision, we must first understand the classical definition of *semicha*. The word itself is derived from the Hebrew word that means 'to lean upon,' and also has a connotation of authority. It implies that the scholar who is granting *semicha* rests his hand on the candidate's head and pronounces him a rabbi (though in practice this may simply be an oral declaration). Genuine (or 'classical') *semicha* is an entirely different concept from what we mean by the term today.

Rabbinical ordination was initiated at the giving of the Torah, when *semicha* was conferred on Moses at Mount Sinai. Moses later ordained Joshua and the seventy elders in the wilderness and they in turn ordained others. The one prerequisite for conferring genuine *semicha* on a scholar – besides his proven knowledge of Torah – is that the rabbi who gives the *semicha* must himself have been ordained by a ordained rabbi, thus continuously forging new links in the ancient chain. This genuine, Divinely initiated *semicha* continued without interruption until the end of the Babylonian Academies in the fourth century C.E.[10]

The power of this *semicha* surpasses our imagination. If the members of a court of Jewish law were to receive genuine *semicha*, they would thereby be invested with the power to preside over cases which we have been unable to decide in our courts for over 1,500 years. The most important worldwide effect of such *semicha* would be the ability once again to declare the beginning of the new months based on eye-witness testimony.

Until the fourth century C.E., each month was sanctified by a rabbinical court of ordained rabbis in *Eretz Yisrael*. People who had seen the crescent of the new moon would go before the court and attest to the sighting. The rabbis, who had previously calculated when the new moon should appear, examined the witnesses. Once the testimony was accepted, the rabbis would declare that day the first day of the new month. If no witnesses had come by the end of the 30th day, the following day automatically became *Rosh Chodesh*. Messengers were then sent to notify every Jewish community of the day which had been proclaimed *Rosh Chodesh*. In that way, every Jew in every community could keep the same day for Yom Kippur, and begin Passover at the same time. Those communities which could not be notified in time kept Yom Tov for two days.

This monthly procedure continued for more than 1,500 years, from the time of Moses until the time of Rabbi Hillel in the middle of the 4th century C.E. Rabbi Hillel, a descendant of Rabbi Yehuda the Prince, together with his rabbinical court, calculated a predetermined calendar which would be binding on all Jewry without witnesses or ordained rabbis. This extraordinary move suddenly froze the holidays and leap-years into predetermined positions. Rabbi Hillel took this remarkable step to safeguard Torah since, due to the growing dispersion of Jewry, it had became increasingly difficult to inform distant communities of the dates of the various festivals. Were it possible to reintroduce *semicha*, however, ordained rabbis would once again renew *Kiddush HaChodesh*.

Other areas of Torah jurisprudence which have lapsed because of the lack of genuine *semicha* would likewise become a reality again. For instance, a punishment of lashes *(malkos)* could be meted out by the court. Therefore, someone who refused to obey a court ruling against him could be sentenced to lashes, or, perhaps even more importantly, someone who had transgressed a Torah precept punishable by Divine excommunication *(kares)*, would then be freed from divine retribution if lashed. All felonies in Jewish Law punishable by death may be executed only by a court of ordained rabbis. Thus, a person who openly desecrates the Sabbath, and has been admonished by eye-witnesses of the severity of his act and had also been forewarned of the consequences of continuing such behavior, would no longer go unpunished. Also, all monetary cases involving penal fines would once again be judged by rabbinical courts.

For over a thousand years these cases had no place in rabbinical courtrooms. Now, suddenly in the sixteenth century, the Safedean rabbis reintroduced *semicha* and gave an undreamt of boost to Torah jurisprudence.

R' Yaakov Berav

The originator of the idea of reintroducing *semicha* was the undisputed leader of the Safed community and the leading Torah sage in Israel, R' Yaakov Berav. Among his disciples were some of the greatest Torah luminaries of all time: R' Yosef Karo, the author of the *Shulchan Aruch*, R' Moshe Cordovero, a young genius who later became a great Kabbalist, R' Moshe Metrani, a close learning associate of R' Karo who later replaced R' Berav as Chief Rabbi of Safed, and R'

Moshe Galante. (The Arizal was a child living in Egypt at the time, and R' Chaim Vital was a youngster in Safed.)

Who was this unique giant whose foresight reached far beyond his own time?

As a teenage fugitive from the Spanish Expulsion of 1492, R' Yaakov Berav had wandered, homeless, in Northern Africa. Wherever he went, however, his greatness in Torah shone forth. When he was a mere eighteen years old, R' Berav was appointed Chief Rabbi of Fez, Morocco, a Jewish community of over five thousand families. He later settled in Egypt where he was a member of the Cairo court of law for many years. From there he moved to Safed and established a yeshiva.

As a survivor of the Spanish Inquisition, R' Berav naturally felt an empathetic warmth toward his Spanish brethren. Not all those who survived the catastrophe kept to the Torah path. Some were so materially and spiritually impoverished by their wanderings that they were happy just to be alive, even if Torah played almost no part in their lives. Those who remained in Spain were even less fortunate. They succumbed to threats of torture and became Marranos, Jewish converts to Christianity. Many only ostensibly renounced their faith in order to remain alive, but continued clandestinely to cling to Torah practice. From all points of view, the expulsion from Spain was one of the greatest tragedies in the history of the Jewish people.

Background for Reintroducing Ordination

As time passed, some of the Marranos repented, escaped from Spain, and returned to their faith. According to Torah Law, their act of renunciation of Torah was punishable with Divine excommunication *(kares)*. Their heartfelt repentance alone was not sufficient before the Law to heal the wound they had caused by forsaking Judaism.

R' Berav was heartbroken over their predicament, and searched for a means to annul their decree of *kares*. Were there a rabbinical court of ordained rabbis, he knew, the repentant Marranos could be sentenced to lashes and thereby be freed from kares. The *Mishna* clearly states, "Anyone who deserves the punishment of excommunication, once lashed by the court, is freed from his Divine punishment, as the verse says, 'then your brother shall be dishonored before you' – once he has been dishonored by receiving lashes, then he is your brother."[11]

But how could genuine rabbinical ordination be reinstated? Where could one find a rabbi whose *semicha* was connected directly to that of Moses, an individual who was himself a link in that unbroken chain? Tradition attests that Elijah the Prophet, who ascended to heaven without dying, was ordained, and in the time of the *Mashiach*, he will return and reinstate *semicha*.

Yet, R' Berav was convinced that there must be a more tangible means available. To this end, he scoured and searched the texts of Law until he found another means of reinstating ordination. The Rambam, in his famous *Mishna Torah*, rules that by scrupulously following certain guidelines *semicha* may be reinstated in any generation. He writes, "Should all the rabbis living in Israel agree to appoint judges and ordain them, then their declaration of *semicha* is official. These newly ordained rabbis have the power to judge cases of fines and lashes, and also to ordain others."[12] At last, R' Berav had found a source which would help save the repentant Marranos.

Furthermore, the implications of reinstating *semicha* would be even more far-reaching. *Semicha* would empower the judicial courts with a central role throughout the Jewish world. Cases from all corners of the world would come before its judges, and dissension between religious factions would slowly cease as the questions that separated them were resolved. Most of all, it would be a vanguard to the Messianic period, as prophesied by Isaiah, "I shall restore your judges as they once were... afterwards you shall be called the city of righteousness."[13]

These positive reasons for reinstating *semicha* had to be carefully weighed against possible dangers. First of all, R' Berav was concerned that the Rav of Jerusalem, R' Levi ben Chaviv, and his associates, might oppose his plan. Even though the rabbis of Safed were greater in number and authority than the rabbis of Jerusalem, R' Berav feared that a negative influence from Jerusalem could jeopardize the strong solidarity that existed among the rabbis of Safed.

Secondly, such a move was liable to endanger him personally, as well as the entire Jewish community, with the new civil government. Twenty-five years earlier, the Turkish army had defeated the medieval Egyptian Mamluk rulers and a new era in the rulership of Israel had begun. For the Jews, this was a great improvement and engendered a new security. Yet if the authorities were to learn of the power which *semicha* would invest in Jewish courts, they might interpret it as an act of rebellion on the part of the Jews to free themselves from civil law. It could cause harsh repercussions, especially to its instigator, R' Berav.

Semicha is Revived in Safed

During 1538, R' Berav and his associates made their decision. This historic event took place in the Yossi Bannai Synagogue and R' Yaakov Berav was unanimously given *semicha* by all the rabbis of Safed. He, in turn, ordained four other rabbis: R' Yosef Karo, R' Moshe Metrani (known as the Mabit), R' Moshe Galante, and R' Moshe Cordovero.[14] In order to prevent any backlash from Jerusalem, R' Berav promptly dispatched a letter to R' Chaviv, notifying him of the dramatic event and solemnly ordaining him rabbi.

R' Chaviv's reaction was forceful and immediate. No! *Semicha* could not be reintroduced into Jewish law until the time of the *Mashiach*, he declared. There were soon aligned with him the rabbis of Jerusalem and Egypt, and a wide schism

Rabbi Yossi Bannai Synagogue, where semicha *is believed to have been reinstated*

between Jerusalem and Safed was the woeful result.

R' Chaviv, who had also fled Spain in 1492, wrote a long reply to support his position. The Rambam admits, he contended, that this is not a clear *halacha* (point of Jewish law) and needs more investigation. Among his numerous points of opposition, one was particularly pertinent: the incomparable importance of Jerusalem. A halachic decision of this magnitude, R' Chaviv contended, must come from Jerusalem, as is clearly stated in the verse, "Torah shall go forth from Zion, and the word of God from *Yerushalayim*" (Isa. 2:3). Jerusalem may under no circumstance be secondary to Safed, even if at that time more rabbis resided in Safed than in Jerusalem.

Later, R' Berav wrote a defense of his position and answered every point of contention. He reassured everyone that he had no intention of misusing the power of ordination. Under no circumstances would capital punishment be administered, nor would the calendar revert to its original state of monthly verification by eye-witnesses. However, the tension between him and R' Chaviv continued to burgeon. It became so personal that threats were made on R' Berav's life by dissident groups.

The sages of Safed, in an effort to support R' Berav's position, issued a statement backing his decision and officially approved it with the seal of the rabbinical court, but to no avail. The momentum against R' Berav's initiative had gained supremacy.

The increasingly virulent controversy between the leaders of Safed and Jerusalem finally reached the ears of the Turkish governor, who quickly issued a warrant for R' Berav's arrest. The Rav of Safed made a narrow escape and fled to Damascus, where he died eight years later at the age of seventy-two.

His body was brought back to Israel for burial in the old cemetery of Safed.[15]

R' Yaakov Berav is buried in a large cave located in the lower half of the ancient cemetery of Safed

A Question of Timing

The vision of R' Yaakov Berav had been to instill a new dimension into the framework of living Judaism. His singular

Safed Versus Jerusalem

foresight that *semicha* was the key to the future, and his entirely selfless efforts to attain his goal led to a hard-won victory that was apparently never actualized. No cases of lashes were recorded, and the chain of ordination continued for only two more links before ceasing. R' Yosef Karo ordained R' Moshe Alshich, who later ordained R' Chaim Vital. Why the rabbinical court of Safed never used its power of *semicha*, and why it ceased to exist only fifty years after its revival is today a matter for mere speculation.[16]

Those vivid hopes and secret expectations of so many, of the establishment of a Sanhedrin as a preparatory step in bringing the light of the *Mashiach* out of its hiding place, had not been realized. Or had it? Some thirty years later, in 1570, R' Yitzchak Luria arrived in Safed and revealed some of that hidden light.

NOTES
1. Letter cited in *Eden Tziyon*, pp. 104-106   2. *ibid.*
3. *Chesed l'Avraham*, 3:13   4. *Zohar*, 2:220
5. *Kaftor v'Ferach*, p. 284
6. Responsa *Chasam Sofer, Yoreh Deah*, no. 234. According to *halacha* there is a practical difference. *Orech Chayim* (561) discusses the laws regarding tearing one's garment when seeing the cities of Israel and Jerusalem. If Safed is greater than Jerusalem, then one would rend his garment twice, once in Jerusalem and again in Safed.
7. Cf. Rambam, *Hilchos Beis HaBechira* 6:16, where he explains that Jerusalem and the Temple are sacred for all time. Cf. *Yevamos* 6b, which compares the reverence one must have of the Temple to Shabbos. Just as Shabbos is eternal, so is the reverence of the Temple forever.
8. *Toras Moshe*, end of *Emor*
9. Responsa *Chasam Sofer, Yoreh Deah*, no. 234   10. Num. 11:16-25
11. *Makos* 3:15, Rambam, *Hilchos Sanhedrin* 17:7
12. Rambam, ibid. 4:11   13. 1:26
14. There are different opinions who is included in the four. Cf. *Seder HaDoros*, 5298, p. 241, who says he ordained ten rabbis
15. His burial site is in a large cave near the grave of R' Yosef Karo. Buried in the same cave is R' Moshe Alshich. Cf. *Eden Tziyon*, p. 85, who suggests that the grave is located much higher up, very close to the Arizal's grave.
16. Cf. *Iyr HaKodesh*, vol. 4, p. 128, for a full discussion

Safed

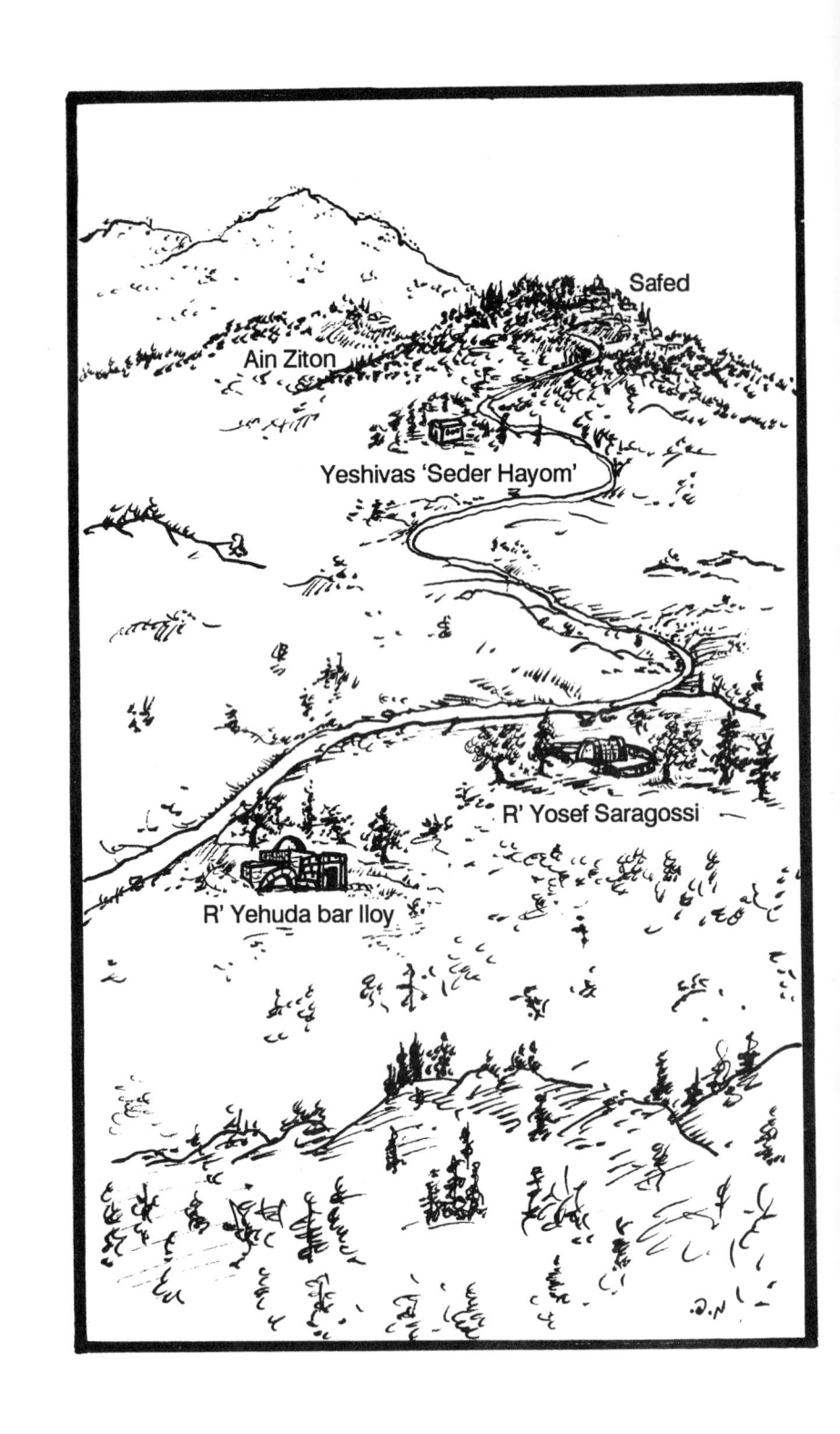

Ain Ziton

Yeshivas 'Seder Hayom'

R' Yosef Saragossi

R' Yehuda bar Iloy

3
The Mountaintop City

Safed is located in the Upper Galilee in the Biblical portion of Israel allotted to Naphtali. From her elevated vantage point, Safed commands a panoramic view of the entire area: the Sea of Galilee (the Kinneret) to the east, Mount Tabor to the south, and Meron to the west. This mountaintop city, strategically located along the main road between Acco on the coast and Damascus far-off to the northeast, would naturally be the choice of any military professionals to establish a stronghold, and its natural resources would seem to make it a foregone conclusion that it has long been a place of human habitation.

However, surprisingly little is known about Safed's early history. Nowhere in the Books of the Prophets, the consecrated annals of Jewish history, is Safed mentioned, while dozens of other cities whose locations are unknown to us today played a dynamic role in the chronicles of our forefathers.[1] Furthermore, throughout the entire Talmud and *Midrashim*, that vast repository of Talmudic debates, history and exegetical stories, we find only two obscure references to Safed.[2]

SAFED: THE MYSTICAL CITY

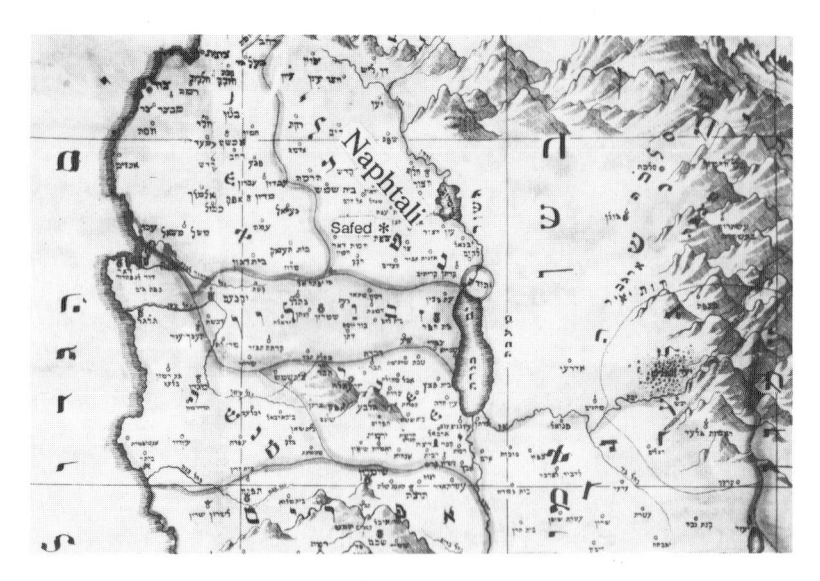

A map of the Galilee designating the territory of each Tribe. This map was drawn by the famous researcher of Eretz Yisrael, R' Yosef Shwartz, who lived in Israel during the first half of the 19th century

In the first reference, the Talmud refers to a certain place in which an abundance of prize honey was produced in the 'city of Sufim.' The word *'sufim'* is derived from the Hebrew word *sofeh* (צופה), to observe. We have already noted that Safed's location at the top of a mountain permits a commanding view, an extensive field of observation, of the surrounding countryside.[3]

Our second reference is found in the Jerusalem Talmud, where one priest's hometown is identified as Safed. This reference led one commentator to believe that Safed may have been a city of priests.[4]

Both Talmudic references are cryptic at best, and add very little color, let alone hard facts, to Safed's early history. However, to claim that Safed was nonexistent as a center of human habituation until the Middle Ages, based merely on this lack of information would be ludicrous. In the first place, her natural water supply and strategic location almost certainly guaranteed her an important role in the history of *Eretz Yisrael*. Then again, the spiritual oasis that is the essence of Safed must surely have attracted untold numbers of great sages to bask in her splendor.

After examining all available sources, we remain almost as baffled as when we started to research Safed's earliest history, and therefore hesitate even to speculate, with one exception. Because of her location high up on a Galilee mountain, it is quite possible that Safed was one of the fire-top mountain sites from which were relayed the messages announcing the day which had been proclaimed *Rosh Chodesh*.[5]

Place names almost always reflect the essence of their nature. The first reference we discovered in the Talmud was that the name Safed refers to *sufim*, which implies the ability to see far off into the distance. Another possible source for the city's name stems from the name of its ancient citadel. This fortress, destroyed by the Romans during their conquest of Israel in the middle of the first century of the common era, was called the Citadel of Yorafas (יורפת).[6] The Hebrew letters *resh* and *tzadi* are interchangeable, and the first two letters, *yud* and *vav*, may have fallen away with the passage of time, leaving (צפת), *Tzefat*. This latter meaning appears to refer to the city's physical nature, the location of the citadel, while the former, *sufim*, offers an insight into her nature as a site particularly conducive to spiritual enlightenment.

Safed is not mentioned in any of the Mid-eastern chronicles until Medieval times. In 1187, Saladan, the King of Egypt, conquered Israel, which had been under the governorship of the Islamic Caliph and the ruling Christian crusaders, who were led by Goydon. Goydon, in his attempt to escape from Saladan's siege of Jerusalem, fled to Safed, where he was captured and he and his army slain.[7]

Saladan returned from the Galilee and continued his siege of Jerusalem. After having been deprived of their leader, the Christian population chose to ransom their lives rather than continue the fight, and were granted safe passage out of the Land. With regard to the Jews, King Saladan maintained a benevolent policy and honored the site of the Holy Temple.

Around the time of Saladan's conquest of Israel, R' Benyomin of Toledo passed through the Land, and made note in his Travels of the size of the Jewish population of each town through which he traveled. According to his records, Safed at that time had no Jewish inhabitants; nor did Hebron. Safed did have a fortress manned by a large garrison of troops which was supported by a gentile population.[8]

Around the year 1260, the Ramban, R' Moses Nachmanides, arrived in Israel where he dedicated the last years of his life to writing his famous commentary on the Bible. Although it is known that he visited Jerusalem, Hebron and Acco, whether or not he also visited Safed is open to conjecture.

Throughout the fourteenth and fifteenth centuries Safed did not play an active role in Jewish history.[9] For various reasons, few Jews ventured to settle there. Jerusalem held the crown, and cities like Acco, Tyre, and Sidon also had significant Jewish communities. Safed's sole mark of distinction was her cemetery. A number of Talmudic Sages and even prophets were buried on her western slope. These grave sites were a symbol of her dormant holiness which was only awaiting an auspicious time to reveal itself to the world.

Revival of Torah in Safed

The first recorded election of a Rav of Safed was in 1490. This was R' Yosef Saragossi, the mentor of R' Dovid ben Zimra (the Radbaz). R' Saragossi's constant love of his fellowman, even to the extent of making peace between gentiles, was proverbial. He passed away in 1506.[10]

Some generations later, there occurred an amazing incident which earned him the somewhat unlikely title of 'The *Tzaddik* of the Hens.' It seems that the presiding gentile governor, a blatant anti-Semite, one day demanded that the Jews

In the foreground is the tomb of R' Yosef Saragossi, surrounded by olive trees. Safed is in the background.

of Safed bring him several hundred pure white hens. If they failed there would be the gravest of consequences. The Jews were panic stricken. How could they possibly fulfill such a request? After hurried and desperate consultations, they recalled how R' Saragossi had been known as a peacemaker even among gentiles, and decided to pray at his grave. Maybe, in his merit, the Almighty would heed their prayers and save them from tragedy.

R' Saragossi's grave was located not far from Safed on the road to Meron, a good hour's walk from the Jewish Quarter.

SAFED: THE MYSTICAL CITY

The Jews of Safed walked along the mountain road with an air of uncertainty about them, and when they reached the tomb they fervently prayed for salvation. Their faith and devotion notwithstanding, they returned home with heavy hearts.

The next morning a Jew hurried to shul to tell his companions of his dream the previous night.

"R' Saragossi came to me," he said excitedly. "He told me not to worry. All we have to do is to bring the required number of hens to his grave site, regardless of their color."

The following day the townspeople took several wagon loads of hens to the grave site. Suddenly, in a revealed miracle before the eyes of everyone present, all the hens turned white! They offered praises and thanks to the Almighty who, in the merit of the *tzaddik*, had saved their lives.

When they returned to the city and handed over the hundreds of white hens to the gentile governor's office, he and all his aides were speechless.[11]

Slowly, Safed was becoming renown as a place of holiness, and more and more families began to settle there. In 1523, a traveler from Italy recorded that close to three hundred Jewish families were then living in Safed. The population of Safed at that time thus equalled that of Jerusalem.[12]

During this time Safed boasted three synagogues. One was for the Sephardim, another was called Morisko, whose congregants were of Greek-Oriental descent, and the third, the oldest, was called Eliyahu's Shul because according to tradition it was the place where Elijah had prayed. Eliyahu's Shul was later renamed after the Arizal, and is today known as the old Sephardi Ari shul, and is located at the bottom of the Jewish Quarter.[13]

Ottoman Influence

The Turkish conquest of the Middle East ushered in a new era of peace for the Jews. In 1518, the Sultan's army conquered Israel and Egypt from the Egyptian Mamluk dynasty.

The Mountaintop City

The Ottoman empire stretched along all of North Africa and even controlled a large section of Europe.

Sultan Selim I was a unique monarch. He was a brilliant warrior with a deep philosophical bent. He recognized in the Jewish faith a noble ancestry and a rich history dating back several millennia. He therefore maintained a benevolent policy toward his new subjects.

He made significant improvements throughout the country. The most monumental project was the construction of a new wall around Jerusalem. Over the long history of our people, walls around the Holy City had been built, destroyed, and rebuilt numerous times. As the Sultan marveled at the city's majestic history, he was aghast at its current degraded state. For over three hundred years it had remained unprotected by a wall. He felt duty-bound to rebuild the walls, and construction began in 1527. When the wall was completed in 1544, the Holy City was once again cloaked in the dignity that was its heritage, and this same wall stands to the present day as a tribute and gift from Sultan Selim I to the Jewish people.

Sultan Selim I, enamored of the Jewish way of life, commanded his personal physician, a Jew, to translate the Bible and prayer book into Arabic. Selim I studied these works eagerly and with great respect, and became a lifelong friend of his Jewish subjects.

Eretz Yisrael entered an era of peace and affluence. Food was plentiful and cheap. The trade route between Safed and Damascus was alive with commercial caravans. Although the Jews of Safed were not rich, jobs for merchants, weavers, silversmiths and tailors, for example, were readily available. Those who chose to live a life of Torah learning rather than one of commerce, also found it a perfect setting.

The next Torah leader of the city (after R' Yosef Saragossi) was R' Yaakov Berav, with the attendant controversy over rabbinical ordination in 1538. He was elected *Rosh Beis Vaad*, head of the rabbinical council, but declined the post. He instead chose to support himself as a spice merchant, but remained the undisputed leader of the community.

R' Yosef Karo, author of the *Shulchan Aruch*, accepted the post R' Berav had declined after he arrived from Turkey in 1536. Later, R' Moshe Metrani was *Rosh Beis Vaad* until he passed away in 1585. During this jubilee period between 1530 to 1580, Safed reached her zenith and retrieved the crown from Jerusalem.

Safed Flourishes

The sixteenth century was a time of spectacular growth for Safed. Population swelled as an influx of new immigrants chose to make Safed their new home. The great majority of the immigrants were Sephardim from the Mediterranean basin, although some were refugees from Spain and Portugal, and there were also some of Persian and Turkish descent. In addition, a small minority of Ashkenazi Jews immigrated during this period.

In response to the growing needs of the community, more and more synagogues and yeshivos were built. By the end of the century there were thirteen shuls, where in the early 1500's there had been only three.

Although many men supported their families by engaging in various occupations, for the layman as well as the scholar, the main concern was the acquisition of Torah wisdom and striving for the path of righteousness. Certain groups even wrote ordinances pledging to rectify bad behavior, and to honor their fellow man in spite of personal differences.

Yeshivos hummed with the music of Torah learning from early in the morning until late at night, as both layman and scholar dedicated their time to Torah study. Even everyday conversations were elevated by a sincere concern for self-betterment. It is not an exaggeration that several hundred students filled R' Yosef Karo's yeshiva. The yeshivos of R' Moshe Cordovero and R' Moshe Alshich were also extremely prominent. The influence of this Torah-centeredness spread

The Mountaintop City

R' Mose Machir, author of Seder HaYom, had a yeshiva in this building some 450 years ago, in the time of R' Yosef Karo. The building stands on the roadside between Safed and Meron.

from Safed to nearby Ain Ziton, where the author of the *Seder HaYom* had a large yeshiva. Great scholars and communal leaders were produced by all of these outstanding yeshivos.

Torah reigned on every street corner. Today, it strains our imagination to picture what it must have been like: Such a great luminary as R' Yitzchak Luria strolling along the lanes of the Jewish Quarter with his chief disciple, R' Chaim Vital, whispering the secrets of creation; R' Yosef Karo, the venerable sage and author of the *Shulchan Aruch*, sitting at the head of the rabbinical court and pronouncing a halachic decision which would be heard around the world; the Shabbos discourses of R' Moshe Alshich which captivated his audience and inspired preachers for generations to come.

There were other *tzaddikim* who sought to camouflage their greatness. One such hidden *tzaddik* was R' Elazar Ezkari who, as beadle of a local shul, was considered a simple, common man. Only years later was his greatness revealed

SAFED: THE MYSTICAL CITY

Cover to the first printing of Sefer Charedim, *Valancia, 1601*

when he published a masterwork on the commandments, *Sefer Charedim*.

In order to acquire a sense of this dramatic era when Safed was at the height of her greatness, and to glimpse the splendor of Torah at such an exalted level, we must make our approach slowly and carefully, feeling our way step by step.

NOTES

1. There is a town called Safed mentioned in Judges 1:17, but that town is located in the portion of Shimon, in southern Israel. Also, in II Chron. 14:9, King Asa fought a battle in the "valley of Safed," which the commentators identify as a valley in the portion of Judah. (*Chibas Yerushalayim*, pp. 67-68). Some commentators claim that Safed was one of the forty-eight Cities of Refuge mentioned in Josh. 21. Cf. *Eretz Chaim*, pp. 92-93
2. while Meron, only a few miles away, is mentioned numerous times. (*Tivuos HaAretz*, p. 476)
3. *Sotah* 48b. Cf. *Kaftor v'Ferach*, ch. 11, pp. 283-284
4. Jer. *Rosh Hashanna* 2:7; *Massaot Moshe*, p. 140
5. Jer. *Rosh Hashanna* 2:1

6. Cf. *Joshephus*, ch. 68, *Tivuos HaAretz*, p. 83; *Chibas Yerushalayim*, pp. 68-69
7. Cf. *Tivuos HaAretz*, pp. 435 and 476
8. *ibid.* p. 442
9. In 1315, the author of *Migdal Oz* (a early commentary on Rambam) lived in Safed
10. *Sefer Charedim*, Introduction to Ch. 8
11. *Chibas Yerushalayim*, p. 106
12. The entire pamphlet by this anonymous traveler is printed in *Otzar Massaot*, pp. 130-139
13. *Chibas Yerushalayim*, pp. 71

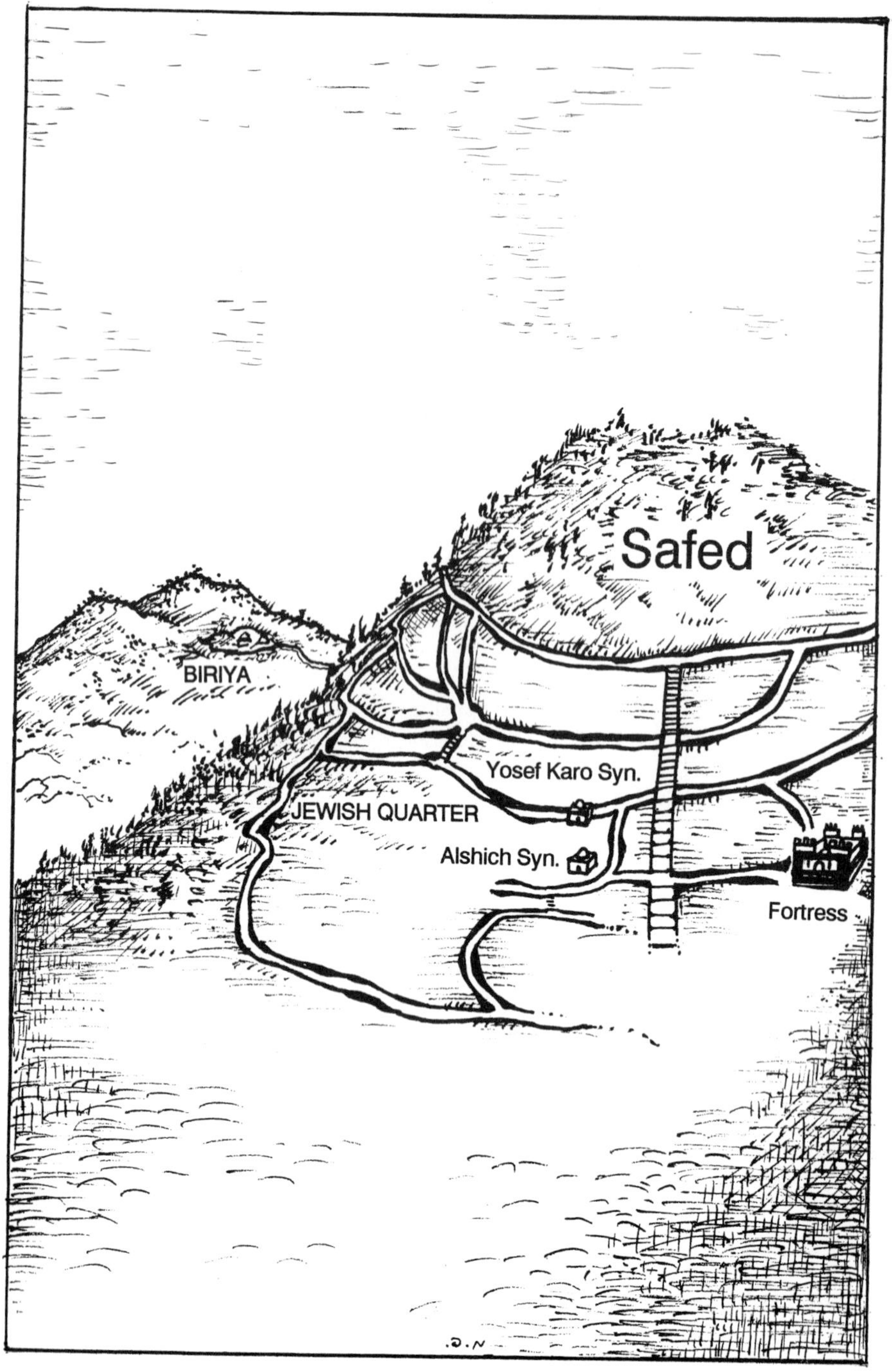
Safed
BIRIYA
Yosef Karo Syn.
JEWISH QUARTER
Alshich Syn.
Fortress

4

The Golden Era

As we have seen, the sixteenth century revealed the grandeur of Safed. The two principle aspects of Torah, the revealed and the mystical, went through a type of rejuvenation in Safed which transformed the living nature of Judaism from that time onward. In great measure, two saintly men shared the responsibility for this new light of Torah. R' Yosef Karo gave the world of Jewish law a new guidebook. And R' Yitzchak Luria revealed the innermost sanctum of the hidden mysteries of the Torah. They became the torchbearers for the future.

By studying their deeds we can best perceive the revolution in Torah which they achieved. It is precisely their noble souls, their living Torah, and their remarkable actions which imbued the stones of Safed with their mystical and spiritual glow.

Torah Jurisprudence

Throughout the process of the codification of the Torah the works of several sages stand out as milestones among the multitude of wise men who lived throughout the ages. Rabbi Judah the Prince organized the *Mishna* in the second century, and Rabbi Ashi as well as Ravina committed the Talmud to writing a few generations later. In the twelfth century, Maimonides wrote his encyclopedic codification of all of Torah Law, the *Mishna Torah*. And a hundred years later, Rabbi Yaakov ben Asher codified applicable areas of Jewish law in his masterpiece, the *Tur*.

By the sixteenth century, however, there was a growing necessity for definitive *halacha*, practical applications of Talmudic law. As we shall see, a very pious and learned man stepped forward to fill that need, and his magnum opus, the *Shulchan Aruch*, became the universally accepted basic text of Jewish law from that time until today.

R' Yosef Karo penned his halachic masterpiece in Safed in the middle of the sixteenth century, while presiding as head of the judicial court. His yeshiva in the center of the Jewish Quarter was the largest in the city. Wherever he went, townsmen paused in deference to his seniority in Torah jurisprudence.

Who was R' Yosef Karo, not only as a Torah sage, but as a man? What was his influence in Safed? Most especially, what equipped him for the unprecedented task of propagating Torah on such a level that millions of Jews over the last four hundred years continue to scrupulously study his *Shulchan Aruch*?

To these questions, it will be helpful to explore a few significant incidents in R' Karo's life, both in Safed and in his native town in Turkey.

A Heavenly Voice

Shavuos is the festival which commemorates the giving of the Torah on Mount Sinai. At that time it is traditional for God-fearing men to congregate in synagogues and study halls and to learn Torah throughout the night. Some choose to learn alone, others prefer group seminars, and still others re-

The Golden Era

cite selections from the Written and Oral Law from a book called the *Tikun*. Each one's goal is to prepare himself psychologically and spiritually for his personal reception of the Torah on this sacred day, as if it were that very first Shavuos.

One Shavuos night in the beginning of the sixteenth century, a group of scholars assembled in a shul in Adrianople on the Turkish-Greek border. Among them were R' Yosef Karo and R' Shlomo Alkabetz. They resolved to recite the *Tikun* together, slowly and with the deepest of concentration. After they finished selections from the Bible, they began reading *Mishnayos* from the Oral Law.

Suddenly an unearthly voice filled the shul, vibrantly and distinctly. "Hearken unto Me, My friends, My beloved."

"*Shalom!* How fortunate you are — both in this world and the next — for on this night you have glorified Me by your learning."

The voice resounded with growing intensity. The scholars were frozen into silence, and prostrated themselves on the synagogue floor in awe.

"Alas," continued the voice, "for so many years My crown has been cast into the dust. But with your deep devotion and learning you have now returned it to its original splendor.

"Be strong, My dear ones, My beloved, and rejoice. Know that you are privileged to dwell in the chambers of the King. The sound of your Torah learning has ascended to the Holy One Blessed Be He, and pierced the firmament. While you recite the *Tikun*, the angels stand in silence and the fiery ones are mute, as all the heavenly Host listen. Had there been ten of you, the effect of your devotions would have been even greater. Nevertheless, rejoice in your good fortune, My beloved, for in your merit I was able to come tonight."

The voice subsided. The study hall reverberated in the momentary silence.

"Never interrupt your learning for a moment," continued the voice. "Your studies weave about you a thread of lovingkindness as a sign that it has been accepted by God. Were it permitted, I would show you the ethereal fire which surrounds the shul now.

"Arise now, My children, and proclaim, '*Baruch shem kavod*...' "

Everyone arose and cried out in unison, "*Baruch shem kavod*... Blessed is His glorious Name forever."

There was another period of silence before the voice continued.

"Return now to your studies, and do not stop even for a second. Know that this is an auspicious time to settle in *Eretz Yisrael*, and that there I shall guard and enlighten you."

Tears of joy streamed down their cheeks as the men realized that they had been privileged to encounter the *Shechina* that night, and to hear her speak to them.[1]

A Call for Excellence

R' Yosef Karo's entire being was transformed by hearing that Divine voice. The acquisition of Torah knowledge was not in itself the goal, he realized, it was a means to total dedication of every cell and fiber of his mind and body as a vehicle for a Godly life. Holding a rabbinic post was not just a communal responsibility, it was a means to facilitate bringing world Jewry under one canopy of definitive *halacha*. And living outside of Israel, in *chutz l'aretz*, had been merely a means to coming closer to God in the garden of His palace in the Holy Land.

R' Yosef Karo labored night and day to rectify and achieve these new goals. Besides studying the Talmud and delving into rabbinical law, he undertook to memorize all six orders of the *Mishna*, the kernel of the Oral Law. After some years, when he had fully mastered the *Mishna*, another incident occurred which forever changed his life: An angel descended from heaven to teach, guide, and rebuke him. The angel, created from R' Yosef's command of *Mishna*, was a constant inspiration for the young rabbi, and humbled him profoundly. For the next fifty years the *maggid*, as R' Karo called him, enriched his life, guided him, and revealed to him mysteries of the Torah.

Maggid Speaks to R' Yosef

R' Yosef Karo kept a diary of conversations with the *maggid*.[2]

Shabbos night, the 27th of Iyar, on the weekly portion beginning the Book of Numbers. I ate and drank sparingly and then began reciting *Mishna*. I must have dozed off, for when I awoke it was already daybreak. I was very upset. How could I have failed to awaken during the night, I scolded myself, so that the voice would come to me in its customary way? Nevertheless, I started reciting *Mishna*. After I finished five chapters the voice began to vibrate by itself in my throat.

"The Lord be with you!" he echoed, "in everything you do. Be sure to cleave at all times to the fear of heaven, Torah and the study of *Mishna*. Do not do as you have done tonight – when, in spite of the way you sanctified yourself by eating in measure, you slept the slumber of the lazy man and did not arise to study *Mishna* as you are accustomed. This was serious enough for me to have forsaken you...

"But in the merit of your knowledge of the entire six orders of *Mishna* by heart, and your austere lifestyle, the heavenly yeshiva agreed that I should continue to communicate with you.

"I converse with you like a man speaks with his fellowman – an achievement which only one person in a generation is worthy of. Therefore, my son, hearken to my voice when I command you to study Torah constantly, without interruption day and night."[3]

Unifying the Codes

At the turn of the sixteenth century, R' Yosef Karo recognized an urgent need to unify all the existing codes and commentaries. Expulsions from Germany, France, Spain and Portugal had reduced the physical and spiritual lives of tens of thousands of fugitives to the minimum requirements of existence. Moreover, even competent rabbis faced the overwhelming task of assessing each law according to a wide array of earlier authorities in order to reach a final decision.

Therefore, before writing his *Shulchan Aruch*, R' Karo wrote a long commentary to the *Tur*. This set the background for his *Shulchan Aruch*. Although his twenty-year project began in Adrianople, it was completed in Safed.

"With the passing of each generation," R' Yosef Karo wrote in his introduction, "the Jewish people have been scattered further apart, and untold trials and tribulations have further weakened us, in fulfillment of the verse, 'for the wisdom of their wise men shall perish' (Isa. 29:14).

"Were it not for the Torah and those who faithfully study it, the Torah would have splintered not just into two, but into a myriad number of Torahs. The problem stems in part from the array of halachic books, which in their admirable endeavor to shed light, actually confound and cast shadows. Each author writes independently, sometimes needlessly repeating what his predecessors have written, and at other times reaching conclusions which diametrically oppose other authorities. Often a writer quotes a *halacha* as if there is unanimous agreement to its interpretation, but when one carefully checks he finds that this is not true.

"Were a person to attempt the project of researching each and every law from its source in the Talmud through the commentators and rabbinical decisions, it would be an overwhelming task. And were he to study all the authorities on one *halacha*, he would still be faced with the delicate task of weighing all of the various factors to decide the final law...

"Therefore, I, the smallest among ten thousand, Yosef ben R' Ephraim Karo, have zealously taken upon myself a call from the Almighty to remove this hindrance by writing a book which will include all the laws, explaining their sources and setting out all the differing opinions.

"I chose to base the law on the opinions of the three great pillars of *halacha*: the Rif, the Rambam, and the Rosh. When two of them are in agreement, then their opinion is the *halacha*..."

At the end of his introduction, R' Karo explained the name of his commentary. "I have entitled this work *Beis Yosef* for several reasons. First, just as our forefathers were physically sustained in Egypt from the house of Joseph *(Beis Yosef)*, so my prayer is that many may be spiritually sustained by this book. Also, this book is the portion of all my labors, and is my *bais* (house) in this world and the next."[4]

In *Eretz Yisrael*

As a young man in Adrianople, R' Yosef Karo's responsa (halachic opinions) were influential in rabbinic circles, and earned him the title of *Maran* (our esteemed Rabbi). Upon immigrating to Israel in 1536, he settled in Safed. It was the month of Elul and the eve of the Sabbatical year, and in every yeshiva and synagogue R' Yosef was impressed by the serious countenance of each and every man, reflecting the sanctity of the time. The intensity of that month of repentance and the sound of the shofar blowing moved him deeply.

The then-leader of Safed, R' Yaakov Berav, offered the forty-eight year old scholar the position of *Rosh Beis Din*, head of the Rabbinic Council. R' Yosef accepted and was immediately immersed in forming halachic decision-making policies in Israel.

It was two years later that the sages of Safed unanimously voted to reinstate *semicha*. In an unprecedented move, R' Yaakov Berav was ordained a full-fledged rabbi, the first to be so ordained in a thousand years. He ordained others, among them R' Yosef Karo and the eighteen year old prodigy, R' Moshe Cordovero.

SAFED: THE MYSTICAL CITY

Interior view of the Rabbi Yosef Karo Synagogue

Around the year 1540 R' Yosef opened a yeshiva, probably at the site of the present synagogue on Beis Yosef Street. It met with great success and attracted brilliant students, some of whom were to be the future leaders of Torah Jewry. In the course of the next thirty years, the yeshiva bustled with the sound of hundreds of students studying Torah. R' Yosef lectured regularly, sitting near the Holy Ark, while his disciples sat on cushions in the crowded study hall and listened attentively.

R' Moshe Alshich

R' Moshe Alshich, a great rabbinical authority and preacher, was one of R' Karo's leading disciples. In recognition of his superb command of Torah, R' Yosef ordained him rabbi. This is the sole case in which R' Yosef or any other rabbi ordained by R' Berav used the power of his *semicha* to ordain another. Years later, after his mentor's death, R' Moshe Alshich ordained his disciple, R' Chaim Vital.

The Alshich Synagogue

R' Alshich had a shul near the Abuhav Synagogue on Abuhav Street. On Shabbos afternoon townspeople would file down the narrow lane leading to his shul, and soon both the interior and the adjoining courtyard were filled to capacity. R' Moshe was a charismatic speaker and his sermons on the weekly Torah portion attracted the greatest sages of Safed alongside the laymen. R' Yosef Karo attended regularly, as did R' Chaim Vital and the Arizal.

During one of his sermons, R' Moshe stood before the hushed crowd and explicated the ten times Laban deceived Jacob by changing the system of payment which Jacob received for tending his father-in-law's flock.

"Although the verse reads 'ten times'," R' Moshe announced, "it may be reread as ten times ten. Therefore, the wicked Laban actually tried to outwit Yaakov a hundred times!"

As R' Moshe enumerated each method, the Arizal began to chuckle and, during a pause, quietly left the shul.

Later, the Arizal explained his conduct. "R' Alshich's sermons are authentic," he began, "and may be classified as stemming from one of the seventy principal dimensions by which the Torah may be interpreted.

"Heavenly angels descend on Shabbos to listen to his sermons. Thus, how could I not come as well?

"When R' Moshe was describing each sneaky technique of that ruthless Laban, I noticed how the audience was impressed by such craftiness.

"What made me laugh, however, was when I noticed that Laban himself was hovering in the shul and nodding in acknowledgment of each method with which he tried to outsmart Yaakov. At that point, I simply had to leave."[5]

R' Moshe, although famed as an orator, spent the entire week studying *halacha* by day and Talmud by night. Only on Friday would he begin preparing his Shabbos sermon. He published these sermons under the title *Toras Moshe*, and they were acclaimed a masterpiece throughout the Jewish world. He also published sermons on the remaining books of the Bible (the Prophets and the Writings), as well as a volume of responsa.

Other Disciples

R' Moshe Galante was another leading disciple of R' Karo. is surname was given to his father by Roman aristocrats who were impressed by his noble character and stature. ('Galante' has the same root as our word 'elegant.')[6]

When he was only twenty-two years old, R' Galante's mentor deemed him fit to rule on any halachic question which might come before the rabbinical court. He later became a *dayan* (halachic judge) and Kabbalist. His grandson, also called Moshe Galante, became the first *Rishon L'Tziyon* of Jerusalem around the middle of the seventeenth century.

One of the great Kabbalists of this period was R' Moshe Cordovero. As a young man, his mentor in the revealed aspects of the Torah was R' Yosef Karo. R' Karo had a special fondness for his brilliant, young, humble disciple. They exchanged numerous halachic dialogues, as the developing R' Moshe was exceptional for his total immersion in every facet of Torah. In turn, R' Karo mentioned several of his opinions in his book of responsa.

The disciple who remained with R' Karo for the longest time was R' Elisha Gliko. He remained in the yeshiva throughout his mentor's lifetime, and later became the Rosh Yeshiva.

The *Shulchan Aruch*

R' Yosef Karo's commentary to the *Tur*, the *Beis Yosef*, was not conceived as final compendium of Jewish law. It was a cornerstone upon which to construct definitive *halacha*: the masterwork which he named the *Shulchan Aruch, The Set Table*.

The challenge and responsibility of writing the final *halacha* was a major task with enormous implications, and consumed R' Karo's mind and soul for years.

Sometime in the year 1555, when the *Shulchan Aruch* was near completion, a plague broke out in Safed. It was dangerous to remain in the city. R' Yosef moved to a small nearby village, Biriya, and there the *Shulchan Aruch* was completed.

With its completion, the *maggid* informed R' Yosef Karo of a decision of the Heavenly Court. "Since you strove to reinstate the crown of Torah – *semicha* – in its proper place, you shall merit that through your compendium of Jewish law, the *Shulchan Aruch, semicha* as you know it today will reach its widest dimensions. All who wish to be ordained as rabbis will first be tested in their knowledge of the *Shulchan Aruch*."[7]

The Universal Code of Jewish Law

There was one major deficiency in the *Shulchan Aruch*. It did not codify the customs of the Ashkenazi Jews of Europe. This omission was significant because in a number of instances their customs and those of the Sephardim are as different as day and night.

SAFED: THE MYSTICAL CITY

The Rama, R' Moshe Isralosh, supported R' Karo's code of law, and stood up in its defense.

"It appears to me," he wrote, "that the *Shulchan Aruch* was written as authoritatively as if it had been given to us by Moses at Mount Sinai."[8]

In order that the Code could also be used and relied upon by Ashkenazim, the Rama wrote marginal notes. He defined the customs and halachic variations of Ashkenazi Jewry clearly, making hundreds of citations. Eventually, in later editions of the *Shulchan Aruch*, these marginal notes were incorporated into the text. In the end, the *Shulchan Aruch* was whole and acceptable by all Jews of different backgrounds, and became the first universal code of Jewish law in centuries.

The Fortress of Safed

Sixteenth century Safed was a growing city and the well-being of her citizens was a high priority to her Rav, R' Yosef Karo.

The Turkish rulers of Israel endorsed a benevolent policy towards the Jews. The implementation of that policy, however, lay in the hands of the provincial governor, who lived in Damascus. As long as his armies exercised a strong protectorate role in the Galilee, the local Arab population remained passive. But whenever his legions weakened their stance, the Arab settlers wrought havoc on Jewish lives and property.

The Council of Safed, headed by R' Karo, devised a plan to improve the security of their community. A fortress built in the heart of the city would be an immense aid in protecting not only the city, but also her neighboring Jewish communities. The projected fortress would include a military base and an inn for caravans, travelers and merchants.

Before the project could get underway, it was necessary to obtain the consent of the Sultan in Constantinople, both to the idea itself, and for a pledge of economic support. For a number of reasons, their initial efforts were plagued with obstacles, and the plan was abandoned.

Some years later, after several incidents of Arab crime endangered Jewish life, another attempt to improve security was made by the Council. This time, the Damascus governor's senior officer favored the plan and resolved to see it through. Together with a Jewish advisor, an appropriate knoll was selected, the land was bought, plans were drafted, and a contractor was hired.

The fortress-inn was planned to be four stories high and very long. The ground floor, designed as an caravansary, included stables and shops. The middle floors were occupied by the Turkish garrison, and the top floor contained housing for the expanding Jewish population.

With the project only half finished, the builder suddenly

Ruins of Fortress

halted work due to lack of money. The Council sent an urgent request to the Sultan for more funds. Without his support, their labors to date would be for nought. The community of Safed nervously awaited a reply from Constantinople.

Months passed with no reply. Finally, a communique was received. The Sultan agreed to support the project. Relief and gratitude shone on everyone's face. The work continued to the project's completion.

At its dedication, the fortress's bronze plated doors swung open, ushering in a new era of peace in the Galilee.

The Power of the Rabbinic Court

Under the leadership of R' Yosef Karo the power of the rabbinic court grew immensely.

The most outstanding member of the rabbinical court was R' Moshe Metrani, known as the Mabit. He was a genius in his own right, as well as a disciple of R' Yaakov Berav. In 1525, at the tender age of twenty, he entered the rabbinate and was ordained by his mentor a decade later. He remained in Safed for sixty years, except for a brief period during which he lived in Jerusalem, and he wrote a commentary on the Rambam's *Mishna Torah* and a book on ethical conduct, the *Beis Elokim*.

The Mabit differed with R' Karo on a number of issues brought before the court. However, agreement would usually be reached after learned consultation between them.

In 1564, the leaders of the Ashkenazi congregations of Safed imposed a tax on Torah scholars. The court was swift to react by banning the taxation.

The voice of Safed's judicial court was heard throughout the world. "The *Beis Din* of Safed," wrote R' Karo, "is of the highest caliber, both quantitatively and qualitatively. Cases from around the world come before the court, and its decisions are accepted and implemented without dissent."

Sometime around 1570, the Radbaz, R' Dovid ben Zimra, settled in Safed and joined the rabbinical court. The city's dignitaries came out to welcome the venerable Radbaz, including R' Karo and his *Beis Din*. Close to a hundred years old, the Radbaz was a legendary figure, both as a halachic giant, and as one who had been privileged to be visited by Elijah the Prophet. He was the mentor of R' Bezalel Ashkenazi, compiler of the *Shita Mekubetzes*. After forty years as Chief Rabbi of Cairo, the Radbaz decided to spend his last years in the Holy Land.

R' Karo bestowed special honors upon him, placing the Radbaz before himself at every opportunity. By this time, the *Beis Din* of Safed was indisputably world famous.

Protecting Repentant Marranos

The tragedy of the Spanish Inquisition and the expulsion of hundreds of thousands of Jews in 1492 was still an open wound more than half a century later. Jews who had publicly denied their faith, known as Marranos, survived the auto-da-fe but suffered deep pangs of regret. Eventually some managed to leave Spain and, as repentant returnees, openly proclaimed their love of Judaism by attempting to return to a Torah lifestyle in more conducive surroundings.

One such group of repentant Marranos chose to settle on the island of Crete. The flourishing Jewish community of Candia looked askance at these 'renegade' Jews and mocked them, calling them apostates, and generally interfering with their freedom to live as Torah Jews.

When reports of this shameful behavior reached the rabbinical court of Safed in 1568, they reacted swiftly and decisively. A proclamation, signed by R' Yosef Karo, the Mabit, the Radbaz, and R' Yisrael di Koriel, was sent to the Candian community ordering them immediately to cease humiliating the repentant Marranos.

"...You have committed a grave sin by your actions," they ruled. "You have locked the door to repentant Jews. Rabbeinu Gershon decreed a ban against anyone who treated a *baal teshuva*, someone who has returned to his faith, in the manner in which you have been treating these repentant Marranos.

"Therefore, from this day forward be exceedingly cautious not to stumble and repeat what you have done.... If, Heaven forbid, anyone should transgress our decree, he should sit in a one-day long, self-imposed excommunication, orally confess his sin, and vow never to stumble in this matter again."[9]

The strongly worded proclamation was indeed effective. A new attitude developed toward the repentant Marranos, and in the course of time they were harmoniously integrated into the Candian community.

A Match for R' Yosef's Son

R' Yosef Karo was over eighty years old when he arranged the engagement of his oldest surviving son.

His first wife and their three children and had passed away in 1535 during a plague in Salonika. R' Yosef's second wife bore him a son, Shlomo, in 1555, while he was completing the *Shulchan Aruch*. After his second wife passed away, R' Yosef married the daughter of one of the sages of Jerusalem, who bore him a son whom he named Yehuda.

Shlomo was fifteen years old in 1570 when his father felt it was time for him to marry.

Safed was full of respectable families, fathered by wise Torah sages and nurtured by righteous women, some with eligible daughters. Who would not be eager to marry his daughter to the son of the revered author of the *Beis Yosef* and the *Shulchan Aruch*?

As R' Karo considered the potential matches, he learned of a new family who had recently arrived from Egypt with a daughter of the appropriate age. The girl's father was an eccentric Torah giant who sought to hide his greatness from the world. However, in the course of a few months in Safed, his name and deeds had spread rapidly from mouth to mouth. R' Yitzchak Luria's eminence lay in the realm of mysticism, where revelations were commonplace. His insights into the souls of the living and the dead captivated many. Most importantly, his saintly personality made him a vessel of light, humble at all times, a true Torah sage.

The Luria family was a paragon of righteousness, and R' Yosef felt confident that this was the right match for his son. Soon connections were made between the two Torah giants, and the city of Safed buzzed with the news of this exceptional *shidduch*.

The engagement party was held at the Luria home. R' Yosef returned home late that night and told his wife, who had been unable to attend, what had happened.

"My dear wife," he told her excitedly. "What can I tell you! What can I say of the inner dimensions of Torah and the commandments!

"I never would have imagined what fortune was in store for me tonight when I listened to such profound words of Torah as emanated from the mouth of the saintly R' Yitzchak Luria. It is absolutely unimaginable that a human being has such depth of perception. Even an angel does not know what he knows...."

R' Yosef stopped to catch his breath, his face glowing with excitement.

"Truly," he continued, his eyes aglow, "his soul must be descended from one of the early prophets, for even the greatest of Talmudic Sages could not attain that which he has.

"And yet, my beloved wife, on that very account I am greatly afraid for him. Our generation has fallen too low to absorb the radiance of his saintliness, and I fear that he might all too soon be taken away from us."[10]

The marriage was in 1570, with the whole city participating in the festivities.

Happy Parents

The wedding was memorable. Not only was it the joyous beginning of the formation of a new home in Israel, but in a less tangible way, it was almost as if the two aspects of our

SAFED: THE MYSTICAL CITY

One Torah, the hidden and the revealed, were united. R' Yosef Karo, blessed with secrets of the Torah which the *maggid* had revealed to him, was the paragon of the revealed Torah. He succeeded in uniting the Jewish people through a codified *halacha* in a way that had not been achieved since the time of Rambam. R' Yitzchak Luria, for his part, gave the esoteric, mystical side of Torah a new direction and dimension that it had not known since the Tanna, Rabbi Shimon bar Yochai.

Together, the two different, yet inseparable aspects of Torah were revealed to the world by these two Torah personages, and symbolized by the marriage of their children. Safed, in turn, reached a pinnacle of grandeur that would endear it forever to the heart of every Jew.

A cobblestone lane in Safed

The Golden Era

NOTES

1. Letter by R' Shlomo Alkabetz, cited in *Shelah HaKodesh, Shavuos*
2. R' Karo recorded many of their conversation. It was published posthumously under the title *Maggid MeYesharim*. The Chida (*Shem HaGedolim*, Part II, *Maggid*) feels that the amount R' Karo wrote down was only a fraction of the dialogues which actually transpired between them.
3. *Maggid MeYesharim*, p. 6
4. Introduction to *Beis Yosef*. The Chida writes (*Shem HaGedolim*, Part II, *Beis Yosef*) that prior to his writing the *Beis Yosef*, the Heavenly court debated who should author such an important commentary. Three candidates were found eligible, all great Torah scholars. R' Karo was selected because of his profound humility.
5. Cf. *Massaot Yerushalayim*, pp. 190-191, *Sifsei Tzaddikim*, p. 152. The verse is in Gen. 31:41.
6. *Shem HaGedolim*, Part I, p.93 (no. 111)
7. *Maggid MeYesharim*
8. Cited in *Anaf Etz Avos*, pp. 230-231
9. Cited in *HaBayis shel R' Yosef*, pp. 95-97
10. *Shivchei Ari*, based on interview of R' Karo's widow by R' Shlomo Shlimel, a young immigrant from Europe, in 1603.

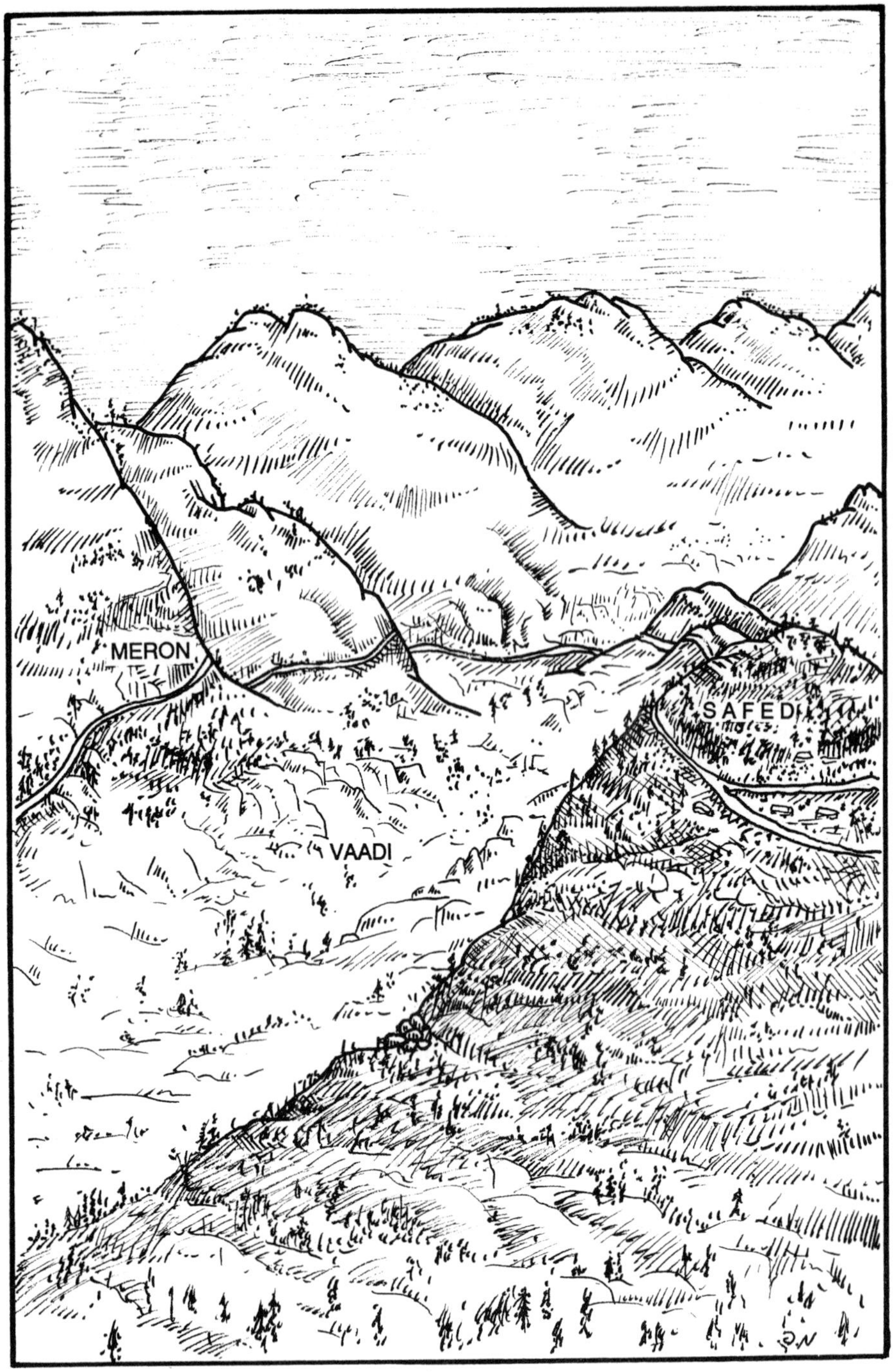
MERON
SAFED
VAADI

5
The Mystics of Safed

Before we can hope to achieve even a glimmer of understanding into the lives and achievements of the great mystics of Safed, we must pause and try to gain a general perspective of Kabbalah and Jewish mysticism. The concept of higher worlds which extend into infinity can cause even the greatest of minds to reel. The holy Names of God, each signifying one of the various emanations of His Oneness, reveal lofty secrets of Creation when arranged in various combinations. The *Zohar* and other mystical books cloak esoteric meanings under disguising layers of veiled wording and parables, and only the initiated are masters at uncovering their true significance. Kabbalah, in its deepest and richest sense, is utterly beyond our ken.

This being the case, we must admit that we cannot truly fathom the essence of the great mystics. Their souls were derived from lofty places and only for their sojourn on this planet were they garbed in mortal flesh. How can we even try to compare ourselves to them! Have not the Sages proclaimed, "If the righteous men of earlier times reached the level of angels, then we are at best but mortal men, and if they were mortals, then we are nothing more than donkeys."[1]

Therefore, before we turn to look at the study of Kabbalah, we must redefine our perceptions both of this sublime area of Torah and of its masters. These mystics, as we shall see, are in a class by themselves, and we cannot measure them by our standards, any more than we can judge ourselves by theirs. As pure vessels for hidden wisdom, they were capable of entering the innermost sanctums of Torah knowledge and were privileged to transmit its essence to the Jewish people.

In the following pages we will glimpse into their daily lives, record some of their remarkable deeds, and taste a small sample of their wisdom. In this way, we will begin to feel a relationship with them, and perhaps a new dimension of Safed will open up to us as we follow in the footsteps of the righteous.

The Light of R' Moshe Cordovero

It was a hot summer day in Tammuz, 1570, when the community of Safed was suddenly thrown into mourning. R' Moshe Cordovero, their beloved *dayan* and mystic was dead at the age of forty-eight.

The townspeople were stunned. R' Moshe had been like a pearl which gleamed in the hearts of all. The layman knew him as a most pious man who nevertheless always had time to greet him and share a simple word. Scholars stood in awe at his sharp command of Talmud and law. His yeshiva was known to be among the finest in Safed, and his students joyfully toiled at their learning day and night due to his inspiration.[2] Students of mysticism soon discovered his depth of soul, and flocked to him as a gazelle races to a flowing brook.

As the funeral procession was about to get underway, the head of the rabbinical court, R' Yosef Karo, solemnly stepped forward to eulogize R' Moshe. This was not a simple task for the eighty year old sage. R' Karo had known R' Moshe for thirty years, since the eighteen year old prodigy had sat and discussed halachic issues with him. R' Moshe, known by the acronym Ramak, had become his disciple, and together they had spent many hours studying the Talmud and its many commentaries. As the years passed, R' Moshe opened his own yeshiva, but he remained active on the rabbinic court and close to R' Karo.

"Today," R' Karo announced, "we have hidden away an Ark of the Torah."[3]

This was high praise indeed, of which only a very few were worthy.

Pillars of Fire

The cortege made its laborious was down the cobblestone lanes toward the cemetery on the mountain slopes below. The entire Jewish community attended: young and old, scholar and layman.

Suddenly, one of the mourners raised his voice, "Did anyone see something unusual just now?"

People looked at him questioningly, silently. Curiosity grew as he repeated his question.

On the left is the grave of R' Moshe Cordovero. The large tomb with a lantern on top is that of the Arizal.

Finally, a fifteen year old boy stepped forward and said he had seen something.

"What," pursued the questioner, who was none other than R' Yitzchak Luria, "did you see?"

"I saw two pillars of fire escorting the coffin."

"Yes," confirmed R' Luria. "That is true. We should know," he explained, turning to those around him, "that a pillar of fire is a divine sign of a man's greatness, and it is only sanctioned to one or two *tzaddikim* in a generation. We are privileged to have seen that R' Moshe Cordovero is ones."[4]

When the procession reached the grave site more eulogies were delivered. R' Yitzchak Luria was among the speakers.

"The verse states," began R' Luria, " 'If a man committed a sin punishable by death, and he is put to death, you shall hang him on a tree.' A sin implies a deficiency in the totality of the person. And when the Sages say that death is caused by sin, they were not referring to R' Moshe, *zatzal*, for there was no deficiency in R' Moshe to warrant his death.

"So how, then, can we explain his passing? This same verse alludes to an explanation. The words, 'you shall hang him on a tree,' may also be read to imply that we 'hang' the reason for his death on the primordial serpent who caused Adam to eat from the 'tree' of good and evil."[5]

That Wednesday afternoon, the 23rd of Tammuz, the mourners returned home saddened, but also intrigued by the Rav who saw the pillars of fire.

The Ari Comes to Safed

Only a few months before Ramak passed away, R' Yitzchak Luria had settled in Safed. Although born in Jerusalem thirty six years earlier, he had lived in Egypt since early childhood. His greatness had been recognized only by the Torah sages; laymen knew almost nothing about him. For seven years following his marriage, he isolated himself throughout the week in a house built over the Nile River, returning to his home only on the Sabbath. He then immersed himself in Talmudic studies for an additional seven years, learning with R' Bezalel Ashkenazi, compiler of the *Shita Mekubetzes*. Throughout this fourteen year period, R' Luria studied Torah constantly day and night. He attained a magnificent degree of purity of mind and spirit, and delved into untold depths of the secrets of the hidden Torah. Elijah the Prophet was his mentor, and most probably Elijah purified his disciple by sprinkling him with holy water mixed with ashes of the red heifer. R' Luria's greatness in hidden Torah was and remains unmatched.[6]

In spite of all this, when R' Luria moved with his family to Safed at the age of thirty-six, he was virtually unknown.

Ramak's System of Kabbalah

R' Yitzchak Luria attended the yeshiva of R' Moshe Cordovero, which specialized in the study of Kabbalah, the mystical aspects of Torah. R' Moshe lectured before a select group of scholars, always striving to unravel and systematize the coils of mystical thought.

A vacuum in the oral transmission of Kabbalah had begun after the death of the Ramban in the mid-thirteenth century. Until then, the hidden aspects of Torah had been conveyed verbally from generation to generation by saintly and learned men. They were careful to commit to writing no more than minimal key phrases and concepts, lest the uninitiated or uneducated misunderstand or misuse this most precious and powerful knowledge.

Significantly, there had never been any misunderstanding or controversy regarding the purity of that verbal transmission. Just as the ancient esoteric writings – the *Zohar*, *Sefer Yetzira*, *Sefer HaBahir* and others – were themselves free from all dispute and argumentation, so this later verbal transmission was untainted by doubt or error. The ancient works cloaked mystical concepts in parables and homilies on Scriptural verses. The keys to unravel the secrets were left in the hands of these pious *tzaddikim*.[7]

SAFED: THE MYSTICAL CITY

After the passing of the Ramban, when the chain of transmission of this mystical knowledge had nearly ceased, a new generation of mystical thinkers began to record their interpretations of the earlier sages and the cryptic references in the ancient works. Each of these sages devised his own system, and controversy arose among them. For two hundred years the mystical aspect of Torah was under constant threat from misconception and lack of structure.

The greatness of the Ramak lay in his ability to alleviate this controversy to a great degree. His exceptional qualities of wisdom, humility, and piety particularly fitted him for this task. His mentor, R' Shlomo Alkabetz, had initiated him into Kabbalah with a special sensitivity to the search for ultimate, divine truth.

R' Cordovero called his masterpiece on Kabbalah *Pardes Rimonim, The Orchard of Pomegranates*. He first scrupulously organized all existing material on Kabbalah, based on the earlier and most authoritative sources. Then he closely examined the post-Ramban writings and meticulously determined which ideas were compatible with genuine Kabbalah and which ones had unfortunately gone astray. Thus, the Ramak succeeded in systematizing Kabbalistic thought and greatly reducing error and dissension.

The Ramak also wrote the *Ohr Yakar, The Precious Light*, a colossal commentary to the *Zohar, Tikunnim* and *Sefer Yetzira*. This unique manuscript, tens of thousands of pages long, was a monumental work, but remained virtually unavailable for study until R' Menachem Azariya of Pino, Italy, a Kabbalist of the next generation, offered R' Moshe's widow a fortune for the right to make a copy of it.

Although R' Yitzchak Luria held variant opinions and favored a different system of Kabbalah, he deeply respected R' Moshe.

"R' Moshe," proclaimed R' Luria, "is the epitome of truth, and his Torah is genuine in the supernal worlds."[8]

The Perfection of Man

R' Cordovero spoke always of the perfection of man, and he himself strived with every breath to achieve it and to assist others in their own quest for perfection.

His book on the perfection of self, *Tomer Devorah*, was the first guideline on ethical behavior based on Kabbalistic concepts. It became a classic throughout the Jewish world.[9]

"It is proper for a man to emulate his Maker," opens *Tomer Devorah*. "In so doing one binds himself to the secret of the Divine configuration, its image and likeness.

"Should one emulate the attributes of his body alone, and not the outgrowth of his actions" – feel holy yet not abide by Torah Law – "he simply falsifies the supernal configuration, and of him it is said, 'What a beautiful image, but with such despicable actions!'

"It is a fact that the real supernal image and likeness are visible in one's actions. How will it help a man that he physically possesses a Divine image in the formation of his limbs, while his character traits do not reflect his Maker?

"Therefore, it is wise to emulate the lofty characteristics of the Crown. These are the thirteen attributes of Divine mercy alluded to in the secret of the verse (Micah 7:18-20), 'Who is like You, O God, who pardons iniquity, and forgives transgression... You shall cast all their sins into the depths of the sea... as You have sworn to our fathers from days of old.' "[10]

The Ramak stressed the importance of humility.

"For a man to emulate his Maker in the secret of the attribute of crownship, it is necessary that he internalize his physical actions, which are the essence of his interrelationship with others.

"Foremost is the all-encompassing trait of humility. Crownship is contingent on humility, because crownship dwells above all other Divine attributes, but never seeks to ascend or to exalt itself. Instead, crownship descends....

"So a man must feel a sense of shame should he want to stare upward in haughtiness. One should cast his gaze downward to undermine his ego as much as possible....

"Likewise, a man under no circumstances whatsoever, should deny spreading goodness to others. The sins and bad deeds of others should not enter his mind and prevent him from doing a good act. As we know, the Almighty constantly sustains everything in creation, and does not regard any creature with contempt (for if He did the world would instantly cease to exist). He supervises everything and gives mercifully to all. So, too, a person must give wholeheartedly to others and never despise anyone. Even the smallest creature should have importance in one's eyes, and he should think how he can benefit it....

"A person should integrate all the attributes slowly into his being. The most important attribute to acquire is humility. It is the key to all the others since humility is, spiritually speaking, located in the head and is related to the first attribute of crownship. Therefore, everything below crownship is bound up in it.

"The essence of humility is to have no self-importance whatsoever. One should think of himself as a nobody, as did Moses, the humblest man of all, when he said "What are we..." (Ex. 16:7), until one will appear in his own eyes as the most insignificant creature, despicable and loathsome.

"As one constantly toils to attain this trait, all the other traits will automatically rectify themselves within him."[11]

R' Cordovero next offered some practical steps whereby one could successfully enter the 'gates of humility.'

(1) Accustom oneself to flee from honor;

(2) Mentally picture one's own shame, how one's body is full of waste products;

(3) Constantly recall one's past sins, and one's desire to purify oneself of them. "What better way is there than to

accept embarrassment, which has no physical affliction and does not waste time that should be devoted to Torah," he wrote. "Rejoice, too, when you are insulted."[12]

Meditation

To emphasize the importance of deep meditation when praying, R' Cordovero made the following analogy:

> The prayers of one who utters his words without *kavanna*, deep meditative concentration, are not heeded by the King from within His palace. Instead, it is like a mortal king who hears the incoherent cries of one of his subjects standing outside the palace walls and making noise. The king can respond only indirectly. He will forbid the man entry to his palace, preferring to send one of his servants to attend to such a one's needs. Similarly, prayer without *kavanna* simply cannot ascend into the palace of the King of Kings. Prayer without *kavanna* lacks wings to fly through pure and holy air, and cannot break through the refined firmament and heavenly hosts.
>
> One who prays with *kavanna*, however, affixes wings to his prayers, and they will be guided heavenward. His prayers will ascend all the way to the palace of the King. There they will be received within the palace, and their ascending influence will be answered by the King Himself with a reciprocal descending influence, earthward from Heaven.[13]

The Author of *Reshis Chachmah*

Ramak's closest disciple was R' Eliyahu di Vidas, author of the *Reshis Chachmah, The Beginning of Wisdom*.

Reshis Chachmah, published around 1575, quickly became a standard work, praised for its novel approach to self-perfection. It was the first work to integrate Kabbalistic thought as an integral part of a systematic path to the full service of God. The author quoted extensively from the *Zohar* and other mystical writings, along with *Duties of the Heart* and *Menoras*

HaMeor. What *Tomer Devorah* described in microcosm, *Reshis Chachmah* achieved in macrocosm.[14]

The closeness between R' Eliyahu di Vidas and his mentor has best been expressed by the Arizal. The Arizal knew the secrets of the roots of men's souls, and he testified that R' Cordovero and R' di Vidas stemmed from two aspects of the same lofty soul.[15]

After his mentor died, R' Eliyahu studied Kabbalah under the saintly R' Yitzchak Luria until the latter's death two years later. He then moved to Hebron where he passed away around 1580.

Cover to the Amsterdam edition (1708) of Reshis Chachmah

Another disciple of the Ramak was R' Avraham Galante, the brother of R' Moshe Galante. R' Avraham's achievements in the world of Kabbalah may be measured by the status he received as one of the four greatest mystics of that era. The other three were his mentor, the Arizal, and R' Chaim Vital.[16]

Gerushin: Self-imposed Exile

The Ramak reintroduced *gerushin*, self-imposed exile, a unique means of coming closer to God.

"When one wanders from place to place in self-exile, with pure motives," he explains, "one creates a bond with the Divine Presence which is itself in exile. One should exclaim, 'What has become of the honor of heaven since the *Shechina* is in exile!' Thus, one should reduce as much as possible the content of his travel bag, and with a humble heart set forth into galus. While journeying, he should bind himself to Torah studies, and thus the *Shechina* will travel with him."[17]

The Ramak learned about *gerushin* from the author of the *Zohar*, Rabbi Shimon bar Yochai, and his disciples, who would frequently wander away from home to study Torah together. R' Cordovero walked with his disciples in the forests around Safed and taught Torah. Sometimes they spent only a few hours in the fields and valleys, and at other times they traveled for days on end. They were often known to travel to Meron where the Rashbi's tomb is located, and study the *Zohar* there.

The Ramak told of wandering with R' Shlomo Alkabetz, his brother-in-law, the sage who initiated him into the world of Kabbalah. He recorded many Torah interpretations which arose spontaneously while walking in the valleys and hills, although they were beyond their normal realm of comprehension. They traveled with the exalted feeling of having the *Shechina* hovering over them.[18]

R' Shlomo Alkabetz

R' Shlomo HaLevi Alkabetz was renowned for his wisdom and piety. His poetry was superlative. Most famous is his

SAFED: THE MYSTICAL CITY

Lecho Dodi, "Let's go forth, my beloved," which quickly became universally incorporated into the *Kabbalos Shabbos* prayers, where even today it is as beloved as ever.[19]

As time went by, his saintliness aroused jealousy among some of the gentiles. One day R' Shlomo was ambushed by an Arab farmer and murdered. The farmer buried him in his courtyard under a fig tree. The following day the tree blossomed and bore fruit – exceptionally large and delicious figs... yet it was out of season!

Soon news of the miraculous occurrence reached the ears of the Turkish provincial governor. He summoned the Arab farmer.

"What is your secret of outstanding horticulture?" he asked. "This is the first I've ever heard of a tree bearing fruit before its appointed time."

The farmer remained silent. He was afraid of the consequences should he confess.

The governor asked again, more firmly this time, more demanding of an explanation. The farmer remained mute. Finally, the governor ceased to tolerate the farmer's insolent silence, and ordered that he be tortured. The Arab finally confessed to killing R' Alkabetz, and admitted that from the day he had buried him the fig tree had begun to bear fruit.

Startled and impressed by this revelation, the governor commanded that the farmer be hung from that very fig tree as punishment for slaying a holy man of Israel.[20]

The World of Kabbalah

Through the piety, devotion, and saintliness of such men as these, the world of Kabbalah was now perched on the verge of its greatest reorientation in thousands of years. R' Moshe Cordovero and his disciples had set the background for the light of R' Yitzchak Luria to shine forth in all its splendor. Now, the Arizal could come out of his self-imposed hiding and reveal the ultimate system of Kabbalah.

NOTES

1. *Shabbos* 112b
2. Its location is unknown
3. *Anaf Etz Avos*, p. 147. It is unknown whether he spoke before the funeral procession began or later at the cemetery.
4. *Shem HaGedolim*, Part I, p. 101
5. Cf. *Anaf Etz Avos*, p. 149; the verse is found in Deut. 21:22
6. Chida, *Midbar Hadamos, Alef:* 26
7. This background discussion is based on *Shomer Emunim (HaKadmon)*, Part I:17
8. *Shomer Emunim*, I:17
9. First published in 1589, and reprinted numerous times
10. *Tomer Devorah*, ch. 1
11. *ibid.* ch. 2
12. *ibid.*
13. *Pardes Rimonim, Shaar HaKavanna*, ch. 1, p. 78b
14. It is divided into five gates: Fear, Love, Repentance, Holiness, and Humility; recently republished in an annotated, three volume set.
15. *Shaar HaGilgulim*, ch. 36, and *Sefer HaGilgulim*, ch. 65.
16. *Kiryat Arba*, intro., R' Avraham Azulai's commentary to the *Zohar*
17. *Tomer Devorah*, ch. 9, pp. 37-38
18. Cf. *Sifsei Tzaddikim*, p. 142
19. He was a contemporary of R' Yosef Karo in Adrianople, and was with him on the Shavuos night when the *Shechina* spoke with them. He also wrote the *Bris Levi*.
20. *Kav HaYashar*, ch. 86: 3-4

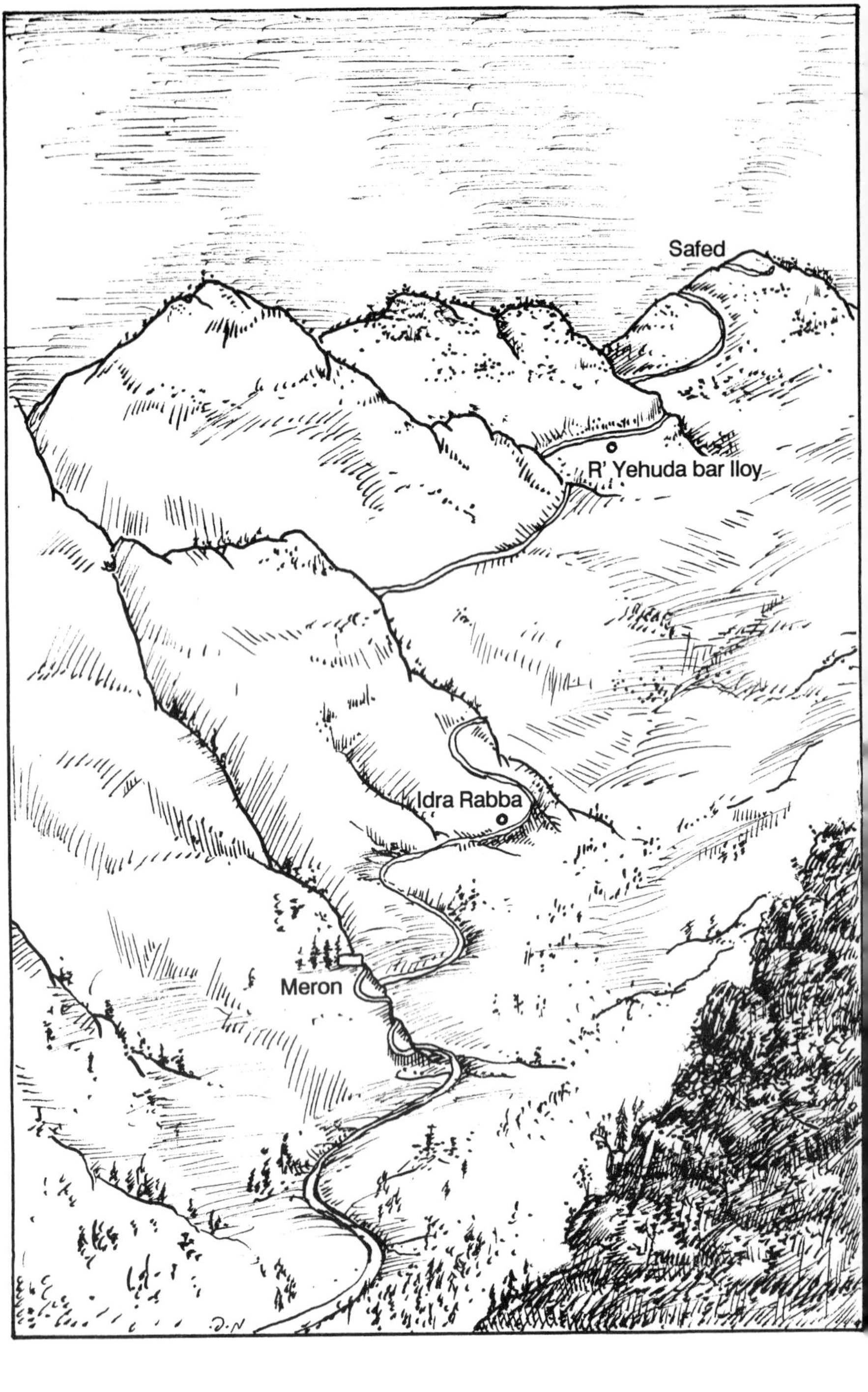
Safed
R' Yehuda bar Iloy
Idra Rabba
Meron

6
Arizal and His Disciples

The Arizal lived in Safed for six months before he revealed his greatness to his divinely predestined disciple, R' Chaim Vital. Their union as mentor and disciple/scribe would radically alter the dimensions of mystical thought. Although they had met in the early months of 1570 at R' Cordovero's yeshiva and discussed subjects in Kabbalah, R' Vital felt at the time that he already had a profound grasp of this lofty wisdom without the need of a new mentor. The Arizal knew otherwise, though he kept silent and waited.[1] R' Vital's tutelage under R' Moshe Cordovero ended with the latter's sudden death that summer.

R' Chaim Vital Finds a Master

One day R' Chaim went to the Arizal's house to discuss with him a certain section of the *Zohar*, pretending that he did not understand it. His real motivation, however, was to obtain a sense of exactly where the Arizal was holding – the level he had attained – in depth of soul and command of Kabbalah. R'

Yitzchak Luria, of course, immediately understood R' Chaim's purpose, and commenced to reveal lofty secrets hidden beneath every word of the *Zohar*. As R' Chaim listened, his head began to reel and his soul nearly left him.

R' Chaim then asked for an interpretation of a second portion from the *Zohar*. Immediately the Arizal opened before him a treasure chest of mysteries. R' Chaim was spellbound.

When R' Chaim asked for the meaning of a third *Zohar*, R' Luria said, "You have reached your limit. You are not yet prepared to receive more revelations than those which I have already made to you."

Stunned and brokenhearted, R' Vital left the Ari's house. As soon as he got home he put on sackcloth, rolled in the dust, wailed and cried out bitterly. He implored God, "Let me find favor in the eyes of R' Yitzchak Luria. Oh, Lord, let me be worthy that he should initiate me into the mysteries of Your Torah."

The following morning, R' Chaim returned to R' Luria's house. He prostrated himself before the Arizal, kissed his hand, and beseeched him, "For the sake of Heaven, I beg you. Do not send me away empty-handed. Don't forsake me. Don't separate me from you."

R' Yitzchak Luria gazed at him intently. "The dust in which you rolled yesterday benefited you greatly. That was the reason I told you I would not teach you. Now that you have implored God from the depths of your soul, your prayers have been accepted. From now on do not fear, I shall teach you everything, God willing."[1a]

The News Spreads

R' Luria cautioned his neophyte disciple not to disclose his greatness to anyone. His sole purpose in coming to Safed, he divulged, was to perfect R' Vital, who in turn would disseminate Kabbalah to the world.

The Arizal and His Disciples

After a while R' Moshe Alshich heard rumors that his disciple in Talmudic studies, R' Vital, was studying Kabbalah under a great master. Intrigued, he cornered R' Chaim one day and asked him if the report was true. When R' Chaim endeavored to evade his query, R' Alshich demanded a full confession. R' Vital divulged everything.[2]

He explained that R' Luria, who had studied with R' Bezalel Ashkenazi in Egypt, had a firm grasp of Talmud, *Mishna*, and *Aggada*, all of which he knew by heart. And in *Pardes HaTorah*, Kabbalah, he was unmatched. The mysteries of the *Zohar* were unveiled to him beyond human penetration. He understood the chirping of birds,[3] the rustling of leaves, and the speech of angels. He could tell everything that happened in a man's lifetime and what type of damage he had caused in the upper worlds. He knew the source of a man's soul, and his purpose in this world, as well as his

The wise men of Safed

earlier *gilgulim*, and thereby would prescribe guidelines to rectify one's soul.

Even while sleeping, he studied Torah with the souls of *tzaddikim* in *Gan Eden*. For every secret that was revealed to him, R' Luria confessed that he had cried out to the Lord until tears flowed down his cheeks and into his beard. All this R' Yitzchak Luria had earned by perfecting himself from his youth, little by little, until he reached the level of divine spirit and was privileged to study with Elijah the Prophet.[4]

In no time at all, the wondrous news spread throughout Safed and scholars and laymen alike came to R' Luria's house for advice. The Arizal selected ten outstanding scholars as his inner circle of disciples. Each one was God-fearing and thoroughly conversant in the *Zohar*. As time went by, the number grew to over thirty disciples.[5] Instead of opening a yeshiva in the city, R' Luria chose to teach in the forests outside of Safed and in the Galilean mountains. There he divulged the mysteries of creation and unraveled the parables of the *Zohar*. He also revealed the grave sites of many Talmudic Sages, whose marking stones had fallen into obscurity over the generations. Most of the time, however, the Arizal spent with R' Chaim Vital.

Many who knocked at R' Luria's door were not searching for a mentor in Kabbalah. They sought a spiritual guide and advisor, who recognized the depths of their soul, its past *gilgulim*, and its present strengths and weaknesses. They asked him to set forth a path of rectification, whereby they could serve the Almighty to their fullest. R' Luria refused no one.

R' Vital looked favorably on his master's role in the center of the public eye. Not only was R' Luria sought out by citizens of Safed, but soon people from distant places came to see him. Now, thought R' Chaim, many will benefit from my master. R' Luria, however, disagreed.

"You have caused us great harm," he confided to his disciple. "Because of all the people who come to me I do not have the necessary time to teach you properly – which is, after all, my real purpose here. But I can not refuse them entry for by nature I am very humble.

"However, if this continues," R' Luria pleaded, "it will endanger my life."

R' Vital dismissed the Ari's words. He could not imagine that wrong could possibly come from broad exposure of such a holy man to the world.[6]

Radbaz Reprimands R' Luria

Soon after R' Luria began teaching Kabbalah, Radbaz, R' Dovid ben Zimra, summoned him to his house. The Radbaz, who had moved to Safed from Egypt a few years earlier, had been concerned that R' Luria was propagating Kabbalah without having first attained the necessary prerequisites. So discreet was the Arizal in all his ways that even the leading rabbi of his home town was unaware of his greatness. They had both lived in Cairo for many years and the Radbaz, as Rav of the city, had known R' Luria to be a gifted scholar. R' Bezalel Ashkenazi, a leading student of the Radbaz, had been R' Luria's teacher in Talmud for seven years. Yet, the Radbaz knew nothing of his stature in Kabbalah.

"I order you not to teach Kabbalah publicly," the venerable Radbaz commanded.

The Arizal nodded.

Later, the Radbaz heard that R' Luria had resumed lecturing publicly, and again summoned him to his house. As R' Luria complied and began making his way through the alleys and lanes of Safed, Elijah appeared before the Radbaz and revealed to him the magnitude of the Arizal's soul and his real mission in Safed. By the time R' Yitzchak arrived, Radbaz's attitude had changed.

"Go forth, my son," said the revered Radbaz, "and disseminate Kabbalah. You are truly groomed for it!"[7]

Ramak Comes in a Dream

Shortly after R' Chaim Vital began studying the mystical system of Kabbalah based on the Arizal's teachings, he grew curious about the system propagated by his first mentor in Kabbalah, R' Moshe Cordovero. Although both systems were based on ten sefiros and four supernal worlds, on closer examination the teachings of the Arizal were of a completely different nature.[8]

One night R' Cordovero came to R' Chaim Vital in a dream. R' Chaim spoke with him and made him vow not to conceal anything from him.

"In the heavenly worlds where you reside," he asked R' Cordovero, "is Kabbalah taught according to your system or according to the system of R' Yitzchak Luria?"

"Both systems are true," he answered. "Nevertheless, my system is geared for novices in Kabbalah while the teachings of your master reach to the essential, inner dimensions of Kabbalah.

"Now that I dwell above in the world of souls," the Ramak confessed, "I study only according to R' Luria's system."[9]

Most of Ramak's writings were published by R' Menachem Azariya of Pino, Italy. Although he was their contemporary, he never traveled to Israel to meet the *mekubalim* (Kabbalists) of Safed. Yet he viewed the Ramak's writings as the most important breakthrough in centuries, and bought the original folios of *Pardes Rimonim*, the Ramak's system of Kabbalah. R' Menachem Azariya wrote a commentary to *Pardes Rimonim*, entitled *Pelach HaRimon, A Slice of the Pomegranate*. Later, when the teachings of the Arizal reached Europe, many took a new attitude towards R' Cordovero's writings.

"I have to admit," wrote R' Azariya, "that after I was privileged to study the smallest amount of the writings of the Arizal from folios sent to me by righteous men of *Eretz Yisrael*, I guarded myself against a sense of haughtiness when thinking of R' Cordovero. To the minds of many, the Ramak's writings were tainted and outdated by the Arizal's all encompassing approach. Yet these people are mistaken.

"It is public knowledge that I always quoted R' Cordovero

fondly whenever I delivered a sermon in synagogue. Furthermore, I can genuinely say that he was my mentor. Although I never met him, R' Cordovero's writings were a pathway into the world of mysticism. The Ramak opened the gates to understanding the basic foundations of Kabbalah no one can deny. Yet there lies beneath that foundation a deeper side which the Arizal has revealed.

"Therefore, I shall always regard the Ramak with awe, and shall honor his name in this world and the next."[10]

The Arizal Turns Away Great *Tzaddikim*

The city of Safed was ablaze with Torah. The Arizal had awakened people to yearn for self-perfection and to kindle the inner sparks of their divine soul. Disciples of the Ramak, already on the path, sat easily at R' Luria's feet. R' Eliyahu di Vidas and R' Avraham HaLevi were among them.

A number of other *tzaddikim* sought entry into the inner circle of R' Yitzchak Luria's group. They also desired to study his system of Kabbalah. However, the Arizal refused them.

One was R' Moshe Alshich, the teacher of R' Vital since the latter's youth. R' Alshich recognized the greatness of his disciple, and from the moment R' Chaim divulged to him who his master in Kabbalah was, he thirsted to study mysticism under the Arizal.[11]

One day R' Moshe visited R' Luria's house and broached the subject. R' Luria answered that his teachings were to be disseminated by R' Chaim Vital, not by himself. R' Alshich implored him to teach him Kabbalah directly.

"I have only come into this world," explained R' Luria, "to teach R' Chaim. Only he is capable of spreading Kabbalah."

"But how can I study under R' Chaim?" pleaded R' Alshich. "After being his Rav, I should become his student?!"

"Yes," answered R' Luria. "Were I not his mentor in Kabbalah, I would be privileged to be his student. I would be jealous of what he will accomplish in his lifetime."[12]

Another sage who sought to study Kabbalah with the

Arizal was R' Yosef Karo, the revered head of the rabbinical court of Safed and author of the *Shulchan Aruch*. Although R' Luria was not altogether in favor of it, they did study together a few times. R' Karo, a truly humble man, never let his forty year seniority interfere with his goal of acquiring ever greater Torah wisdom.

"Your soul," R' Luria finally disclosed to him, "is not capable of comprehending this wisdom through my system. You will succeed best by studying the teachings of R' Moshe Cordovero.

"As a sign that what I say is true," continued the Arizal, "as soon as I begin revealing mystical secrets you shall begin to doze off."

And so it happened. Every time R' Luria divulged a Kabbalistic thought, R' Karo's head nodded and his eyes closed.[13]

But There are Greater Men than Me

Something perplexed the twenty-eight year old disciple of the Arizal. Why had he, R' Chaim Vital, been singled out as the sole person in his generation to receive and disseminate the Kabbalistic system of R' Yitzchak Luria? There were outstanding scholars who towered above him and great *tzaddikim* living in Safed to whom he felt absolutely subservient. Yet, R' Luria agreed only to bequeath his divine wisdom to him. "Why?" R' Chaim asked his mentor.

"There is no connection between us," answered R' Luria. "In fact, you are inferior to all the great *tzaddikim* of Safed. Had I chosen one of them, I would indeed have been highly esteemed by the community.

"Therefore, let this be a sign to you. This was not based on a chance calculation of your worth. That you were chosen in heaven makes it clear to me that the greatness of your potential surpasses theirs.

"Furthermore," R' Luria revealed, "do not think that the greatness of a man is measured by how he is esteemed by his fellowman. If you could see the hidden blemishes that people have, you would be astonished.

"Know that I have weighed all of these *tzaddikim* on the scale of truth, and not one of them is as pure and suitable to receive my teachings as are you."[14]

Well of Miriam

R' Chaim Vital was born and raised in Safed. After his Bar Mitzvah, he studied Torah under R' Alshich.

One day R' Yosef Karo came to caution R' Alshich.

"Your student Chaim is a very remarkable young man. In the name of the *maggid* who comes to me, I request that you be exceptionally careful in supervising every stage of his development, particularly in Torah."[15]

R' Chaim quickly gained a deep understanding of Talmud and *halacha*, and was later ordained by R' Alshich.[16] He soon turned to the mystical side of Torah and avidly studied the *Zohar*. In due course of time, he was initiated into the select circle of R' Moshe Cordovero's disciples.

When he began studying with R' Luria in 1570, his mentor set out a two-fold program for him to constantly follow. The first directive was to restrain himself at all times from any bad character traits. He should never get angry, depressed, haughty, or impatient, nor should he even discuss trite matters. Instead, he should maintain a low-keyed image of himself, filled with inner joy and fear of sin. The second directive was an order of learning, a detailed curriculum. Every day he should study Bible, *Mishna*, Talmud and Kabbalah, especially the *Zohar*.[17]

R' Luria stressed that man's ability to ascend the spiritual ladder depends greatly on one's *kavanna*. Besides the necessary *kavanna* when fulfilling a commandment, the Arizal cautioned his disciple to be very meticulous when reciting blessings on food. All foods, he explained, possess *kelipos* which 'desire' to create a negative affect on the eater. Only by reciting the blessing with the proper *kavanna* can one annul that adverse affect, thus purifying one's body and cleansing one's thoughts.[18]

Next, R' Luria delineated a path of repentance for R' Chaim to follow to correct sins he had committed earlier in his life. For instance, as an atonement for cursing his parents when he was a child, R' Chaim was to fast for three consecutive days, meditating on certain holy names. The fast ended on Shavuos night.

"The whole night of Shavuos," wrote R' Vital, "I studied Kabbalah with R' Luria. He informed me that I had succeeded in atoning for that sin."[19]

Both the intensity of their learning and its tremendous quantity and complexity began to affect R' Vital. He realized that he could not retain all of the vast wisdom his mentor was bestowing on him.

The situation worsened. When R' Chaim confided his concern to his mentor, R' Luria simply told him not to worry. He had a plan. Together they went to Tiberias and walked through the town until they came to the fishing dock by the banks of the Kinneret (Sea of Galilee). There they rented a small boat and rowed southward into the lake in the direction of the Tomb of Rabbi Meir Baal HaNess. About halfway there, the Arizal slowed the boat and carefully scanned the water, searching for a certain spot, using an ancient synagogue on the shoreline as a landmark. When he reached the exact spot for which he had been searching, which appeared no different from the rest of the lake, he lowered a flask and filled it with sea water.

"Drink this!" he ordered his disciple as he handed him the flask. "It is water from the well of Miriam from which our forefathers drank in the wilderness. They were called the Generation of Knowledge, and once you have partaken of this water, it will cure you and you shall forget nothing I teach you."

So it came to pass. From that day R' Chaim Vital both

View of the Kinneret shoreline from Tiberias in the foreground to the Tomb of Rabbi Meir Baal HaNess. Somewhere in this area lies the Well of Miriam.

comprehended the wisdom of the Kabbalistic system of his mentor, and became its principal disseminator and author of the *Kisvei Ari*, the authoritative writings of the Arizal.[20]

Why the Arizal Never Wrote

The Arizal's disciples once asked him why he did not write down his own teachings.

"Were all seawater ink," R' Luria answered, "and all the vast firmament paper, and all stalks quills, it would still not be enough for me to write down my wisdom.

"When I start to reveal to you a single secret," he confessed, "I feel a downpour of divine influence like the gushing rapids of a waterfall. At first I am at a loss how to pass on even the smallest amount of this wisdom to you. Then I devise a way to channel it in such a manner that I can divulge to you a minute part of that secret.

"It would be dangerous," he cautioned, "were you to receive too much at one time – like a nursing infant who could strangle to death were his mother's milk to flow too quickly into his mouth."[21]

One summer afternoon a disciple of the Arizal, R' Avraham HaLevi, entered his master's house. It was Shabbos afternoon, and he found R' Luria napping on his bed. Upon looking more closely, R' Avraham noticed the Arizal's lips moving, murmuring. He was intrigued and bent over to listen. R' Luria awakened.

"What are you doing?" asked R' Luria.

"Please forgive me, "apologized his disciple. "I noticed your lips moving and wanted to hear what you were saying."

"Let me explain," the Arizal said as he sat up. "When I sleep my soul ascends heavenward via clearly defined pathways. Ministering angels meet me and escort my soul to the highest angel. He asks me which yeshiva in *Gan Eden* I desire to attend that day. I choose one and am immediately brought there. There in the yeshiva I study mysteries of the Torah that have never before been taught on earth."

R' Avraham HaLevi listened breathlessly.

"Please, could you tell me what you were learning now while you were napping?"

His mentor laughed. "I call the heavens and earth as witnesses that were I to expound for eighty consecutive years what I learned today, I would be unable to finish explaining the secrets that I heard about *parshas* Biliam. Believe me, this is no exaggeration."[22]

The Arizal Honors a Youngster

One day R' Luria was in his house discussing Torah with his chief disciple when a teenage boy knocked at the door.

"Come in."

The boy, Shemuel, opened the door and bashfully entered.

Immediately R' Luria stood up and greeted him. "*Baruch Habo!* Welcome." He shook the boy's hand and invited him to sit beside him.

"What can I do for you?" asked R' Luria politely.

As they spoke, R' Chaim Vital gaped in amazement. His mentor had never acted like this. Why did he stand up for a young local boy? And why did he give him a chair to sit on?

As soon as the boy left, R' Chaim's could no longer contain his curiosity. "I've never seen you act in this manner with anyone before. What is the reason for it, if I may ask?"

"By your life!" called out his mentor. "I never stood up for this youth, nor did I greet him with '*Baruch Habo.*'

"What really happened was this. I saw the soul of the *Tanna*, Rabbi Pinchas ben Yair, hovering over the boy's head — a merit this boy earned today by performing a commandment for which Rabbi Pinchas ben Yair was famous when he was alive. I stood up for the *Tanna*, and greeted him with '*Baruch Habo.*' "

R' Vital marveled at this revelation. What commandment, he wondered, had the boy done to deserve such a handsome reward? With permission, he dashed outside in search of the youth.

"Shemuel!" he called out, "Where are you? Wait!"

Soon he found him in one of the cobblestone lanes, and asked, "Tell me, Shemuel, what extra commandment did you do today?"

"The only thing I did out of the ordinary today," he answered hesitantly, "happened this morning while I was going to shul. I left my house at the crack of dawn and walked through the dark lanes in the direction of the synagogue. As I turned a corner, I suddenly heard crying from one of the windows. Why would adults be crying, I wondered?

"I decided to find out. When I entered the house, I saw a few pieces of furniture turned over and the family undressed, sobbing. A band of thieves had taken everything of value, they told me, even their very clothes.

"I gave the father my clothes and dashed home to put on my only other garments, my Sabbath clothes. As you see, I'm still wearing them."

Delighted, R' Vital kissed him and returned to his master.

"In the merit of this *mitzva*," grinned R' Luria, "Shemuel certainly deserved that the *tzaddik's* soul should envelop him. Rabbi Pinchas ben Yair had been famous precisely because he redeemed captives and helped forsaken people whenever he could."[23]

The Arizal's Method of Teaching

Most of the Arizal's teachings were delivered outside the walls of a yeshiva. He chose the uninhibited surroundings of the valleys and mountain slopes around Safed. Sometimes they walked to Meron and studied by the tomb of Rabbi Shimon Bar Yochai and his son. Along the way they would occasionally stop at the grave of Rabbi Yehuda bar Iloy, the Rabbi most often quoted in the *Mishna*.[24] Closer to Meron, they would study at the site of the *Idra Rabba*, the site at which the Rashbi had revealed many lofty secrets of the Torah.

At the *Idra*, R' Luria pointed to a rock and said, "Here sat Rabbi Elazar, and over there," he pointed to another rock, "is where Rabbi Abba sat when the Rashbi revealed mysteries of creation nearly fifteen hundred years ago."

The Arizal knew that on a mystical level his own disciples correlated to the disciples of Rabbi Shimon bar Yochai. Accordingly, he told R' Vital, who was to disseminate his teachings, to sit in the place of Rabbi Abba. Rabbi Abba was the scribe who wrote down the teachings of Rabbi Shimon bar Yochai. This is the famous *Book of Splendor,* the *Zohar*. The Arizal sat on the same rock upon which Rabbi Shimon bar Yochai had sat, and one by one, the Arizal directed each disciple to his particular spot. Then he began his discourse.[25]

The Idra *is near Meron*

R' Luria's method of teaching was unique. He would introduce a topic and then walk away without delving into it.

R' Chaim Vital would then continue the discourse in depth to the other disciples.[26]

Although this system proved successful, it once caused some friction. R' Yaakov Arazin was one of R' Luria's outstanding disciples, and he was some years older than R' Chaim, who was at the time thirty years old. One night R' Arazin went, distraught, to the Ari's house.

"I admit that I do not have a clear heart," he confessed to his master. "I am R' Chaim's senior. Why must I listen to him deliver the discourse? It does not seem fair."

R' Luria looked at him. "Of all my disciples only R' Chaim is able to understand my wisdom. I have come into this world only to teach him."[27]

The Goal

The goal of the Arizal's life and teachings was three-fold, yet all encompassing. First was to bring the light of Kabbalah into the world through a select number of disciples, with comradeship and peace being their common purpose. The next

SAFED: THE MYSTICAL CITY

Rabbi Yehuda bar Iloy's cave is located on the Safed-Meron road

step was to awaken Jewry from their slumber and backsliding in their fulfillment of the commandments by arousing them to complete repentance. Then, God willing, they could ignite the sparks of *Mashiach*, unite God's Name in the world, and hasten the final redemption.[28]

Unity among the disciples was paramount to R' Luria. It was imperative that there be a genuine spirit of love between them.

"Every morning before praying," he said, "be sure to consciously fulfill the commandment of 'Love your friend as yourself.'[29] Meditate with the aim of engendering within yourself a genuine love for every Jew that naturally matches your love for yourself. This *kavanna* will enable your prayers to ascend unhindered and produce the proper affect in heaven."

The Ari paid special attention to his disciples.

"It is essential that my *chaverim*, (my companions)," as he called his disciples, "fulfill this commandment to the extent that they bind themselves together, each one becoming a limb of a united body. Should one of them be suffering or a member of his family be ill, all the other *chaverim* should empathize with him and pray wholeheartedly for his recovery."[30]

Of course, this comradeship applied to their families as well. In the spring of 1572 a plague struck the Galilee. The surest means of protection was to remain inside as much as possible. In order not to disrupt their lives, R' Luria found a large courtyard with an appropriate number of rooms in which his disciples and their families could live together. The invisible menace of the plague stalked the Galilee for months. Finally, after five months a quarrel broke out between two wives on the eve of the Sabbath. Their husbands also became involved, and it worsened and worsened.[31]

Later, the disciples went to receive the Sabbath in the fields with their mentor, as was their custom. When they returned to shul for the evening service, R' Luria sat with a frown on his face. R' Vital became concerned, for he had never seen his mentor cloaked in mourning at this time. The Sabbath is a spiritual delight, where all grief and worry disappears.

"Our master," R' Vital asked after the evening service. "Why are you so sad?"

"When we went to receive the Sabbath," R' Luria spoke in a hushed voice, "I saw the angel of death. He quoted to me the verse in the Book of Samuel, 'Both you and your king shall be swept away.'[32] I realized that the decree of death had already been pronounced against me and some of my disciples.[33]

"The final stamp," he turned and looked at his disciples, "was sealed today when some of the chaverim quarreled. So long as there was *shalom* among you, there was no gateway through which the negative powers could enter and endanger us. But now it is too late."[34]

Shortly thereafter, on Friday, the first day of Av, R' Luria was stricken by the epidemic, and five days later he passed away. Five of his disciples also lost their lives in the plague.

Shabbos in Jerusalem!

Every Friday afternoon R' Luria and his disciples would pray the *Kabbalos Shabbos* service together. They would walk outside the city and sing praises of the Lord and receive their additional soul of Shabbos. According to tradition, the spot where they welcomed in the Sabbath Queen is where the two present-day Ari Ashkenazi synagogues are located, below Meginim Square. In those days the upper half of the Jewish Quarter consisted of open fields.

One Friday afternoon at dusk, in the midst of their singing, R' Luria suddenly raised his voice and asked, "My comrades, would you like to come with me now to Jerusalem and have the Sabbath there?"

Some immediately responded affirmatively. But others hesitated.

"We are willing, *Rabbeinu*," they answered, "but let us first tell our wives that we won't be here for the Sabbath."

The sparkle in the Arizal's eyes disappeared. He began to tremble. He hit his hands together and cried out, "Woe unto us that we lacked the merit to be redeemed! Had you all answered 'yes,' joyfully and without any second thoughts, the Jewish people would have been redeemed. Alas, it was precisely at that moment that the opportunity was opened to us. But as soon as you tarried, the moment passed and galus once more spread its veil over us."[35]

Power to Bring Everyone Back in Repentance

There was something that disquieted R' Luria in his last months, though it was not his eminent death. To him, death was merely a transition out of his body into a spiritual world of souls and continued Torah revelations. He was, however, deeply concerned over the state of world Jewry. This material world needed rectification, both in the study of Torah and in the deeds of man. Were he to live another five years, he said, he would be able to correct both of them and bring about the final redemption.[36]

The Arizal and His Disciples

With more time, the Arizal would have been able to elucidate the entire Torah according to the *Zohar*. The revelations of the inner meanings of the Bible, Mishna, Talmud, and Midrash would emit a new light of Torah into the world, and thereby cast away the shadows of doubt. The *Shechina*, wandering in exile for generations, would return home again. For example, *Pirkei Hechalos*, one of the most antiquated mystical writings known, had intentionally been printed with numerous errors in order to safeguard it from charlatans. If it could have been read without any flaws, the Arizal explained, anyone would be able to create worlds with it. This would bring about untold dangers if left in the wrong hands. He knew how to correct it, but refused. Man was not yet ready for it, he said.

R' Luria had within him the potential to stir world Jewry to repentance. When news reached a community that a great *tzaddik* lived in Safed whose purity and light of Torah allowed nothing of this world to be hidden from him, people would crowd together to hear more details. A tangible awe would fall upon them. R' Yitzchak Luria needed merely to glance at you to know every detail of you life, no matter how personal and private. He knew the transgressions you had made in a previous *gilgul*, an earlier lifetime, and for what particular purpose you had been brought into this world.

Many sinners were as afraid of him as of a wild lion. Yet, many others journeyed to him in order to learn how to rectify their souls. The Arizal gave each one a series of *kavannos* upon which to meditate, and guidelines on how to cleanse the stains which his sins had created, in order to rectify himself completely in his lifetime.[37]

Even dead souls begged the Arizal to rectify them. These were souls so soiled with sin that even the fires of purgatory were unable to cleanse them. They were therefore condemned to wander around the world in bondage. When the Arizal walked in the fields and forest, myriads of these tormented souls would appear before him.

"What are you doing here?" he asked them.

"We have heard of your saintliness," they answered, "and of your lofty nature. We have come to beg you to rectify us — for this is within your means."

"If the Lord will grant me life," answered the *tzaddik* unhesitatingly, "I will rectify you and all the world."[38]

This process of rectification would take time, which is perhaps the most precious commodity to a *tzaddik*. R' Yitzchak Luria needed more time to achieve this goal. But the generation was not found worthy, and the Arizal was taken away in his prime. He was only thirty-eight years old when he died.

Death of the Lion

On Friday, the first of Av, 1572, R' Luria was stricken with cholera, the plague that had been stalking the Galilee. Day by day, his condition worsened. By Tuesday, the fifth of Av, he was critically ill.

His disciples took turns around-the-clock keeping watch at the bedside. When R' Chaim Vital left that morning, he was replaced by R' Yitzchak HaKohen. R' Yitzchak had never seen his mentor look so pale and weak.

"Alas," he cried, aghast, "is this the hope we've been waiting for? As long as you were with us our sole aspiration was to see the spreading of goodness, Torah, wisdom, and greatness in the world."

"Had I found a single perfect *tzaddik* among you," said the Arizal, "I would not have had to pass away from this world prematurely."

As they spoke, R' Kohen noticed that his master began to glance about the room.

"Where is R' Chaim?" R' Luria asked nervously. "At a time like this, he left my side!"

The Arizal was perturbed. He knew his last breath was near, and he wanted to reveal a particular Torah secret to his foremost disciple before leaving the world.

"What should we do from now on?" asked R' Kohen.

"Tell the *chaverim* in my name, that as of today they are to stop studying Kabbalah. They might misunderstand it, thus falling into heresy and destroying themselves. Only R' Chaim may continue, in secrecy, to study this wisdom."

R' Kohen was stunned. "But is there no hope for us?" he pleaded.

"If you are all worthy of it," the Arizal said quietly, "I shall come and teach you again."

"How will you return when you are about to pass away from this world?"

"You do not understand the mysteries of creation. I shall return, whether it be through dreams, or in your waking state, or via other means."

Suddenly, the Arizal looked at his disciple.

"Quickly, get out of the house. You are a *kohen*, and my time has come. I'm not free to explain any more."

R' Kohen jumped up and ran outside. When he reached the threshold, he heard his mentor breath a deep sigh as his soul departed from him.[39]

Piecing the Broken Vessel Together

A veil of darkness covered the earth. The flow of Divine light for which the Arizal had served as transmitter in this world for two and a half years suddenly ceased. Revelation of Torah of this magnitude would now remain locked in the heavenly abodes for lack of a pure vessel to receive and disseminate it.

R' Chaim Vital's mission was to piece the fragments together into a cohesive system of Kabbalah. First he collected whatever the other disciples had heard from their master and then made them sign a declaration of secrecy. R' Vital's writings, called *Kisvei Ari*, were entitled *Shemona Shearim*, the *Eight Gates of Mystical Wisdom*. His son Shemuel took a leading role in their publication.[40]

Cover to Shaar HaKavannos, *one of the* Eight Gates of Mystical Wisdom *by R' Chaim Vital*

R' Chaim spent the next forty-seven years of his life refining his mentor's teachings. He became a Rav in Damascus, wrote prolifically, and encouraged his fellow Jews to repent. Best known among his other writings are *Shaarei Kedusha, The*

Gates of Holiness, a work of ethics, and homilies on the weekly portion, *Etz HaDaas Tov*.

Thirty years after the passing of the Arizal, worldwide Jewry's yearning for access to the Kabbalistic system of the Ari was still very intense. A close-knit circle studied the available, handcopied writings. It was forbidden for the writings to be printed and sold like other books. Kabbalah was a sacred treasure chest, and access to it was confined to select *tzaddikim*.

Burning Embers

In 1607, R' Shlomo Shomiel, a Jew of European stock who immigrated to Safed around the turn of the century, wrote that R' Vital and other *tzaddikim* were still awaiting daily the fulfillment of the Arizal's last words that he would return and teach them. R' Vital admitted that during the first twenty years after his mentor's death, R' Luria visited him in his dreams every night and taught him Torah.[41]

Safed had lost the last of these blazing torchbearers by the beginning of the seventeenth century. Yet the embers were still hot. Every morning after the prayer service, congregants would remain to study. Some chose *Chumash*, others *Mishna* or Talmud, and others the *Zohar*.

Thursday morning after praying, the men would congregate in one of the large synagogues to recite *selichos*, a special prayer of supplication. Before beginning, R' Moshe Galante, one of the leaders of the community, would stand up on the podium and speak. His charismatic personality, coupled with his brilliant Torah knowledge, aroused his listeners to *teshuva*. During the *selichos* many would cry over the destruction of the Temple, the exile of the *Shechina*, with an intense yearning for the redemption.[42]

Although the torchbearers had passed away, the living imbued their lives with their Torah and saintly deeds. Even when great *tzaddikim* like R' Vital, R' Alshich, and R' Eliyahu di Vidas moved to other cities, Safed continued to attract new inhabitants, and grew in size.

By the turn of the seventeenth century, writings from Safed were illuminating the world. The *Shulchan Aruch* was now the international code of Jewish Law. The Kabbalistic systems of the Ramak and the Arizal lifted up a new generation of seekers after Torah wisdom, and embellished their lives with a fuller sense of dedication to serving God.

The Arizal's House and Synagogue

The Arizal's house was located near the Ari Sephardi synagogue at the bottom of the Jewish Quarter. Long after his passing, the sanctity of his house was still respected by everyone. Once, however, generations later, someone started to build a new house on the ruins of the Arizal's house. An old man warned him, "How dare you profane the place which was sanctified with such holiness. Stop or you will surely face the consequences!"

The man brushed aside the old man's words and continued building. On the day of the inauguration of his new house, a fire broke out and destroyed everything, killing several people. Ever since that tragedy, the site has remained an undeveloped mound.[43]

The Arizal Sephardi Synagogue was located, as we have mentioned, at the bottom of the Jewish Quarter. Sometime before the first earthquake of 1759, the beadle of the shul was R' Benyomin. He had been ill for months. One night he dreamt that he entered the synagogue and walked over to the Holy Ark to light the *ner tamid* candle. He was surprised to find someone sitting there quietly, draped in a *tallis*.

"Who are you?" he inquired.

"I am Yitzchak Luria."

Recalling that he was ill, R' Benyomin asked the Arizal to pray for his recovery.

"Why haven't you fixed the roof?" interrupted R' Luria.

"There are some leaks and rain comes in."

"I've been sick for sometime now," the beadle answered apologetically.

The Ari Sephardi Synagogue

"I have come to warn you," the *tzaddik* spoke sternly. "I want no one to sit on the place where I am now sitting. This was the spot where I sat when I was alive, and it has holiness."

"Yes, yes, of course, but please, I beg of you to pray for me..."

"Give me your hand," said the Arizal.

R' Benyomin gave him his hand and immediately awoke. He was completely cured.

One of the first things he did the following day was to have a huge stone rolled into the shul and cemented to the spot where the Arizal had sat. He then ordered the roof to be repaired.[44]

Today, after two major earthquakes, the stone is no longer in the rebuilt synagogue, and the precise spot is unknown.

On the left side as one enters the main shul is a small room with a very low entrance. Tradition says that it was in that enclave Elijah the Prophet appeared to the Arizal and revealed mysteries of the Torah to him.

107

SAFED: THE MYSTICAL CITY

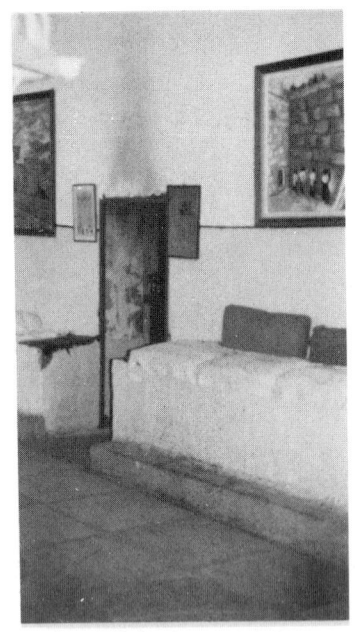

Left: *Inside the Ari Sephardi Synagogue is a small, low ceiling, chamber where Elijah appeared to the Arizal.* Right: *The Arizal* mikve

The Arizal *Mikve*

Nestled in the crevice between two mountain slopes is the Ari *mikve*, a cold water immersion pool. It is located below the Jewish Quarter, just above the cemetery. Natural spring waters come out from a rock wall and flow several feet along a stone canal into the immersion pool. The pool, which is barely large enough for two men at one time, is carved out of solid stone.

A large structure has been built over the *mikve*, extending forty feet to the west with a low entrance way. It dates back hundreds of years. Whether or not it stood in the time of the Arizal is unknown.

The Arizal was accustomed to immerse in this pool every morning before praying, summer and winter. During his last immersion something extraordinary occurred.

The Arizal mikve is fed with a continuous flow of spring water which issues out of the mountainside (arrow), and flows along a carved stone slab several feet before spilling into the immersion pool.

"My master commanded," wrote R' Chaim Vital, "that after he passed away his body should be immersed one last time before burial. The day he passed away we carried his body to the *mikve*. As we were about to immerse him, we said, 'Master! Please forgive us,' and then we started to slip his body into the water. To our amazement, he bent over and immersed himself!"[45]

Light of *Mashiach*

The revelations of mysteries of the Torah from the mouth of the holy Arizal were intended to usher in the era of *Mashiach*. That is, however, they were to do so providing that world Jewry was found worthy. The time passed and the God-given gift to mankind was snatched away. Yet, the Kabbalah of the Arizal has remained as an inheritance to His children. It has continued to increase Divine light in the world. And for the great *mekubalim*, the Jewish mystics of each new genera-

SAFED: THE MYSTICAL CITY

tion, it continues to contain the keys to the treasure chest of the secrets of the Torah, and the renewed hope of the coming of *Mashiach*, soon, in our days.

Likewise, the stones of Safed were imbued with a glow of holiness sparked by the presence of the saintly Arizal. The Divine Presence surrounded him at every moment, and like a pillar of fire it impregnated the ground on which he tread and the synagogues in which he prayed and learned. Who today doesn't sense the connection of Safed with true Jewish mysticism? Who doesn't feel a particular spiritual freedom when wandering about Safed? This enchantment we have today is in part kindled by the lingering vestiges of the light of the *Shechina* which hovered constantly around the pious Arizal. And if we recount some of his deeds and study some of his wisdom, we will surely be able to tap into even more of the essence of Safed.

NOTES

1. *Shivchei Ari*, pp. 25b-26b. *Toldos Yitzchak*, ch. 15, writes that their first meeting was three months after Arizal came to Safed. Elijah the Prophet had ordered the Arizal to leave Cairo and settle in Safed with the intention to teach R' Chaim Vital.

1a. *ibid.*

2. *Shivchei R' Chaim Vital*, pp. 12b-13a

3. This is the secret of the verse, "the birds of the sky will carry the voice, and the sound of their wings shall tell a matter" (Eccl. 10:20). (*Shivchei Ari*, p. 11a)

4. *Toldos Yitzchak*, ch. 6, and *Shivchei Ari*, pp. 10b-11a

5. *Shaar HaGilgulim*, p. 69a

6. *Shivchei R' Chaim Vital*, pp. 12b-13a

7. *Shem HaGedolim*, Part I, p. 73 (no. 332); some say the Ari was student of the Radbaz (ibid.)

8. Cf. *Kitavim Chadashim of R' Vital, perush* to *Bris Minucha*, pp. 2-4. R' Safrin, in his introduction, cites a number of places where Arizal quotes Ramak.

9. *Shivchei R' Chaim Vital*, p. 19b

10. Introduction to *Pelach HaRimon*. Cf. *Anaf Etz Avos*, p. 126, where he quotes a letter of a contemporary, written in 1582, which says, "This wisdom propagated by the Arizal is as different from other systems of Kabbalah as day is from night."

The Arizal and His Disciples

11. Cf. *Shaar Hagilgulim*, p. 69 a-b. R' Alshich was among the second group of ten disciples of the Arizal. Chida brings that the Arizal told R' Alshich that his purpose in this gilgul was only to perfect the level of *drash*. The higher level of sod, the secrets of the Torah, the Arizal told him, he had already perfected in an earlier *gilgul*.
12. *Shivchei R' Chaim Vital*, p. 3b
13. *Shivchei Ari*, p. 37b
14. *Shivchei R' Chaim Vital*, p. 12a; R' Chaim Vital was a *gilgul* of Rabbi Akiva. His soul descended directly from Cain.
15. *Shivchei Ari*
16. 20 Elul, 1590
17. *Shaar HaGilgulim*, p. 63b
18. *ibid*. p. 51b
19. *Shivchei R' Chaim Vital*, p. 28a-b. For other steps in his *teshuva*, see *Shaar HaGilgulim*, p. 51a
20. *Pri Etz Chaim*, Gate of Learning, p. 361
21. *Shivchei Ari*, pp. 6b-7a. Cf. ibid. 32b. The Arizal wrote a commentary to *Zevachim* in the style of *Shita Mekubetzes*. The only known copy was destroyed in a fire in Izmir, Turkey. (*Shem Hagedolim*). He composed Shabbos songs, and some prayers for the three meals of Shabbos.
22. *Shivchei Ari*, pp. 5b-6a. R' Avraham Halevi studied under both the Ramak and the Arizal. The Arizal taught that a nap on Shabbos benefits one's soul, while napping during the week is detrimental (ibid.). Cf. *Shem Hagedolim*, Part I, p. 73 (no. 332), where he cites *Midrash Shemuel* on the verse, "He and Samuel went and dwelt in Nayot" (I Sam. 19:18). That night, says the Midrash, David learned more than the sharpest student could learn in a hundred years.
23. *Shivchei Ari*, pp. 14b-15b. Cf. *Toldos Yitzchak*, no. 30, for similar story of the soul of Beniyahu ben Yehoyada hovering over R' Chaim Vital. The youngster was R' Shemuel Azida, author of *Midrash Shemuel* on *Pirkei Avos*. *Chazal* hint to the connection between doing a special commandment and the soul of a *tzaddik*: "One who endeavors to purify himself is assisted from heaven" (*Shabbos* 104a). As soon as one resolves to do an important *mitzvah*, the soul of a *tzaddik* who excelled at that same percept in his lifetime binds himself to that person and helps him to fulfill the *mitzvah*. *(Shivchei Ari,* pp. 14b-15a)
24. Cf. *ibid*. 29a, for story that occurred when the Ari and R' Moshe Galante were at Rabbi Yehuda's grave
25. *ibid*. p. 26, and *Shivchei R' Chaim Vital*, p. 28a
26. *Tur B'rekas,* introduction
27. *Shivchei R' Chaim Vital*, p. 29a. R' Vital asked his mentor the same type of question. For the Arizal's Kabbalistic answer, see *Shaar HaGilgulim*, bottom of p. 66b
28. R' Luria was *Mashiach ben Yosef (Shivchei Ari* p. 9b)

29. Lev. 19:18
30. *Shaar HaGilgulim*, p. 53a
31. *Shivchei Ari*, p. 34a-b
32. I Sam. 12:25
33. Cf. *Shivchei Ari*, p. 33b, where Ari informs R' Vital of the heavenly decree of his own death within a year for revealing to his foremost disciple mysteries of Torah which were not yet permitted to be taught. This, too, was the cause of the Ari's son's premature death.
34. The instigator of the quarrel was expelled from the group, not so much for the fit of anger, but rather because the root of his soul was tainted. The anger brought out his negative side and shifted the balance of his deeds against him. (Cf. *Shaar HaGilgulim*, p. 69b)
35. *Shivchei Ari*, pp. 9b-10a
36. *ibid*. pp. 30b-31a
37. *ibid*.
38. *ibid*.
39. *Shivchei R' Chaim Vital*, pp. 25b-26a, and *Shaar HaGilgulim*, p. 71a-b
40. The story of how some of his writings were copied while he was ill, and how others were taken from his grave by righteous men, is discussed in *Shivchei Ari*, p. 35a.
41. *Shivchei Ari*, p. 38b
42. ibid. pp. 16b-17b
43. *Chibas Yerushalayim*, p. 75. In 1765, the author of *Ahavas Tziyon* writes that a wayfarer's lodging for the poor was built on the site. The ground floor was unoccupied – in keeping with its holiness – and a second floor housed the wayfarers (ibid.). Today, Kiryas Breslav acquired the surrounding land for a housing development project. When told that Ari's house was located there, they agreed not to touch the site. Thus, even today, the mound remains as testimony to the Arizal's saintliness.
44. *Chibas Yerushalayim*, p. 72
45. *Anaf Etz Avos*, p. 78

Arizal's grave

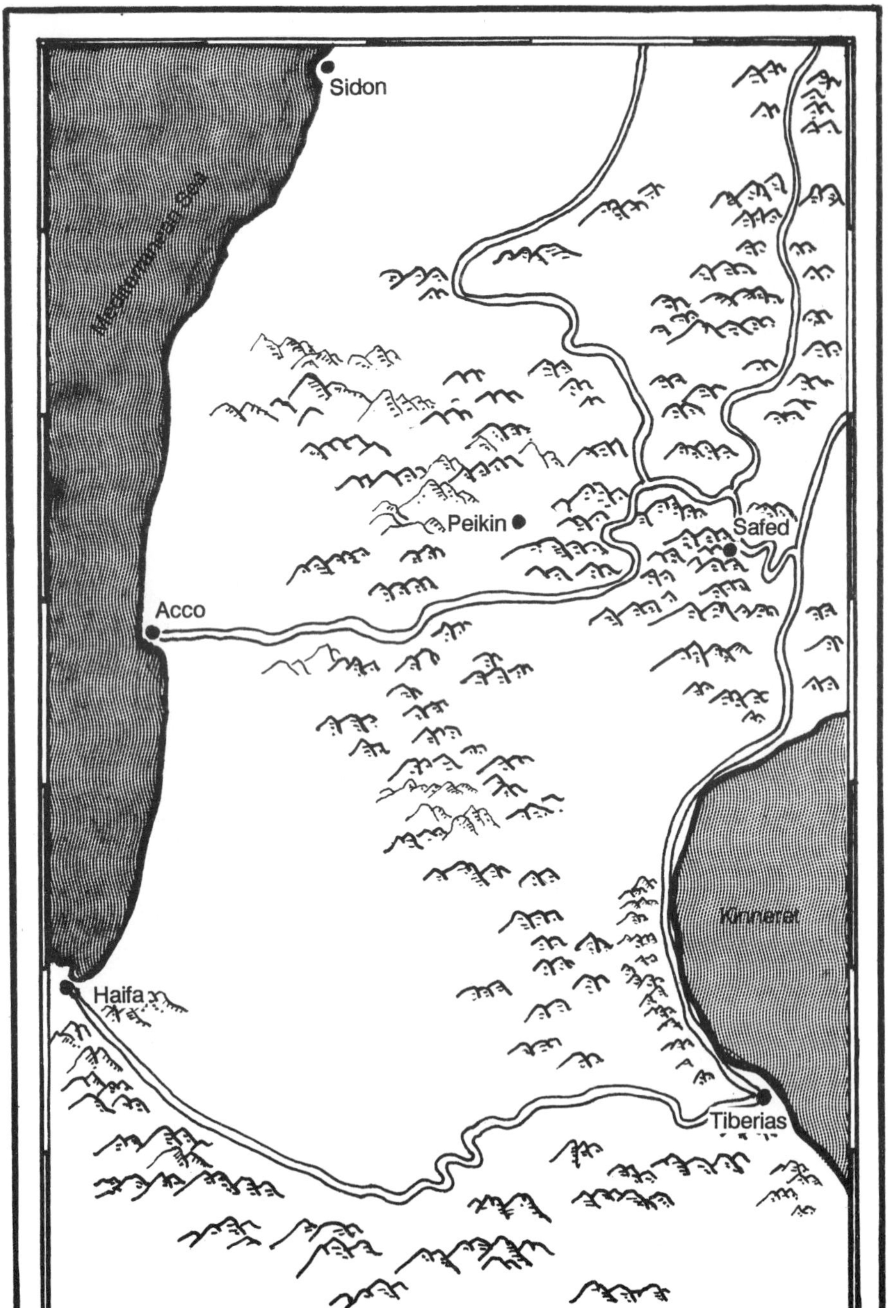
Sidon
Mediterranean Sea
Peikin
Safed
Acco
Kinneret
Haifa
Tiberias

7
Influx of Chassidim

By the end of the sixteenth century, Safed had reached the pinnacle of her grandeur. With the passing of the great luminaries of both Kabbalah and the revealed Torah, Safed gloried in the memory of her golden era like a widow recalling her most precious moments with her departed husband. She still retained her status as the largest Jewish community in Israel, with more than six thousand Jewish residents. Yet a spiritual vacuum had set in. Kabbalah, for instance, was studied only behind closed doors, with the writings of R' Chaim Vital and the Ramak as the only guide. No longer would an Arizal or a R' Cordovero reveal to them new pathways in mysticism. True to the Kabbalists' traditional concern that these powerful truths not fall into the hands of those unprepared or unworthy to possess them, these writings were kept hidden under a cloak of secrecy, and only much later did they appear in print.[1]

SAFED: THE MYSTICAL CITY

Change in the Ruling Power

By the 1620's, a hundred years after the Ottoman Empire had conquered the Middle East and ushered in an era of relative peace, a wave of insecurity and danger engulfed the Jews. One story from among many will suffice to show the heroism of Jews in the clutches of a ruthless tyrant.

R' Yeshaya Horowitz immigrated to *Eretz Yisrael* in 1622, and accepted the post as Chief Rabbi of Jerusalem. Three years later a despot named Even Paruch illegally bought the right to rule Jerusalem from the provincial governor in Damascus. With a legion of three hundred soldiers, he stormed the Holy City and loosed a reign of terror. Most of his cruelty was directed at Jews. For example, one day in Elul he and his henchmen suddenly burst into the two central synagogues, arrested fifteen leading rabbis, and threw them into a dungeon. R' Horowitz was among them. Only with great difficulty and considerable sacrifice did the community succeed in ransoming them for an exorbitant sum.

The city gates were kept closed and barred day and night. The one-eyed Even Paruch wanted no one to escape from the city and to tell the sultan in Constantinople of his criminal deeds. He squandered the money of his Jewish subjects and forced them to borrow from wealthy Arabs at high interest rates. He beat them mercilessly.

Clearly, this unendurable situation had to be terminated. R' Horowitz and a group of other rabbis devised a plan. They managed to escape the city by lowering themselves by rope over the wall under the veil of night. They raced for their lives far to the north and took refuge with the Jewish community of Safed.

Once news of Even Paruch's excesses reached the Sultan, he commanded the provincial governor to expel the tyrant. The governor, however, was afraid to go to war. Finally, a message was dispatched threatening Even Paruch with armed intervention if he did not abandon Jerusalem peacefully, and of his own accord.

Influx of Chassidim

The tyrant, of course, was not daunted by the communique from Damascus. However, he did have a disquieting dream. He dreamt that an old man of good stature approached him and started to choke him to death.

"Who are you?" the despot cried out.

"I am King David! You shall die a bloody death if you do not leave this city."

Even Paruch awoke from his dream very distressed indeed. Not long afterwards, in Kislev, 1627, he left the Holy City.[2]

R' Horowitz's stay in Safed was temporary. Although the community welcomed him with open arms, he decided to settle in Tiberias, at that time an undeveloped town with an insignificant Jewish population. He passed away there in Nisan, 1630.

A few years later, in 1632, Sultan Amrad declared war on Persia. In preparation for the upcoming military campaign, he wanted to base his army in Lebanon and Israel for the winter. The Sultan dispatched a communique to every major city in his commonwealth demanding that the citizens feed and shelter his legions for a period of three months. In the spring the troops would set out eastward to begin their campaign. Safed was among the cities selected as a base camp.

Despair gripped the Jewish community of Safed. For more than a year there had been a crop failure in the Galilee and Judah, and the price of food was exorbitant. The situation had reached near-famine proportions. How could they possibly feed thousands of soldiers when there was not even enough bread for themselves? Alarm and dismay gripped the heart of every Jew.

The regent in Acco was sympathetic to the needs of his subjects in the Galilee, especially the Jews. His reaction to the royal edict was daring and immediate.

"Why are you sending troops to Safed and Sidon at a time like this?" he wrote Sultan Amrad. "It could prove fatal for both your soldiers and my citizens. I warn you, therefore," he ended, "not to come here. No matter how many infantry are sent, not one will return alive!"

To back up his word, the regent amassed an emergency corps of forty thousand men and stationed them at key positions on all the major roads. Several thousand were sent to protect Safed.

"No one is to take anything from the Jews," he commanded his men. "Nor are you to sleep in their homes or in any of their Houses of Worship."

When the commander-in-chief in Damascus heard of the regent's vow to protect his subjects and his readiness to back his word, he acquiesced and retained his army in Syria for the winter.[3]

Decline of Safed

On a superficial level, one could not distinguish between the golden era of Safed and the decades immediately following. Safed bustled with activity, commerce, yeshivos, and spiritual leaders. With a Jewish population of more than six thousand inhabitants, Safed was larger than Jerusalem. Yet to the sensitive observer something intangible was lacking. Although there were capable scholars in the city, great luminaries were absent. The spiritual crown, as it were, which had adorned Safed for more than a jubilee of years, had returned to its traditional abode on Mount Zion.

More and more Torah scholars of the seventeenth century chose to settle in Jerusalem. The Chief Rabbi of the Holy City during the last half of the seventeenth century was R' Moshe Galante the Second.[4] Known as *Rav HaMagen*, his genius and sterling qualities appealed to the younger generation of Torah scholars. His yeshiva was one of the largest in the Land, and produced a number of leaders and Torah scholars. After his death in 1689, his chief disciple, known as the Pri Chadash, became Rosh Yeshiva, and R' Moshe Chaviv was installed as Chief Rabbi of the city.

Influx of Chassidim

The Rav of Safed at that time was R' Avraham Galante, the uncle of *Rav HaMagen*. He labored assiduously for the needs of the community, and his personal integrity was beyond reproach. Whenever there was a doubt as to whether it was permitted to use community funds for a specific purpose, he chose instead to pay from his own pocket.

As was often the case, the financial needs of the Jewish community exceeded their resources. Having recently returned from a fund-raising campaign for the city in Turkey, R' Galante borrowed money from Jews and gentiles alike for communal needs. He relied on the promised donations from the Diaspora to repay the loans. During the next three years an increasing solemnity fell upon the Rav of Safed when only a fraction of the promised monies had trickled in. This minor sum could not begin to offset the astronomical debts which had accumulated.

Communal leaders were in an uproar, and some demanded his immediate resignation. R' Galante stood his ground. Under mounting pressure, the Rav of Safed agreed to go before an arbitration board of three rabbis in Hebron. After a thorough investigation, the board unanimously absolved him of all responsibility. Furthermore, they declared that the personal money which R' Galante had lent for communal projects was to be repaid to him.

Despite this vindication, R' Avraham Galante resigned shortly following this incident, and moved to Damascus where he died in 1696.[5]

A New Generation of Kabbalists

R' Chaim Vital survived his master, the Arizal, by some forty years. For reasons that remain obscure, he left Safed and spent the greater part of his life in Damascus. There he continued to refine the Kabbalistic system of his mentor. He also lectured and penned treatises on a wide array of subjects to stir his fellow man to repentance, such as his masterpiece, *The Gates of Holiness*.

SAFED: THE MYSTICAL CITY

R' Vital taught Kabbalah to a select circle of disciples. The most prominent were his son R' Shemuel Vital, and R' Chaim Kohen. His son was the mentor of a young genius and doctor, R' Yaakov Tzemach. Assembling the authorized writings of R' Chaim Vital became the lifelong task of these two men.

R' Yaakov Tzemach, who immigrated from Portugal in the early 1600's, settled in Safed, where he studied Talmud and Jewish law for six years. When he then turned to the study of Kabbalah, he was unable to find a mentor in Safed, and was compelled to move to Damascus, and later to Jerusalem. After eighteen years of intense study, R' Yaakov Tzemach became the leading Kabbalist of the seventeenth century and the greatest exponent of the writings of R' Chaim Vital. He organized and published the collected works of R' Vital, and made the writings of the Arizal accessible to initiated students of Kabbalah.[6]

"The reason that this wisdom was revealed," wrote R' Tzemach, "in a generation as low as ours, was to provide a shelter within which we could harbor and cleave wholeheartedly to God. The earlier generations were protected from evil forces by their righteousness, but today we are too far away from our supernal source. Only by studying this exceedingly deep wisdom can we be safeguarded."[7]

Refugees from the *Churbah*

In 1721, a tragedy befell the Jews of Jerusalem which caused the Ashkenazi community to flee for their lives. Many of these refugees resettled in Safed.

The story begins in 1690 when the hundred-member group immigrated to *Eretz Yisrael* and settled in Jerusalem. Tragically, their leader, R' Yehuda HaChassid, died three days after their arrival. Because they had a weak economic base to begin with, they became entangled in an endless cycle of debt to the wealthy Moslems of the city.

In the fall of 1721, an Arab mob stormed their synagogue and burned the Holy Ark, Torah scrolls, holy books, and all

Influx of Chassidim

the furnishings. Only the stone edifice remained standing. Because of the total devastation, the synagogue was called the *Churbah*, the Destroyed Synagogue.

The Arabs expelled the Ashkenazi Jews and forbade them reentry until their debt would be paid in full. The Moslems did not distinguish between the Jews who had actually borrowed the money and other Jews of Ashkenazi descent who might want to live in Jerusalem. The ban was applied indiscriminately, and consequently no Ashkenazi Jew lived in the Holy City for the next hundred years. Ashkenazi immigrants, finding the gates of Jerusalem locked to them, settled instead in Safed, Hebron, and Tiberias.[8]

Some of the refugees from the *Churbah* resettled in Hebron, and some in Safed. These formed the first Ashkenazi community of Safed.[9]

First Half of the Eighteenth Century

In the eighteenth century, most new immigrants to Israel chose Jerusalem as their home. R' Chaim Attar, known as the *Ohr HaChayim*, settled in Jerusalem in 1740 and opened a yeshiva. His disciple, the Chida, wrote that as profound as the *Ohr HaChayim's* written works were, "they revealed but a tenth of his wisdom... and wherever he went an aura of holiness enveloped him."[10] Later, another mentor of the Chida, the great mystic R' Shalom Sharabi, immigrated to *Eretz Yisrael* and settled in Jerusalem.

The sleepy little village of Tiberias came to life when a new *yishuv* was established there by the venerable R' Chaim Abulafia in 1740. A number of families from Safed were attracted to the now growing town and became part of the new Jewish settlement.

Safed, however, did not rank as first choice for establishing a home by new settlers at this time, nor was it known as a unique Torah center.

SAFED: THE MYSTICAL CITY

R' Chaim Abulafia's shul, called Etz Chaim, is renowned for its sancity until today.

First *Aliyah* of Chassidim

The Baal Shem Tov's love of the Land of Israel was like an unquenchable thirst. It burned within him and his disciples.

In 1740 a small group of his disciples and their families set out for the Holy Land. They were led by R' Nachman of Horodnak, the grandfather of R' Nachman of Breslav. Their destination was Safed. The Baal Shem Tov's own ill-fated journey a year or two later ended before he ever reached *Eretz Yisrael*.

The following year the venerable R' Eliezer Rokeach joined them. As Rav of Brody for over twenty years, he had made many close ties with Chassidim of the city, and was revered as a Kabbalist and wonder-worker.[11] At the age of seventy-five he left his post as Chief Rabbi of Amsterdam to fulfill his dream of serving God in the Holy Land. Upon his arrival, he became the undisputed leader of the Ashkenazi community of Safed.

Influx of Chassidim

The reason for the Chassidim's choice of Safed over Jerusalem was twofold. In their eyes, Safed was the "City of *Mekubalim* [Kabbalists]." All the original yeshivos and synagogues were still standing. The graves of the *tzaddikim* of that golden era were but a stone's throw away. The second, and unavoidable, reason was that Jerusalem was still closed to Ashkenazim since their expulsion twenty years earlier.

The potential of this nucleus *aliyah* of Chassidim was great, yet it was quickly marred by a backlash of senseless hatred on the part of some of the already resident Ashkenazim. Their primary target was R' Rokeach. Cursed and defamed publicly, his life was made miserable to the point that he would have returned to Europe had his health not failed him.

The following Succos, 1742, the two principal instigators of this hate campaign mocked him, saying, "Here in Safed you put on airs to be Prince of the community, yet in Poland you would not be accepted as Rav of even the smallest Jewish community."

A few days later he passed away and was buried in a cave among other *tzaddikim*.[12] He vowed that the two assailants would be punished from heaven: that they would be stricken in a plague and then killed by the sword.

That very winter a plague broke out, and these two men were among those stricken. They were then sent out of the city where marauders ambushed and killed them.

With the passing of R' Rokeach, the spirit of the Chassidim was broken. Most returned to Europe.

R' Gershon Kitover, the Baal Shem Tov's brother-in-law, left Israel and returned to Europe with a heavy heart. He sincerely prayed to be able to re-immigrate at the first opportunity. The Baal Shem Tov, however, detained him in Europe for several more years.

Only in 1747, did R' Kitover succeed in resettling in *Eretz Yisrael*. This time, out of necessity, he lived in Hebron. His heart lay in Jerusalem, but for the time being his desires were thwarted by the Moslem exclusion of Ashkenazi Jews. During that winter a plague claimed the lives of two hundred inhabitants of Jerusalem. This heartbreaking disaster was a sign to R' Kitover not to try to force his way into the Holy City. Six years later R' Kitover moved to Jerusalem incognito, studying Kabbalah in the famous Beis El Yeshiva of R' Shalom Sharabi. He died in 1761, and was buried on Mount Olives.

First Earthquake: 1759

Late one night in 1759, the residents of Safed were jolted awake by the eerie sound of the stone walls of their houses creaking as they shifted from their foundations and came crashing down. Rafters, beams, and stones were flung from their places and hurled in all directions. The earth itself had opened up for a split second and mankind was thrown, helter-skelter, into catastrophe.

On 9 Cheshvan, 1759, the first major earthquake in the Galilee transformed the majestic city of Safed into a pile of rocks and rubble. Over two thousand inhabitants died, including one hundred and fifty Jews. The number of injured and lame was even greater. Within a matter of minutes the crown of Safed had been smashed to shards.[13]

"A few hours before dawn," wrote a contemporary Jerusalemite, "we were suddenly awakened by the tremors of an earthquake. Fortunately, no one in Jerusalem was hurt.

"Later, we heard that at the same time there had been a violent earthquake in Safed... We lamented the disaster for a full week; eulogies were delivered and many cried openly."[14]

A month later, on 6 Kislev, a second intense tremor killed twenty more Jews and destroyed six more synagogues of the city. Only two or three shuls withstood the massive geological upheavals. Over a dozen *batei midrash* vanished on that chilly, terrifying night.

The roads were filled with stunned, empty-handed refugees traveling to Jerusalem, Peikin, Acco, Sidon, and other cities of refuge. Safed became almost a ghost town,

Influx of Chassidim

populated by only a few staunch residents who were determined to remain under any circumstances, a mere echo of the vibrant city of only a few short weeks earlier.

The fifty Jewish families girded themselves with trust in God, and took stock of the situation. Their first concern, after saving human life, was the sanctity of the synagogues. Salvaging the Torah scrolls and other holy objects buried under mountains of debris was a major task.

The magnificent Abuhav synagogue had collapsed, but miraculously the southern wall containing the Holy Ark had remained intact. The Torah scroll, penned in the fifteenth century in Portugal by R' Yitzchak Abuhav, author of the classic *Menoras HaMeor*, was unmarred. Because of its sanctity, this Sefer Torah was removed and read on the *bimah* only three times a year – on Rosh Hashanna, Yom Kippur, and Shavuos. R' Abuhav never left Portugal, but had sent this Torah scroll to the Jews of Safed. It was venerated as a most illustrious Torah scroll.[15]

In order to move the *Sefer Torah* to a safe lodging in one of the surviving synagogues, ten men volunteered to carry it 'not in its proper time.' They first purified themselves in a *mikve* before solemnly marching with it to its new abode. Strangely, all ten men passed away within a year.

The Ari synagogue, located at the bottom of the Jewish Quarter, was badly damaged. However, the small room near the entrance where the Arizal had studied with Elijah the Prophet withstood the shock waves, and the elevated *bimah* stood undamaged under the open skies, almost as if it were crying out the city's distress to the Creator of heaven and earth.

The oldest synagogue of Safed, the Rabbi Yossi Bannai synagogue, survived the cataclysm with but a minor insult to its sanctity. Rabbi Yossi Bannai, a *Tanna*, had been buried high on the western slope of Safed during the Roman rule of Israel. Eventually, a synagogue was built at that site, and his

Left: *Tomb of Rabbi Yossi Bannai.* Right: *The synagogue in which his tomb lies*

grave was located in the women's gallery on the ground floor. It was called *Kever haTzaddik*, the tomb of the righteous, and according to tradition a Torah scroll was buried alongside him.

The few remaining devoted townsmen took stock of their losses and ambitiously began to rebuild the shuls and yeshivas. It would take years, but, God willing, they would succeed. So, with uplifted hearts they embarked on their holy task.

1764: Second *Aliyah* of Chassidim

When the Baal Shem Tov passed from this world in 1760, some of his disciples yearned to fulfill the Besht's dream of settling in *Eretz Yisrael*. In the summer of 1764, about twenty families undertook the arduous journey. R' Nachman of Horodnak, who was on the first *aliyah* a quarter of a century before and had long yearned to return to the Holy Land, led the hardy pilgrims.

The cruise from Constantinople was uneventful, and the ship anchored safely at the Jaffa port. A group of Sephardim debarked and set off for the Holy City. The Chassidim, however, continued on the ship to Acco, a six hour's journey up the coast. Suddenly, gale winds swept the ship off course. The rudder and sails were useless. For nine days the ship floundered at sea out of human control. With their food supply exhausted and water rationed, they could only wait with bated breath to see whether the heavenly court would hearken to their prayers. Finally, on 12 Tishre, the sea subsided and, with prayers of thanksgiving, they landed at Acco.

After recuperating from their harrowing experience, the group of Chassidic families parted ways. Most went with R' Nachman to Tiberias, while a few traveled to Safed. Those who settled in Safed were welcomed with grave faces by the few remaining Jewish residents. The formerly noble city was devastated and impoverished. Rebuilding was in progress, but the raw scars from 1759 were visible at every turn. For example, there was only one Babylonian Talmud in the city, an old edition from Amsterdam, full of errors.

The Chassidim prayed at the Rabbi Yossi Bannai synagogue, and joined in the reconstruction efforts. Yet circumstances sabotaged their intentions to establish a meaningful foothold in the city, and after an unbearable winter they withdrew and sadly returned to Europe.

R' Simcha ben Yehoshua, author of *Ahavas Tziyon*, was one of the last to depart. He had hoped to support himself as a scribe and was disappointed to learn that there was little need for yet another *sofer*. The local market was closed since a surplus of Torah scrolls filled the Holy Arks of every shul. Nevertheless, he had been commissioned to write a *Sefer Torah* for someone in his home town, and he believed he would support himself from this work. His spirit was broken when he was informed that there was a ban against selling

Torah scrolls, *tefillin* and *mezuzos* abroad. Crestfallen, impoverished, and with a dim outlook for the future, he returned to Europe.[16]

The abortive efforts of these early settlers, however, were not in vain. Without this trickling of aliyah from Europe, there might not have been the major influx of Chassidim in the coming years. In another decade the largest single influx of Jews in over five hundred years would succeed in planting permanent roots in the ground these settlers had prepared.[17]

The Great Chassidic Influx of 1777

Every morning R' Menachem Mendel of Vitebst stood on the shores of the Bosphorus and gazed out across the waters. He scanned the horizons for a suitable ship to escort him and his three hundred followers to *Eretz Yisrael*. Sailboats of all types, flying flags of all nations, anchored daily in Constantinople, one of the largest port cities on the Mediterranean basin. Yet, such a selection of seaworthy vessels notwithstanding, R' Menachem Mendel returned silently to his lodgings.

Weeks passed and still the leader of this large group remained reticent. Although his followers' loyalty in him was unshaken, their curiosity was peaked.

R' Menachem Mendel was their gifted leader and the undisputable inheritor of the crown of Chassidus. The Maggid of Mezeritch had inherited it from Baal Shem Tov, and in 1773 when the Maggid passed away, R' Menachem Mendel became his successor. During the next few years, the charismatic, thirty-six year old genius strove to extinguish the wild fires of bitter anti-Chassidic sentiments in Europe. In a daring move, he traveled to Vilna with his chief disciple, R' Shneur Zalman of Liadi, and vigorously petitioned for an audience with the Vilna Gaon. The G'ra, well-known as an opponent of Chassidism, refused.[18]

Thousands flocked to R' Menachem Mendel's side. His deep love of his fellow Jew endeared him to the common man, and his profound wisdom and wise leadership marked him as the new Chassidic leader.

Most of all, R' Menachem Mendel was a lover of peace. Chassidus blossoms best in an environment of shalom. After the failure in Vilna, he reconsidered his mission in life. Man was created to rectify himself and perfect his soul by awakening the holy sparks which lie dormant in the world. Torah, *mitzvos*, and *avodas HaShem* (the service of God) arouse these sparks. Since the menacing fires of *hisnagdos* (opposition to Chassidism) ravaged the young forests of Chassidic avoda in Europe, R' Menachem Mendel sought another garden in which to replant his saplings.

The dream of the Baal Shem Tov glowed in his heart. *Eretz Yisrael* was the place in which to unite the lower and celestial worlds and truly serve God. The bonfires of Europe were nonexistent there. And most of all, the Land of Israel was the ideal place to help bring about the ultimate redemption which every Jew secretly awaited.

A Ship of Ships

One spring day, R' Menachem Mendel pointed to an old schooner sailing into the Bosphorus.

"That's our ship!" he declared.

Some of the Rebbe's party were aghast to see such a weather-beaten old sailboat hailed as the long anticipated absolutely perfect transport for the arduous journey to the Holy Land. Their apprehension was partially stilled by the skipper's attitude. He was overjoyed to take Jewish pilgrims to their ancestral homeland.

At the very onset of the voyage, the captain told R' Menachem Mendel and his party of the incident which had colored his whole life.

"Some thirty-seven years ago," he began, "I took an elderly Jew to Palestinia. In the midst of the voyage we were suddenly swallowed up by a huge tempest the likes of which I've never seen before and hope never to see again. The crew and I did everything possible to keep her afloat, but the gale winds and pounding waves were about to overpower us. Just as we were about to go under, I remembered that there was a Jew on board. I somehow clamored down below deck and burst into this old Jew's chamber. He was sitting there just as if nothing was the matter. I yelled for him to do something. He looked at me with serene eyes, stood up as best he could, took a ram's horn, whispered some incantations and blew it with all his might.

"Suddenly, and you can believe me or not, but it's true, suddenly the sea became as calm as a sleeping baby. It was unbelievable! It was a miracle! That wonder-worker of an old man just blew that horn and heaven harkened to its sound."

"That old man," said R' Menachem Mendel, "was surely R' Eliezer Rokeach, who came to Israel in 1740. And he blew the *shofar* on Rosh Hashanna after whispering the necessary blessings."

The old skipper grinned. "Well, I don't remember his name, but I relive that storm when the old Jew saved my ship each and every day of my life."[19]

Realities of Safed

The Chassidim landed at Acco on 5 Elul, 1777, five months after setting out from Reisen.

Before the caravan left for Safed, R' Menachem Mendel met with the new governor of the Galilee. Achmad-El-Gajar Pacha had recently been sent from Constantinople to replace the ruling tyrant, who had mercilessly devastated the economy, especially crippling Jewish enterprise.

Achmad's finance minister, Chaim Parchi, was a well-to-do Jew from Damascus. Chaim Parchi influenced the incoming governor to inaugurate a new policy of benevolence towards the Jews. R' Menachem Mendel was informed that they would be exempt from taxation, and that the mayor of Safed would allow them to rebuild synagogues and private houses as they wished.

Influx of Chassidim

With a growing sense of destiny, R' Menachem Mendel's party set out for Safed. As the colonists traveled along the twisting mountain roads, the vista revealed itself to them. With high spirits they gazed across the wide valleys and distant mountain peaks. Here, at last, in the Land chosen by the Creator of the universe for His people, they would continue the divine work of serving God and spreading the Torah of Chassidus.

The realities of Safed, however, were less heartening. The outlook was bleak in every respect. Renovation and reconstruction after the earthquake seventeen years earlier was still minimal. Poverty was acute, and indeed the future of the Jewish population was in question.

The Chassidim were enthusiastic idealists. The very air of Safed invigorated the settlers and they set to work to establish a thriving Chassidic community.

"How difficult it is for me to sleep at night," wrote their leader. "When the crystal air of Safed sings, one can hear the heavenly voices calling out to repent."[20]

A few months later one of R' Menachem Mendel's Chassidim asked him a personal question.

"I always imagined it would be easier to serve God in *Eretz Yisrael*," lamented the chassid. "Now that I live here, however," he admitted, "I find in myself bad traits that I never had in *chutz l'aretz*. How can this be?"

"You are mistaken," answered the Rebbe. "In *chutz l'aretz* you had the trait of arrogance, and consequently you never felt your smallness and worthlessness. You simply did not recognize yourself.

"But now, *Baruch Hashem*, you have settled in *Eretz Yisrael*, the Land which naturally purifies a man and humbles him. Now you are capable of discerning your true nature, and have found that you are 'ill' in certain areas of character development.

"Don't be afraid," the *tzaddik* consoled him. "This recognition is half the cure. Now you know what you need to work on to perfect yourself."[21]

First Year

Within the first year, the Chassidic foundation stones were nearly uprooted. The Chassidim were menaced by a wave of anti-Chassidic backlash that stunned and nearly broke the spirit of the young colonists.

Three factions opposed them. First, the existing Ashkenazim, who "lacked all intelligence," harassed them and foiled their efforts at every turn.[22]

A second group of Ashkenazim had immigrated at the same time as the Chassidim. In fact, they had met the Chassidic party in Constantinople and pleaded with R' Menachem Mendel to help them. Their funds had evaporated, and their dream of settling in *Eretz Yisrael* depended on R' Menachem Mendel's kindness to pay their travel expenses to Safed. The hundred member group sought to merge with the Chassidim. R' Menachem Mendel was reluctant to use funds set aside to cover the first two years living expenses in Israel to pay the fare of this group. In the end, however, he acquiesced to their pleas and paid for their entire journey.

However... "Once they saw that we were left penniless," wrote R' Menachem Mendel, "and could no longer assist them, they turned against us and joined the other Ashkenazim in the hostilities towards us."[23]

Finally, some of the Sephardim in Safed united with the growing wave of anti-Chassidism and wrought havoc on R' Menachem Mendel's group. The momentum grew, headed by the local Jewish commissioner, until it reached the point that there was a real threat to life. There were even threats of impending massacre if they did not leave Safed.

R' Menachem Mendel's health was affected by the daily barrage of threats, harassments, and insults. He was bedridden for several months. "One can neither count nor imagine how great was the desecration of God's name."[24]

To save their economic situation, one of the elder Chassidim was sent to Russia to collect emergency funds.

When a plague broke out, the Chassidim evacuated Safed and moved to Peikin, which had a Jewish community of its own. Later, R' Menachem Mendel moved to Tiberias and settled there. There, he was welcomed with open arms, and began to build a Chassidic community.

His leading disciple, R' Avraham Katz of Kalish, however, chose to return to Safed with the majority of the Chassidim.

The True Measure of Things

R' Avraham Katz, as leader of the Chassidim in Safed, withstood the local commissioner and all the other opposing forces until 1784. Finally, he relinquished his dream of living in the city of grandeur, and joined his Rebbe in Tiberias.

During the seven years during which the Chassidim lived in Safed, their influence was limited by the fetters of the constant hostility which surrounded their every move. However, where others had forsaken the Land and returned to Europe, they remained in *Eretz Yisrael*, and built new foundations of Chassidus in Tiberias.

A nucleus of Chassidim, however, did remain in Safed throughout the entire time of tribulation. As the anti-Chassidic sentiments slowly subsided, the enclave of Chassidim regained their composure and openly followed their own unique customs.

Until the beginning of the nineteenth century, quiet reigned. The biggest thorn in the side of the Jews in the Galilee came from Arab marauders. But that was taken for granted; it was intrinsic to living in *Eretz Yisrael* at the time. In 1800, Napoleon's army, stationed in Acco, suddenly invaded Safed and Tiberias. Jewish lives as such were not directly threatened, yet there was a real danger.

SAFED: THE MYSTICAL CITY

The turning point for the Chassidic colony paradoxically came about by the influx of disciples of the Vilna Gaon a decade later. In Eastern Europe, Perushim, as the disciples of the Vilna Gaon were called, and Chassidim were not on speaking terms, to put it mildly. Yet, the common goals of building up and settling *Eretz Yisrael* overcame ideological differences, and the two groups succeeded in working together for common goals. This was living proof that the sanctity of the Land and the immigrants' spirit of self-sacrifice could forge a comradeship unheard of anywhere else.

NOTES
1. The Ramak's work *Shiur Komah*, for instance, was first published in 1883. For a history of the publication of R' Vital's *Shemonah Shaarim*, see *Shivchei Ari*, pp. 35a-b
2. *Tivuos HaAretz*, pp. 455-456
3. *Emek HaMelech*, introduction
4. His grandfather, R' Moshe Galante, received *semicha* from R' Yosef Karo at the age of twenty-two. R' Galante the Second was called *Rav HaMagen* in honor of his responsa which he called *Elef HaMagen*.
5. Responsa *Ganos Veradim* by R' Moshe Chaviv, *Choshen Mishpat*, Kal 2, no. 2
6. *Shem HaGedolim*, Part I, p. 67. He published *Etz Chaim* and *Olas Tamid*
7. Cited in *Toldas Yitzchak*, p. 44
8. There were some notable exceptions. R' Gershon Kitover, the brother-in-law of the Baal Shem Tov, lived there and studied with R' Shalom Sharabi. R' Menachem Mendel, a disciple of the Vilna Gaon, moved there around 1814. Both dressed in Sephardi garb in order to remain incognito.
9. Cf. *Ganos Veradim*, Part I, *Klal* 3, no. 9, who writes that in 1680's there were no Ashkenazim living in Safed
10. *Shem HaGedolim*, Part I, p. 42
11. When he left Brody, he revealed that in his merit and prayers, no mother had ever miscarried or bore a stillborn child. Furthermore, no mother ever had a dangerous childbirth.
12. On 27 Tishre
13. *Tivuos HaAretz*, pp. 411-412, lists fifteen recorded earthquakes in *Eretz Yisrael*. This was number thirteen.
14. R' Raphael Meyuchas, author of *Pri HaAdamah*, Part I, p. 6a

15.*Ahavas Tziyon*, p. 2. According to *Ahavas Tziyon* and *Chibas Yerushalayim*, this southern wall was also the northern wall of the adjacent Ari synagogue. Today, the Abuhav shul is in the center of the Jewish Quarter, while the Ari shul is far below near the cemetery. Some say that the author or publisher of *Ahavas Tziyon* made a mistake, and the author of *Chibas Yerushalayim* copied it. To honor of the Munkacher Rebbe's historic visit in 1930, the *Sefer Torah* was taken out, and he read from it on the *bimah*.
16.*Ahavas Tziyon*, p. 2
17.In 13th century, R' Yonathan HaKohen led three hundred Baalei *Tosefos* to *Eretz Yisrael*.
18.R' Menachem Mendel regretted that he did not break down the door and force an audience with the G'ra. He felt it could have changed the history of the Chassidic movement.
19.Two incidents occurred on their voyage at sea. When they were struck by a violent storm, R' Menachem Mendel stood up on the deck and called out, "May all the embarrassments that I suffered in *chutz l'aretz* stand in my stead." Immediately the storm subsided.

Later, R' Menachem Mendel demanded to be lowered into the sea in order to immerse. He said that in heaven there still remained charges against their party and only by immersing could he reverse the charges. In spite of the danger to his life, he was lowered into the sea and lifted up again. R' Menachem Mendel said: "In the water I saw a venerable old man who helped lift me out of the sea."
20.*Miktavim*
21.*Mishnas Chachamim*
22.*Miktavim*, no. 4, p. 146
23.*ibid*.
24.*ibid*.

Perushim

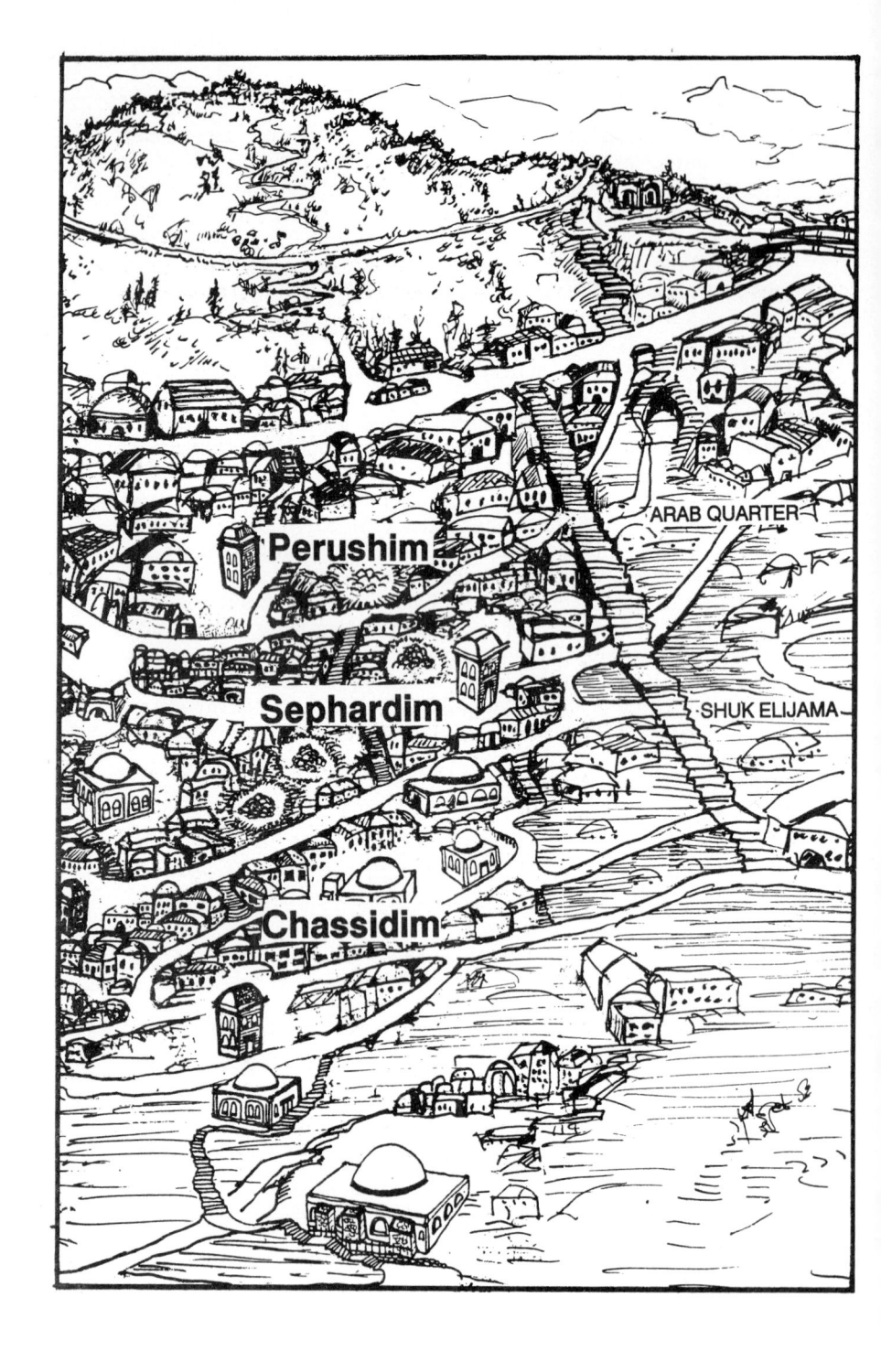

Sephardim

Chassidim

ARAB QUARTER

SHUK ELIJAMA

8
Influx of Perushim

With the onset of the nineteenth century, Safed began once again to rejuvenate herself and thrive. In its first decades, a wave of Ashkenazim, disciples of the Vilna Gaon, immigrated to Safed, and later on more Chassidim and Sephardim settled there. A new chapter in the history of this noble city was about to leave its imprint on the stones and soil of Safed. The momentum which brought about this great influx had started years before in Poland and Russia.

The Vilna Gaon's Vision

The Vilna Gaon had imbued in his students the dream of *Eretz Yisrael*. His vision was to establish a Torah center in Jerusalem and, God willing, transform it into world Jewry's capital of Torah dissemination. In time, the footsteps of the *Mashiach* would stamp that holy ground and awaken man from his lethargy.

Even during the Vilna Gaon's lifetime, steps were being taken to make his dream a reality. The city of Shaklov, Russia, was a stronghold of *Misnaged* sentiment and bustled with religious activity. The *Chazon Tziyon* movement, the pilot project organized to achieve the Gaon's dream, was launched with his blessing. Rabbis delivered orations, committees discussed the practical side of such an influx, and a fund raising network was designed.

Aliyah: 1808-1809

As the nineteenth century unfolded, the first party of seventy souls set out for *Eretz Yisrael*. Called *Iyalas HaShachar*, R' Menachem Mendel of Shaklov led the pioneers. They arrived in 1808, and after a short sojourn in Tiberias, they settled in Safed.

The following year two more parties of Perushim joined them. Together they numbered close to two hundred men, women, and children.

The undisputed leader of the Perushim community was R' Yisrael of Shaklov. A close disciple of the Vilna Gaon, R' Yisrael preserved the call of his mentor in his heart and felt destined to play an important role in the new settlement. His grandfather had been among the first to raise the banner

Safed, the mystical city

some thirty years before, and now R' Yisrael would be the one to see it to fruition.

Why Safed?

The Perushim chose Safed as their home ground partially out of necessity. Many harbored an intense yearning to settle in Jerusalem in order to fulfill the words of their mentor. They felt that their mission in coming to Israel lay only there. Yet, they had to admit that, at least for the time being, Jerusalem was off limits. The Jerusalem Moslems' bizarre ruling of a century earlier banning all Ashkenazi Jews entry because of some Jews' inability to pay outstanding debts was still enforced. Any move to try to settle in the Holy City at this time could prove fatal.[1]

R' Yisrael, however, favored a permanent settlement in Safed. This tug of war between the Jerusalem and Safed factions continued throughout R' Yisrael's lifetime, and was the cause of a number of major decisions concerning the community of the Perushim.

Settling into Safed

The Perushim found the Safed community amiable. Sephardim and Chassidim worked together to help the new immigrants get settled. Housing was the major problem. The reconstruction efforts over the last half century since the earthquake of 1759 supplied adequate housing for the existing community, but an influx of this magnitude could not yet be absorbed. The Perushim were compelled to live in exceedingly cramped conditions in the upper section of the Jewish Quarter, while the Sephardim lived in the middle area, and the Chassidim in the lower streets.

The official language of the land was Arabic. In the first months, none of the Perushim gained enough fluency to hold even a simple conversation in Arabic. The Sephardim spoke Ladino and Arabic, but were able to converse with the Ashkenazim in Hebrew mixed with Aramaic.

SAFED: THE MYSTICAL CITY

Market day was more ordeal than pleasure for the new immigrants. The market place, *Shuk Elijama*, separated the Jewish and Moslem quarters. Peasant farmers from the surrounding villages brought their produce and merchandise into Safed once a week and residents thronged from stall to stall. Everything was hectic, with donkeys and horse carts everywhere. The Perushim, already hampered by the language barrier, were further stymied by the traditional bartering system. Whenever possible, they tried to have a Sephardi act as go-between. Most of all, the Perushim were discomfited to learn that custom dictated that women did not go to the market. So the men, more accustomed to sitting in the yeshiva than to selecting fresh produce, were forced to do the weekly shopping.

The Sephardi Rav of Safed, R' Raphael Yosef Chazon, sat with the leaders of the Perushim, and discussed with them a gamut of halachic issues. He was impressed by their grasp of Torah knowledge and their commitment to the high ideals of a Torah way of life. Together with other Sephardim, he would listen avidly to them discussing the writings of their mentor, the Gaon of Vilna.

The Perushim opened Beis Midrash HaG'ra, and forty men studied there earnestly day and night. They studied Talmud with the relevant laws in the *Shulchan Aruch*, together with the glosses of the Vilna Gaon. R' Sadiya of Vilna lectured on the *Gemora*. In keeping with the dictates of their mentor, they studied *Chumash* with the commentary of Rashi daily. They found, however, that Safed lacked a good library of holy books. Therefore, they requested that new immigrants bring as many *seforim* as possible with them from Russia.

Their relationship with the Chassidim was unique. Knowing that the new *yishuv* was too frail to withstand hostilities and ideological arguments, the Perushim sought a friendly accord with the Chassidim. The small group of Chassidim in Safed happily accepted this new relationship, and in no time a mutual respect began to blossom.

During these years, two great Chassidic leaders journeyed to Safed to spend their last years in the Holy Land. R' Chaim of Chernovitz, author of the classic chassidic commentary to the Torah, *Beier Mayim Chaim*, arrived around 1813 and died in Safed on 27 Kislev, 1818. He was buried in a large cave between the grave site of R' Yosef Karo and the cave of R' Moshe Alshich. While in Safed, he penned a work to inspire his chassidim in Russia. Entitled *Shaar HaTefillah, The Gates of Prayer*, R' Chaim's book thoroughly discussed the power of prayer from the Chassidic viewpoint.[2]

R' Dovid Shlomo Ivshitz, a giant in both the revealed and hidden aspects of Torah, came to Israel in 1809, reportedly on the same ship that was carrying the first *aliyah* of Perushim. In Safed he completed his masterpiece in *halacha*, *Levushei S'rad* on *Yoreh Deah*, and a chassidic commentary to the Torah, *Arvei Nachal*. He passed away on 22 Cheshvan, 1814, and was buried in a cave not far away from the grave of the Arizal.

To the right is the entrance to the cave where R' Chaim of Chernovitz is buried. The grave to the left with the lantern on top is that of R' Yosef Karo.

The Oldest of Problems

The ever present problem of caring for their physical needs loomed heavily before the new immigrants. Their material resources exhausted, they desperately petitioned their European counterparts to send funds. Many subsisted on a near starvation diet.

The distribution of funds sent to the Jewish communities in Israel needed to be renovated. For generations, the Jews in the Diaspora were asked to donate money to support the Jewish communities in *Eretz Yisrael*, especially for those individuals who dedicated their lives to Torah studies. Once these funds reached Israel, their distribution, called *chaluka*, quite literally became the bread and butter of the colonists. The Sephardim periodically sent emissaries to the Diaspora for the purpose of collecting for their communities. The Chassidim, with a more than thirty-year foothold in *Eretz Yisrael*, did the same. The Perushim, however, had not yet organized themselves in this area, and were quick to feel the consequences.

R' Yisrael of Shaklov conceived a plan. Instead of periodic delegates being sent to collect donations in Russia, a permanent network of community-headed charity boxes would insure a steady flow of funds. Each Jewish community would have a representative collect the boxes and forward the money to a central office in Volozhin. From there the funds would be sent to Safed.

In 1810, R' Yisrael left for Europe to implement his scheme. He met with his close associate, R' Chaim of Volozhin, who eagerly gave of his time and energy. The Napoleonic wars, however, intervened. For three years R' Yisrael traveled from town to town, speaking in synagogues and before city councils, stirring people's hearts to the importance of the mission the Perushim colonists had accepted upon themselves. Their mission was really the united mission of all Jews, and the existence of a vital *yishuv* in the Holy Land would have far-reaching repercussions for generations to come. The time to act was now, everyone according to his means: some by donating of their wealth, some by their prayers and blessings, and still others by endeavoring to join them in *Eretz Yisrael*.[3]

With a portion of the money collected, R' Yisrael chose to send a shipment of wheat which the settlers could then sell in Palestine. In this way, he hoped to circumvent the dangers of a human messenger with a moneychest to safeguard from marauders and highway robbers. Later, however, they learned that the ship sank in the Mediterranean Sea.

In the meantime, *dayan* Chaim Katz went to Acco to meet with the most influential Jew in the Turkish protectorate of Palestine. Chaim Parchi had always been sympathetic to the needs of his fellow Jews, and promised Dayan Katz to do what he could for them.

R' Yisrael returned in 1813. The success of his mission engendered new hope in spite of the settlers tenuous situation. Unfortunately, however, the money R' Yisrael came back with was not sufficient even to pay all the debts which had accumulated in his absence, let alone to put the colonists back on a solid footing.

The Plague of 1814

One of the worst plagues in generations raged like wildfire throughout the Galilee. It spared neither the rich nor the righteous. Most of the inhabitants of Safed deserted the city. The Perushim, by that time numbering close to five hundred, scattered.

R' Yisrael traveled with his family and companions to Jerusalem. The journey was filled with tragedy and suffering. First, his wife died near Acco, and other members of his family were struck as they continued the arduous journey under the torrid summer skies. When at last they reached Jerusalem, they found that the angel of death was still on the rampage. It was there that most of his children died, until finally he himself felt the sickness grip and weaken him. Barely conscious, he vowed to write a book on the laws pertaining to *Eretz*

Yisrael if God would spare his life and redeem him from the gates of death.

"I wept until overcome with sleep," wrote R' Yisrael. "I dreamt that someone approached me, and put his hand on me, and that I awoke as if from a long night's rest. He stood over me and said, 'You have been stricken and you have been healed.' I felt God's compassion and loving kindness shine upon me, and I knew then that I would survives."[4]

After the plague dissipated, R' Yisrael returned to Safed. Putting aside his personal losses, R' Yisrael poured his energies into consolidating and revitalizing the surviving Perushim colonists. R' Menachem Mendel and R' Sadiya chose to remain in Jerusalem. They lived incognito; they dressed like the Sephardim, prayed with them, and studied in the famous Beis El Yeshiva.

R' Yisrael remarried. His new wife was from a Chassidic background, which caused quite a flurry in Europe. She bore him a number of sons and daughters, and gave him every opportunity to continue in his role as communal leader, Torah sage, and comforter of his people.

Chaim Parchi Protects his People

Chaim Parchi was the most influential man in the Turkish provincial governorship of the Galilee. For decades he had served as second-in-command to the Pasha, the governor sent from Constantinople, and at times his power even surpassed that of the Pasha.[5]

A conscientious Jew, Chaim Parchi always sought ways to benefit his people. He enacted a law, for instance, which exempted the Jews from taxation, and the needs and causes of the Jewish community were always prominent in his thoughts and deeds.

When one of the Turkish princes died and left an orphaned son, Chaim Parchi adopted the boy, Abdullah, and personally undertook his education. He spared nothing to ensure that Abdullah would one day play an active role in the political arena.

After the plague of 1814, the Pasha died. Chaim Parchi immediately used his considerable influence to have Abdullah appointed Pasha, with the hope that together they would unfold a new era of peace for the Jews in his protectorate. His efforts proved successful, and the Sultan installed Abdullah as Pasha.

A year later a incident occurred which radically changed the relationship between guardian and ward. It happened one day that Parchi reprimanded Abdullah for unethical behavior. Abdullah was infuriated. How dare anyone stand in his way and interfere with his activities, no matter how mischievous! Bent on revenge, he contrived a libel against his mentor, claiming that Parchi was about to incite a revolt against the Sultan, and was therefore guilty of treason and should be put to death.

Friends informed Chaim Parchi of the plot against his life and urged him to flee to Damascus. He refused. Should he forsake his people, he said, Abdullah would unleash a reign of terror against the Jews in the Galilee. His presence was their only shield.

Reign of Terror

This protection, however, was shortlived. One afternoon, on the eve of the first day of Elul, 1819, a militia troop suddenly stormed into the Parchi villa in Acco. The commander read a counterfeit court order sentencing Chaim Parchi to death for insurrection, and ordered him strangled to death on the spot. All of his possessions were confiscated and his body cast into the Mediterranean Sea. His wife and children were able to escape to Damascus.

The news of Chaim Parchi's assassination thrust a dagger of fear and apprehension into the heart of every member of the Jewish population of the province. They no longer had anyone to turn to in the Turkish administration.

SAFED: THE MYSTICAL CITY

Abdullah commenced his dictatorship by levying upon the Jews all the various taxation which they had until then been spared, insisting that all back taxes be paid as well. This demand was patently beyond the ability of the Jewish community to pay. In a show of strength, Abdullah sent his army to Safed and imprisoned a large number of Jews for failing to pay on time. They were forced to sell everything they owned in order to gain their freedom.

R' Yisrael was imprisoned in Acco and prepared to sanctify his life with martyrdom. Enormous bribes raised by members of the community, however, unlocked the dungeon door and returned him to his people.

Chaim Parchi's brothers in Damascus reacted to his assassination by recruiting a private mercenary army. They marched into Israel bent on avenging his blood. They repulsed Abdullah's militia at the Jordan River in 1821, and beseiged his stronghold at Acco for a year. Finally, the tyrant succeeded in having the eldest Parchi brother poisoned. With their leader dead, the campaign collapsed and the remaining brothers retreated with their army and returned to Damascus.

The Jews of the Galilee were thrown into the hands of a ruthless despot. Deliberately imposed hardships and acts of anti-Semitic violence became their daily portion. "From the time that the leader and *tzaddik* Chaim Parchi was taken away from us," wrote R' Yisrael, "we suffered exceedingly, and were constantly in fear for our lives."[6]

The Perushim, still Russian citizens, heard that a minister from Czarist Russia was visiting the Land. After touring Jerusalem, he traveled north to Acco where a representative of the Perushim met with him. The representative explained the desperation of the Perushim's situation, and sought protection from their 'mother country.' The minister agreed to help. A high level meeting was convened and an agreement signed that guaranteed the personal rights of Russian citizens in *Eretz Yisrael*.

A Harsh Reminder

In the spring of 1825, torrential rains stormed the Galilee. Wind and rain whipped the roofs and shutters of homes for days on end. The dome-shaped, stone roofs were held together only with mud and straw mixed with a little mortar. Under normal climatic conditions they stood up well. But this nonstop downpour slowly dissolved the mud-base cement and roofs began to cave in. Tragedy struck randomly, killing and wounding indiscriminately.[7]

R' Yisrael was sitting in his house with his family during the storm. Suddenly the roof collapsed on their heads and buried them alive. *"Baruch Hashem,"* wrote R' Yisrael, "I escaped alive with my family."[8]

A decade earlier, R' Yisrael had vowed to write a compendium of laws pertaining to *Eretz Yisrael* in return for his life. Now he was sharply reminded of that vow and garnered all his strength to fulfill it before there should be another tragedy, when the wrath of God might not be tempered with His attribute of mercy, as it had been this time.

R' Chaim Halevi Horowitz, a descendant of the *Shelah HaKodesh*, was also affected by the tragedy. He had immigrated eight years earlier and aspired to write about the sanctity of the Land. After the tragedy, however, he was compelled to leave Safed, and in 1826, he settled in Jerusalem. He published his guidebook, *Chibas Yerushalayim*, in 1844, and it immediately became a classic.[9]

Cover to first edition (Jer. 1844) of Chibas Yerushalayim, an authoritative guidebook to Israel

A Breathing Spell

In 1831, the Egyptian Pasha, Ibrahim, advanced into

Eretz Yisrael and attacked Abdullah's Acco stronghold. After a brief siege, the city fell into his hands, and Abdullah was captured and imprisoned in Egypt.

Ibrahim's nine-year rule gave the Jews a welcome breathing spell. In an obvious attempt to curry world opinion, Ibrahim dispensed with feudal laws and banished bribery and discriminatory toll booths on the highways. All debts were annulled, and he encouraged a benevolent attitude toward the Jews. He failed, however, to receive favorable international opinion, and in 1840, under mounting pressure, Ibrahim returned to Egypt, not least due to a fleet of British warships off the coast.

In Search of the Lost Tribes

In Cheshvan, 1831, R' Yisrael and the other leaders of the Perushim bade farewell to R' Boruch of Pinsk, a doctor and scholar. He was setting off on the arduous journey to Yemen on the Aden peninsula in search of the ten Lost Tribes of Israel.[10]

The Perushim took this dramatic step in a daring attempt to end the Exile. The *Zohar* revealed that just before the final redemption, the Lost Tribes would return. Furthermore, among the members of the Tribes would be rabbis who had received ordination in an unbroken chain dating back to Moses. They, in turn, could officially ordain other rabbis and reinstate the Sanhedrin. Worldwide repentance and a whirlwind of great expectation would then ensue, and be the forerunners of the coming of the *Mashiach*.

A hundred and fifty years earlier, in 1657, an emissary from Jerusalem to Persia lost his way in the Arabian desert. There he stumbled on the Sambtiyon River and met a shepherd from the Lost Tribes who told him of the well-being of the ten Tribes living on the other side of the River.[11]

Although the emissary was not permitted to cross the River, he was given a letter from the King of the ten Tribes to bring back with him to the rest of world Jewry. The authenticity of the letter was attested to by the great rabbis of that era. The astounding news quickly swept through the Jewish world, and a sense of wonder and excitement abounded.

As he set forth with this incident in mind, R' Boruch carried with him several letters signed by R' Yisrael and other rabbis of Safed. One letter described the state of Jewry over the last fifteen hundred years, and the development of Oral Law from the period of the Second Temple until the time of the Vilna Gaon. Another message contained a number of requests: to pray for them, and to send ordained rabbis back with R' Boruch, and finally to send monetary support for the colonists in the Holy Land.

R' Boruch's two and a half year journey ended, however, with his tragic death. The expectations of many Jews vanished into thin air when the news reached *Eretz Yisrael*. However, R' Boruch had succeeded in contacting one Jew dressed as a Bedouin who apparently knew the location of the Lost Tribes, but refused for any price to reveal it.

Druze Massacre of Safed

The Egyptian hold on Israel in the 1830's relied upon cooperation from the various ethnic groups. An unfortunate example of this occurred when the Druze of the Galilee, upset by their induction into the Egyptian army, sought a means of retaliation. When they realized that Ibrahim's control of the Galilee was minimal, they and the Arab peasant villagers organized themselves into an ad hoc militia. Their target was the Jews of Safed.

On a sunny Friday afternoon in Sivan, 1834, hundreds of armed Druze and Arabs galloped into Safed and inaugurated a month-long pogram. They murdered, maimed, looted, and destroyed everything Jewish. The synagogues were pillaged, Torah scrolls profaned, and furniture burnt. Even *tefillin* straps were desecrated and used to tie their booty in bundles. Jewish homes were ransacked and lawlessness reigned.

R' Shlomo, the Perushim tailor, was caught hiding in an abandoned house. A Druze raised his sword to kill him.

"Don't you remember me?" cried R' Shlomo. "Countless suits I have sewn for you and your family – and this is how you repay me!"

The vandal lowered his sword in a brief moment of human compassion, and quickly dashed off.

Panic stricken, thousands of Jews scattered helter-skelter to save themselves. Some sought refuge in caves in the cemetery. R' Yisrael led a large group to Ain Ziton two miles away and hid there. The Chassidim, led by R' Gershon Margoliyos, received permission to hide in the courtyard of the local Kadi, the Moslem religious leader. Anyone within his courtyard was immune from immediate danger.

When the venerated R' Avraham Dov of Abritish joined R' Margoliyos' group with his own group of two hundred men, women and children, their combined number reached a thousand. After a few days, when their food ran out and the overcrowding became stifling, the Kadi ordered R' Avraham Dov's group to leave and search for another hideout. With no other alternative, several hundred people hurriedly scurried to some ruins at the edge of the city and prayed that their presence would not be discovered. Their only food was a flat *pita* loaf in the morning and one at night, which they were able to secure with money R' Avraham Dov's *rebbetzin* had managed to bring along on her escape.

When Ibrahim heard of the rebellion, he immediately sent his own forces to restore order. Thirteen Druze leaders were executed and some of the Jew's personal belongings were retrieved. The immense human suffering could never be redressed, of course, nor could the ashes of holy artifacts be restored to their sacred wholeness.

Pe'as HaShulchan

R' Yisrael finished writing his masterpiece, *Pe'as HaShulchan*, and planned to take the manuscript to Russia for publication. He wanted to proofread the plates and supervise the printing personally. To his great delight, R' Yisrael Bak arrived in 1832, and set up the first Jewish printing press that had operated in Safed for hundreds of years. Working together, they had the manuscript prepared and ready to go to press by the summer of 1834.

The Druze uprising dashed R' Yisrael's dream to pieces. The Bak publishing house was vandalized, and the labor of years became a heap of scattered metal nuggets. A lone par-

Cover to the first edition (Safed, 1836) of Pe'as HaShulchan

tial copy of the manuscript miraculously escaped the eyes of the evil rebels. From this R' Yisrael would have to begin anew – if he had the perseverance.

Once again R' Yisrael faced the divine elements which confronted his path and said, "I shall go on." In 1836, *Pe'as HaShulchan* was published in Safed. It was the first book pertaining to *Eretz Yisrael* published in *Eretz Yisrael* in generations. More than just a scholarly halachic work, *Pe'as HaShulchan* also delved into the practical laws of farming in Israel, and the complex laws of the Sabbatical year. It was lauded as a masterpiece, and earned R' Yisrael the distinction he well deserved.

First Jewish Settlement

R' Yisrael Bak received land from the Egyptian ruler as compensation for the Druze's destruction of his printing house. Thus, on a stretch of land outside an Arab village near Meron, the first Jewish farm in the Galilee was established. Immigrants from Russia and Poland farmed the land together with the Bak family.[12]

When the Montefiores traveled through the Galilee in 1839, they were impressed by the spirit of the settlers. Now, for the first time in eons, Jews were farming the Land which the Almighty had bequeathed to them on the merits of the Patriarchs. They diligently conformed to all the laws pertaining to the Land, such as *orlah, maaser,* and *shemitah.*

Growing hostility from Arab neighbors, however, forced them to evacuate the farm soon thereafter.

The Perushim Withdraw from Safed

Several factors influenced R' Yisrael to withdraw from Safed, and to re-establish the Perushim *yishuv* in Jerusalem. Although it grieved their leader, R' Yisrael realized that a growing number of Perushim had moved to the Holy City. R' Menachem Mendel and R' Hillel Rivlin were the first to venture there after the plague of 1814.

Two barriers stood in the way of a cohesive Ashkenazi community living in Jerusalem. The first was the problem of the debt of the *Churbah* and the physical danger to life from the hostile Arabs. Second, was the mounting tension with the Sephardim already established in the city. The Sephardim were apprehensive that an Ashkenazi community integrated into their own long established community might deflect the *chaluka* funds coming from Europe which had been designated for them.

At first, R' Yisrael permitted *yichidei segulah*, select members of the community, to settle in Jerusalem. However, as their number increased, a permanent solution had to be found.

Negotiations with the Moslem authorities were opened. The Perushim began by sending presents, then indirectly voiced their petition through emissaries, and finally convened direct talks.

At the same time, the Perushim sent a special mission to the Sultan in Constantinople to request a *firmon*, an official Turkish decree, annulling the debt and demanding the Moslems to behave cordially to the Ashkenazi residents. Finally, an agreement was reached, the gates were thrown open, and Ashkenazim were free to live in the Holy City.

A compromise was likewise reached with the Sephardim, and a new era of an integrated Jewish community in Jerusalem began.

The Final Blow

The final blow to the thirty year old community in Safed was the earthquake of 1837. The city was leveled; the death toll, enormous.

R' Yisrael was in Jerusalem at the time of the disaster for the dedication ceremony of the first Perushim shul, *Succos Shalom*. His family happened to be in Tiberias at the time, and were also saved. As he eulogized the tragedy in Jerusalem, he was overcome with emotion and fainted.

SAFED: THE MYSTICAL CITY

View of the Jewish Quarter with the ancient cemetery below

R' Yisrael, the venerable man of every hour, realized that God had spared his life because of his efforts to create a sound *yishuv* in the Holy City. Therefore, Jerusalem would henceforth be the home base of the Perushim.

He was immediately elected the Ashkenazi Rav of Jerusalem, and strove to unite the community. Every Sabbath he delivered a sermon in the G'ra shul. For the next year and a half, he led his flock faithfully.

In the summer of 1839 he traveled to Tiberias for rest and recuperation. He was nearly seventy years old. On 9 Sivan, R' Yisrael passed away and was mourned by Jews everywhere.

With R' Yisrael's passing, the era of the Perushim's settlement in Safed came to an end. R' Yisrael's courage and foresightedness had been the guiding spirit of the community, and his indefatigable efforts were responsible for its success. The Perushim's subsequent success in Jerusalem grew from the nutrition they had received in the Galilean soil of Safed.

NOTES

1. For other reasons, see *Aliyos Eliyahu*, p. 4
2. Among his other works are *Siduro shel Shabbos* and *Eretz HaChaim*. The date of his passing is uncertain. Some say it was as early as 1814.
3. While in Minsk, R' Yisrael published his commentary to Tractate *Shekalim*, called *Taklim Chadatin*, in 1812.
4. Introduction to *Pe'as HaShulchan*, p. 4b
5. See detailed account by a contemporary, R' Yosef Shwartz, *Tivuos HaAretz*, pp. 462-465
6. Introduction to *Pe'as HaShulchan*, p. 5a
7. Cf. *Orech Chaim* 576:11, "Now, since there are incidents in Safed of homes collapsing from heavy rains, it is permitted to pray for lighter rainfall."
8. *Pe'as HaShulchan*, intro., p. 5a
9. Introduction by publisher, *Chibas Yerushalayim*, pp. 29-30
10. *Aliyos Eliyahu*, p. 63-69
11. Cf. *Keser Shem Tov*, vol. 5, pp. 10-17, for full text of letter
12. *HaRav HaManhig HaRofeh*, p. 215

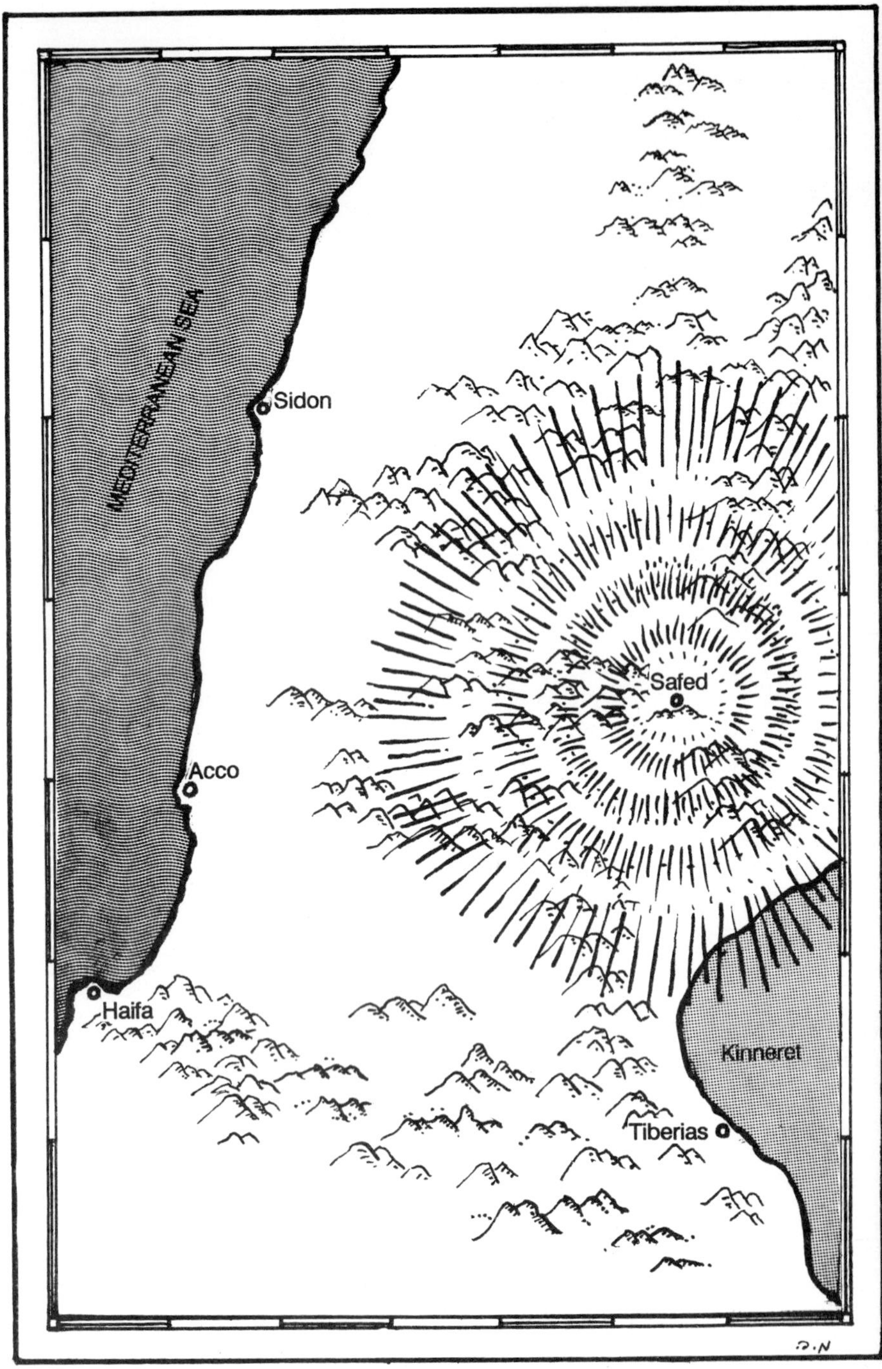
MEDITERRANEAN SEA
Sidon
Acco
Haifa
Safed
Kinneret
Tiberias
N.C.

9
The Terrible Earthquake

Why is Safed such an enigma to us? In large part it is due to the loss of the grandeur of Torah luminaries over the generations. All we have left of them is the record of their deeds and their extant writings. But there has been another irreplaceable loss – the physical structures which housed these Torah scholars, their shuls and their Houses of Study. Two devastating earthquakes within less than a hundred years had completely eradicated the physical remnants of the golden era of Safed. Anything that somehow survived the first earthquake of 1759, was crushed into dust by the gigantic earthquake of 1837. The planet's crust rippled for a few seconds, and the history of an ancient city and her people were forever changed.

A Long Winter's Night

By 1837, Safed and her residents were just beginning to regain their stability in the aftermath of the Druze massacre of 1834. R' Yisrael of Shaklov headed the Perushim community and R' Avraham Dov of Abritish guided the Chassidic community. These two leaders held one another in deep respect and often consulted on communal matters. R' Shemuel Heller, a disciple of R' Avraham Dov, was the Ashkenazi Rav of Safed.

Sunday, 24 Teves, 1837, was coming to a close like any other winter day. With the early sunset, around four-thirty in the afternoon, the Jewish residents closed their shops and returned from the fields. Mothers called their children home for supper. Scholars left the Houses of Study and joined the laymen as they hurried to pray the *Mincha* service in the various synagogues of the city.

As the sun was dipping behind the mountain range of Meron, the earth shook violently, the thick stone and mortar

The scars from the earthquake are still visible today as scores of ruined homes and shuls stand barren where once they had been thriving with life

walls twisted like soft rubber and were jerked loose from their foundations. Heavy roof beams split and collapsed on top of innocent mothers and children. Majestic arched ceilings became unmarked grave stones for an untold number of people.

"The earthquake," writes an eyewitness, "was not like people imagine it to be – a simple splitting of the earth. It was a rippling of the ground, like the sharp twitching of a horse's skin."[1]

"The ground was jarred under our feet," wrote another survivor, "and in a split second the city became a pile of rubble. The death toll was enormous. As the darkness of night quickly fell, the piteous cries and moans of those trapped under stones and fallen rafters could be heard. The survivors were hysterical. 'Daddy! Mother! Can you hear me?' 'My darling wife!' 'My son! Where are you?' "[2]

The avalanche of debris turned the city into a graveyard. Roads and walkways disappeared. Fully ninety percent of the population perished. Two thousand Jews died, and many more were injured and crippled. It was a long dark night in the history of Safed.

The Realities of Daybreak

As the sun rose over the Golan Heights, Safed no longer existed as a city. It was merely a heap of stones.

Survivors rushed about excavating for the living injured and removing them to shelter outside the city. R' Shemuel Heller was discovered alive, buried up to his neck, that morning. He had been standing under the lintel of Beis Midrash Arizal at the moment of the tremendous shock. As the ceiling and walls caved in, the lintel withstood the impact and protected him from debris falling from above. Falling rocks wedged him in place, however, and buried him up to his neck. R' Heller's wounds were so severe that he was bedridden for six months, and he lost the use of one arm for the rest of his life.[3]

R' Nachman Natan Kornel, author of *Teshuvos Ha-Gaonim*, had married in 1835 in Safed, and their firstborn son was the young couple's pride and joy. The infant was crushed to death that night. His mother miraculously survived.[4]

"Now is not the time to cry or deliver eulogies," implored the venerable R' Avraham Dov. "We must do everything possible to aid the injured and rescue those still buried alive."[5]

R' Nachman Natan Kornel (1810-1890)

The moans and whispers of the prisoners of the earth were heard for two and three days under the tons of rubble until, one by one, they were snuffed out. Try as they might, the rescuers had been unable to reach them all in time.

When news of the disaster reached Jerusalem, R' Yisrael broke down in tears. Two hundred Perushim had perished, and hundreds more were injured. He immediately borrowed money from the Sephardim and set up an emergency fund. A team of rescue workers was sent to Safed with food, clothing, and medical supplies. While the caravan made the three-day journey from Jerusalem to the Galilee, the most seriously wounded victims, hovering between life and death, could hold on no longer, and passed away. This earthquake was a tragedy which broke the heart of Jews around the world.

A Miracle in the Night

All the synagogues of Safed collapsed that night with one exception: The *tzaddik*, R' Avraham Dov of Abritish, had a shul in the middle of the Jewish Quarter. On that fateful night, the shul was full of men praying the *Mincha* service.

The Terrible Earthquake

The miraculous hand of God hearkened to the prayers of the tzaddik, R' Avraham Dov, and saved the congregants of the Bas Aiyn Synagogue

While the earth rocked, and it seemed that in seconds the shul would become their common burial pit, the *tzaddik* yelled, "Come to me!" He prostrated himself on the floor near the *bimah* and cried out to God. Congregants scrambled towards him. The domed ceiling over their heads hovered in mid-air as the walls shook under the jolting spasm. The other half of the shul, opposite the *bimah*, collapsed.[6]

Stunned, everyone gaped at the miracle. They had survived. The *tzaddik's* prayers had been accepted by the heavenly court and their lives had been spared. Later, a plaque was hung above the entrance of the Bas Aiyn Shul as a memorial of the miracle.

Who was this *tzaddik* and wonder-worker? And how was he groomed for the task as leader of the *yishuv* during its most trying period?

SAFED: THE MYSTICAL CITY

Rebbe Avraham Dov of Abritish

R' Avraham Dov had grown up among the wellsprings of Chassidus. He had been influenced by R' Levi Yitzchak of Berdechiv, R' Nachum of Chernobel, and R' Nachum's son, R' Mordechai of Chernobel. In 1785, at the age of twenty, R' Avraham Dov became the Rebbe of Abritish and remained there forty years.

His fiery discourses were later written down in Zitomir during the years before he traveled to *Eretz Yisrael*. He refused to have them printed, however, until after they had "breathed the sacred air of *Eretz Yisrael*, and become scented by it." The book was entitled *Bas Aiyn*, the *Pupil of the Eye*, "because I brought the manuscript into the holiness of *Eretz Yisrael* where the eyes of the Almighty constantly gaze."

In 1830, at the age of sixty-five, R' Avraham Dov and his wife left his flock of chassidim and emigrated from Russia to settle in Safed. It was a very timely move.

Safedean Jews, especially the Chassidim, recognized the nobility of soul and greatness of courage which R' Avraham Dov possessed. He immediately became the leader of the Chassidic community, and instilled new vigor in the whole *yishuv*.

When he saw how the *chaluka* system failed to provide for the needs of the Chassidim, he personally restructured it, donating handsomely from his own pocket. Soon, all communal matters pertaining to Safed in general became part of the yoke of service which R' Avraham Dov hefted onto his shoulders. United efforts with the Perushim, especially with R' Yisrael of Shaklov, strengthened the entire Jewish colony of Safed.

R' Avraham Dov's heroism during and after the Druze massacre of 1834, healed and consoled many broken hearts.

R' Shemuel Heller his Disciple

The Ashkenazi Rav of Safed during this period was R' Shemuel Heller, a young, energetic Torah sage. From the

The Terrible Earthquake

moment R' Avraham Dov settled in Safed, R' Shemuel drew close to him and accepted him as his Rebbe.

R' Heller was knowledgeable in medicine, and worked to relieve his fellow Jews of pain and illness. His mentor often sent patients to him. After some years, R' Shemuel decided to withdraw from medical practice. He found that reading gentile textbooks interfered with his meditations while praying.

When R' Avraham Dov heard of his disciple's decision, he was not satisfied with R' Shemuel's explanation.

"But you cure and save so many of our people," said the Rebbe. "And with your practice of treating sick Arabs without charge, as you do your fellow Jews, you are benefiting and protecting the whole *yishuv*."

"I know, but the confusion it has caused in my praying has reached a point where I feel the danger to myself outweighs these considerations and benefits."

Immediately, R' Avraham Dov placed his hand on his disciple's head and blessed him.

"Return to your practice of healing," his Rebbe declared. "You no longer need fear that it will cause any ill effect to your prayers."

From that day onward, R' Heller's mind was cleared and he could study medical books without any interference with his prayers.[7]

First Anniversary of Earthquake

The aftermath of the earthquake was dismal. The Perushim resettled in Jerusalem, leaving the Sephardim and the Chassidim with the overwhelming task of rebuilding fallen stones and broken hearts into a solid edifice with a brighter future.

On the first anniversary of the catastrophe, R' Avraham Dov of Abritish delivered a sermon before the entire Jewish community. He concluded with a word of hope.

"This catastrophe is a sign of the redemption. The Talmud in *Sanhedrin* gives an allusion to the time when the *Mashiach*

SAFED: THE MYSTICAL CITY

Cover to the Bas Aiyn, *R' Avraham Dov commentary to the* Chumash

will redeem us. The *Mashiach* will come when 'this gate shall collapse, be rebuilt, collapse, be rebuilt, again and again, until there shall not be enough time to rebuild it until the *Mashiach* comes.'

"The word gate in Hebrew is שער (*shaar*). These same three letters, when reshuffled, spell the word רעש (*rash*), earthquake. The numerical value of each of these words is five hundred and seventy, which is the same as the *gematria* of צפת, Safed.

"Therefore," the *tzaddik* concluded his speech, "over the last years there have been two major earthquakes, and many Jews have unfortunately perished. May this be the last 'collapsing of the gate' mentioned in the Talmud, and may we soon see the final redemption in our time. Amen."[8]

Massacre of 1838

For decades the danger of Druze attack was a constant threat to the Jews of Safed. Individual incidents of marauders looting wayfarers and tradesman on the roads were not uncommon. The most horrifying and destructive act of violence was the 1834 massacre. Their goal was a lust for money, coupled with a special harboring of anti-Semitic sentiment.

In the summer of 1838, tension mounted when the Druze captured the Egyptian garrison outside of Safed. The local militia, which numbered several hundred men, was greatly outnumbered by the Druze and asked the Jews to pray for them.

On 12 Tammuz, the city was gripped with despair when the news arrived that the Druze were approaching. Dr. Eliezer Loewe, Sir Montefiore's personal secretary, was in Safed at the time.

"We huddled together in R' Avraham Dov's house," he wrote in his diary. "The women were hysterical and the children crying.

"The Rebbe asked me to write a note in Arabic to the mayor pleading with him not to forsake us at this desperate time. I did so, but his answer was mere lip service....

"I sat up most of the night, too afraid to sleep. Finally, I dozed off. Suddenly, I was awakened by screams: 'The Druze are coming!'

"Panic gripped the huddled refugees. R' Avraham Dov's solemn face turned white. 'Let's go to their leader,' he ordered me, 'and ask what they want. You speak fluent Arabic and are protected by the consulate. Perhaps we can save Jewish lives.'

"We met some Druze in the street and, girding myself with courage, I spoke to them. With a savage smile the leader answered me, 'I do whatever I wish. First of all, give me your money.'

"They tore my clothes to shreds searching for hidden money.

"The mayor and his militia fled the city, and the Jews became open prey for the ravenous rebels.

"As we fled helter-skelter, they called after us, 'Don't be afraid! Don't be afraid!' They knew we had precious objects and money on us. The local Arab residents joined them, closing off the last gate of hope.

"I consoled myself by saying that it would be better to die than to see the annihilation of thousands of my Jewish brethren and remain alive."[9]

Many Jews escaped to Ain Ziton, a nearby village, only to discover that the local Arab population had turned against them, and they were beaten and plundered mercilessly.

R' Avraham Dov returned to his house. The rebels first surrounded the courtyard and then stormed inside. They mercilessly beat, looted and stripped the captives. Not satisfied with the amount of booty, they bound R' Avraham Dov hand and foot, and threatened to execute him if twice as much money was not forthcoming.

Unshaken, the Rebbe asked for a glass of water before being put to death. He wished to wash his hands before sanctifying God's Name.

"My children," said the seventy-three year old *tzaddik*, "let me be, and I shall call out the name of God. I shall bless Him for the way He has judged me today."[10]

The Druze held him prisoner and waited for his ransom. Meanwhile, they sat down to eat. An old Arab man came in and startled them by crying out, "Didn't you hear that Ibrahim Pasha and his troops are coming? They'll be in the city any minute! Not one of you will be left alive!"

Unwilling to fight against trained soldiers, as opposed to helpless hostages, off they dashed for their lives. Not only did they leave the booty behind, but even the Rebbe remained untouched.

To Abandon Safed or Not

The three day pillage took a large toll in human life and suffering. Their homes ransacked, dishes and urns broken, and clothes stolen or torn, the refugees' return home was heartbreaking. Worst of all, the precious synagogues had been disgraced and plundered. Their life's breath was knocked out of them, and there seemed no hope for a brighter future.

There was a call by many to abandon Safed and go with Dr. Loewe to Acco, a walled city, and from there to Haifa where they could rebuild the Chassidic community. Due to the number of foreign consulates located there, there was a sense of security in Haifa that was utterly lacking in Safed.

R' Avraham Dov of Abritish voiced his opposition. Should the majority vote to move to Haifa, however, he would feel obligated to follow them because 'the majority determines' is a basic Jewish principle.

"But," he implored, "it is my opinion that we have a duty to remain here in Safed, regardless of what shall befall us."

He explained his reasoning. First of all, their presence would strengthen the not yet stable *yishuv*. Then again, should they abandon the city, their synagogues would be threatened with almost certain desecration and ruin.

Slowly, the ageless *tzaddik* succeeded in inspiring them to work together to rebuild Safed. As the meeting ended, there was no need to call a vote. There was a clear consensus in favor of staying in Safed.[11]

Sir Montefiore's Historic Visit

A year later, in Sivan, 1839, Sir Moses Montefiore and his wife, Judith, visited Safed. The Montefiores were a unique philanthropic couple whose sole mission centered on the needs of the Jews of the Holy Land.

The entire Jewish community welcomed their illustrious guests with song and trumpet blasts.

"While we were still a distance from the city," Judith wrote in her diary, "a large crowd came out to meet us. Young and old, people of all stature, danced and sang before us. Some clapped while others played musical instruments. Such a welcome as this we had never dreamt of!"[12]

SAFED: THE MYSTICAL CITY

As the entourage approached Safed, R' Avraham Dov and the rabbis walked out to greet the honored guests.

"When I saw the revered Rebbe approach, his face glowing with peace," Sir Montefiore wrote, "I descended from my horse and asked him to ride in place of me. I made this gesture not just out of deference to his role as leader of the community. In my eyes, he was greatly esteemed because of the unearthly courage he demonstrated last year in standing before the sword's blade in total readiness to sanctify the name of God."[13]

The grand welcome was made somber by the grave realities of the city. The scars of the terrible earthquake a year and a half ago lay everywhere. The people, downtrodden and feeble, numbered only a fraction of the pre-earthquake population. "Nevertheless," noted Lady Judith, "these unfortunate people appeared happy and full of hope."

The Montefiores lodged in a newly rebuilt house in the Jewish Quarter. They were delighted to hear that the following night there would be the dedication of a rebuilt synagogue. The widow of the former Rav of the city would present a *Sefer Torah*, an old and very expensive one, at the ceremony.

The dedication ceremony was a special event. Among a jubilant gathering, R' Avraham Dov took the *Sefer Torah* from the widow and paraded forth under a white *chupa*. Everyone sang and danced in the candlelit shul. "I was overjoyed to witness this holy event," noted Lady Montefiore.

Since Sir Moses lay sick in bed, the Abritish Rebbe led the procession to his lodging and danced and sang below his window. He was touched and his spirit uplifted. The procession then returned to the shul and the festivities continued until at last the Sefer Torah was placed in the Holy Ark.

"I marveled at the genuine state of joy the people expressed," wrote Lady Judith. "Their voices, hand clapping, and dancing were all dedicated to God alone, and soared above the physical destruction of their city."

The Terrible Earthquake

The next morning, Sir Moses felt better, and together they visited another rebuilt synagogue, this time one of the Sephardim. *Chacham* Mizrachi led them around. Lady Judith, a righteous woman, noticed that in addition to the generally unfinished nature of the shul, there was no provision for a women's gallery.

Later, they met with the Arab mayor, Aved-El-Chalim, who quoted verses from the Bible in praise of their mission on behalf of the Jews of Israel.

They spent days meeting with and presenting a stipend to every Jew of the city, visiting some of the historic sites, and experiencing the uniqueness of Safed.

On their last day, they prayed the morning service in the Bas Aiyn Shul. Afterwards, R' Avraham Dov invited them to eat breakfast with him, together with some esteemed rabbis.

When Sir Montefiore was asked to extend his generosity even further, he did so with an open heart and a generous

Sir Moses Montefiore

hand. He inaugurated a fund to support Torah scholars, so that young men could continue their Talmudic studies without the added burden of economic pressures. He also commissioned the writing of a *Sefer Torah*, and he himself wrote the first words, "In the beginning God created...."

Their sojourn in Safed marked a turning point for the community. The visit instilled in the residents new courage and a sense of destiny. The Montefiores, too, left invigorated by the indomitable spirit of the Jews of Safed, having grown very fond of them and their noble leader.

Death of a *Tzaddik*

In the fall of 1840, yet another plague spread in the Galilee. It skipped from house to house, without warning, and covered the walls with an ugly green mould.

In order to confine the plague, people stricken by the epidemic were quarantined in their homes. This lessened the possibility of it spreading.

The community was heartbroken when they heard that their beloved leader, R' Avraham Dov, had been stricken and his house attacked. Prayers and special *Tehillim* were fervently recited for his recovery, and charity was donated. Somehow, they hoped there would be a way to sweeten the judgement lingering over him, and that at the last moment the verdict would be reversed. A fervent Jew knows that it is never too late.

The seventy-five year old Rebbe lay in bed, weak and ill. He called for his chief disciple, R' Shemuel Heller, to come to his bedside. R' Avraham Dov felt that his time had come, and he wished to relay certain matters to his disciple before leaving this world. These matters included the precious keys of Torah wisdom that one bequeaths only when standing before the heavenly gateway.

R' Shemuel received the message and was about to set out for his mentor's house.

"No!" cried his wife. "I beg you. Don't go. The danger of catching the plague is too great."

Torn between a profound loyalty to his Rebbe and the natural urge to safeguard oneself from imminent danger, R' Shemuel lingered in indecision. Finally, his desire to protect his wife and family dominated and he remained at home.

To his fellow Jews, R' Avraham Dov left this message. "I am the last offering that this epidemic will demand. With my death the plague shall end."

And so it was. On 12 Kislev, the Abritish Rebbe passed away, and the plague disappeared. He was buried in a large cave not far from the Arizal. R' Dovid Shlomo Ivshitz, a Chassidic Rebbe and author, was also buried there.

R' Shemuel Heller lived forty more years, and served the community faithfully as Rav of Safed. He always regretted, however, that he had not followed his innermost feelings and sat by his mentor's bedside and been initiated into vast mysteries of Torah.

NOTES
1. *Koros HaItim*, by R' Menachem Mendel of Kaminetz
2. *Shaarei Yerushalayim*, p. 18
3. Cf. *HaRav HaManhig v'HaRofeh*, pp. 111-112. His wife and three children perished.
4. *M'Gedolei Yerushalayim*, p. 82
5. *Koros HaItim*
6. According to *HaRav HaManhig v'HaRofeh*, p. 118, they had just begun the *tachanun* service at the time the earthquake erupted.
7. *Eden Tziyon*, p. 5; for a full background see *HaRav HaManhig v'HaRofeh*, pp. 262-283
8. *Bas Aiyn*, p. 301. The Talmudic source is *Sanhedrin* 98a
9. Letters of Dr. Eliezer Loewe, cited in *Otzar Massaos*, pp. 288-289
10. *ibid.*
11. *ibid.*
12. *Letters*, cited in *Otzar Massaos*, pp. 308-311
13. *Memoirs*, cited in *Ohr HaGalil*, p. 278

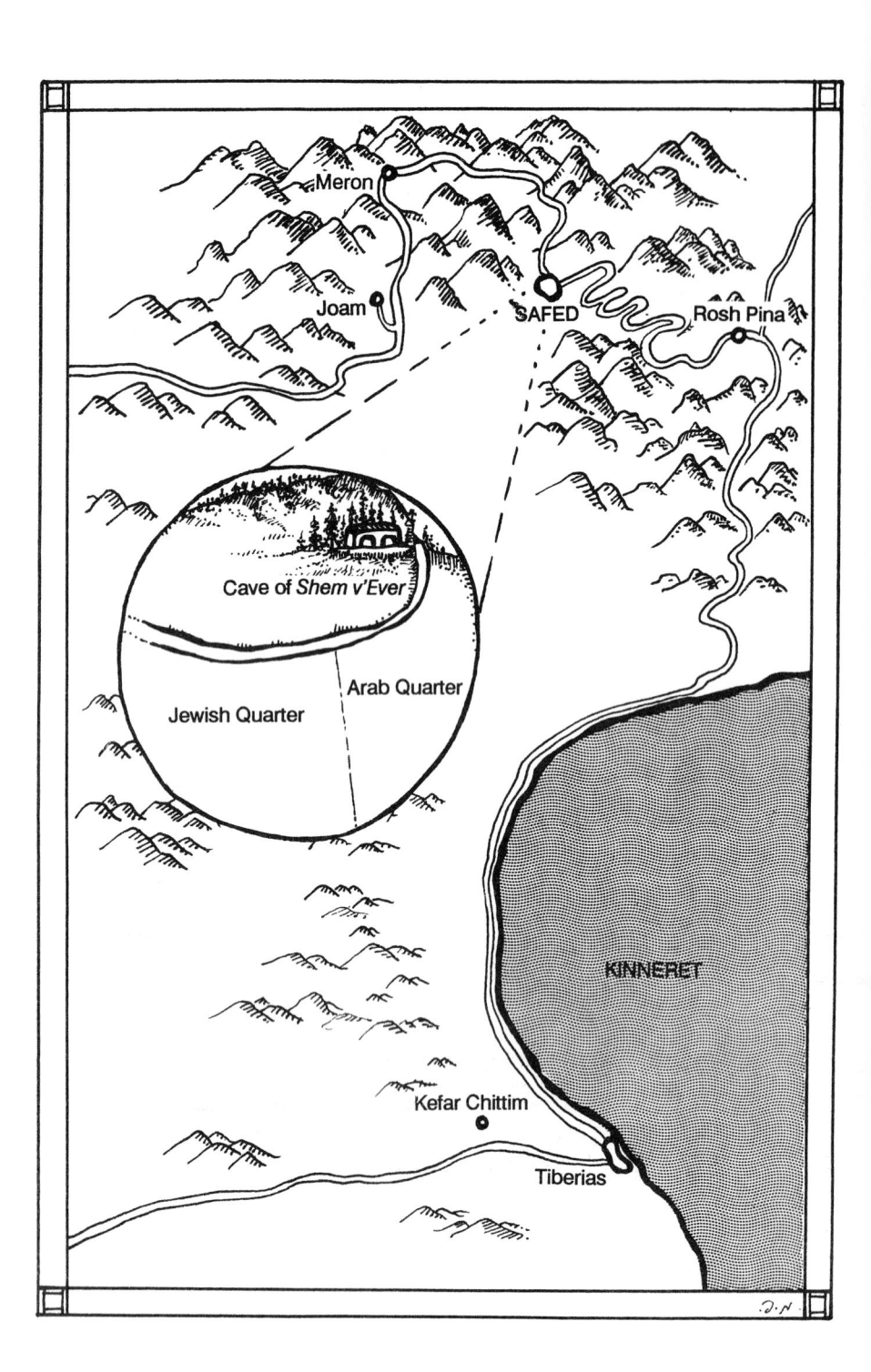

Meron

Joam

SAFED

Rosh Pina

Cave of *Shem v'Ever*

Arab Quarter

Jewish Quarter

KINNERET

Kefar Chittim

Tiberias

10
Rebirth of Safed

Safed was unalterably changed. The great leaders of the previous generation had passed away. The Perushim had moved en masse to Jerusalem. The Chassidim numbered only a hundred and fifty, and the Sephardim even less.[1] The city lay bare and in desperate need of rejuvenation.

Reconstruction of Synagogues

Fourteen synagogues had been destroyed by the terrible earthquake of 1837. Only three were spared the disgrace of total effacement. Half of the Bas Aiyn Shul still stood, a silent testimony to the miracle performed in the merit of the *tzaddik*, R' Avraham Dov of Abritish. The oldest synagogue of Safed, the Rabbi Yossi Bannai Shul, named after the *Tanna* buried there, needed only its roof restored. The Ari synagogue, too, had withstood the shock waves of the cataclysmic upheaval. The southern wall of the Abuhav synagogue, housing the Holy Ark, remained standing. More than a dozen shuls, however, were not so fortunate.

Restoration of the synagogues was proceeding slowly, probably due to the lack both of sufficient funds and of a highly spirited community, itching to see the reconstruction efforts bear fruit. Survivors were still trying to piece together their own lives. R' Avraham Dov had lived, however, to inaugurate one shul.

An Italian scholar and philanthropist, R' Yitzchak Goyatos, visited Safed and was appalled by the state of the once glorious city. He decided to restore the synagogues, and thus return to Safed at least part of her former splendor. Working with architects and builders, R' Yitzchak Goyatos invested his own money and spared nothing to make his dream come true.[2]

The Beis Yosef Synagogue and the Abuhav Synagogue were completely rebuilt. Restoration of the Rabbi Yossi Bannai Shul and the Arizal Sephardi Synagogue also came under his generous ministrations, as did the Alshich Shul. Most of the reconstruction work was completed by 1847.

Abuhav Synagogue, rebuilt after the earthquake of 1837

Jews throughout the country recognized his altruistic motives as a heavenly sign that Safed could once again re-establish herself.

Safed Comes Back to Life

Between 1840 and 1900, the Jewish population of Safed swelled from two hundred and fifty to seven thousand inhabitants.[3] With the reconquest of *Eretz Yisrael* by the Ottoman Empire in 1840, Jews felt safer in the Galilee. A new era in the chronicles of the ancient city was about to begin.

Inside view of the magnificant Abuhav Synagogue

R' Shemuel Heller, the Ashkenazi Rav of Safed during this period, guided the community faithfully. He was highly esteemed for his greatness and loftiness of soul, his profound humility and his genuine love of his fellowman.[4] He wrote a number of books, and republished a number of old books that had gone out of print.[5]

Rebuilding the Ashkenazi Ari Synagogue

The Ashkenazi Ari synagogue stands in the middle of the Jewish Quarter on the right side of the central staircase as you walk down from Meginim Square. On the opposite side of the staircase is Beis Midrash HaAri.

View of the two Ashkenazi Ari shuls from the staircase leading down from Meginim Square. Right: Ari Ashkenazi Synagogue. Left: Beis Midrash Ari

Rebirth of Safed

The Ashkenazi Ari shul, located on the site where the Arizal had received the Shabbos with his disciples every Friday afternoon, was first built in the eighteenth century. At the time, it was an open field. The Beis Midrash HaAri (*HaGadol*) was also located in that field. A stone archway later connected the two synagogues. Both were completely destroyed by the earthquake of 1837.

The rebuilding took time. Only in 1857 was the reconstruction of the Ashkenazi Ari synagogue completed. Later, a master carpenter was commissioned to build a new Holy Ark for the shul. He meticulously carved intricate flowers and clusters of grapes, and also skillfully executed lions and eagles on the border of the Holy Ark.

The Holy Ark of the Ari Ashkenazi Synagogue

A controversy arose over the propriety of these carvings of wild animals on the Holy Ark. R' Heller, as Rav of the city, was asked to decide. He presented an array of halachic sources which forbade such forms of ornamentation and the animal carvings were duly removed.[6]

The Women's Gallery

The women's gallery of the Beis Midrash HaAri has a history of its own. It was originally built after the earthquake as a separate, small House of Study. It was called *Beis Midrash shel Yankel Doktor*, after its main supporter, a physician. This doctor also donated a vast library to the beis midrash, which attracted many scholars of the city to study there.[7] During the First World War, unfortunately, vandalism reduced the library to empty shelves.

In 1937, major renovations of the Ashkenazi Ari shul and the Beis Midrash HaAri included their enlargement. The *Beis Midrash shel Yankel Doktor* was connected to the shul and made into the women's gallery.

Jewish Farm Settlements

For some time there had been a growing desire by scattered individuals to make agriculture their way of life. Until then, the main source of income for most Jews of the *yishuv* came from the *chaluka* system, which was inadequate to support large families and sometimes unfair in the distribution of funds. The major obstacles facing potential Jewish farmers were Arab resistance and open hostility.

In 1856, Sir Moses Montefiore delegated a committee to begin a farm in the Galilee. Thirty-five families from Safed were selected for the pilot project. The obstacles were enormous. Many of the animals died or were stolen. The neophyte farmers, hampered by lack of funds, lived in tents under extremely austere conditions. This initial initiative failed.[8]

Some twenty years later, a group of Safedean Jews calling themselves *Yishuv Eretz Yisrael* bought land outside Safed in the Arab village of Joani. They moved there only three months before the first settlers established Petach Tikva.[9]

The farmers set about their new mission with great enthusiasm. The ground was plowed, and after the first rains, seeds were sown. With every penny spent, they were also investing hope and prayer for a fruitful harvest.

To their great dismay, that year turned out to be a drought year, and the seeds never took root. Furthermore, many of their animals became ill and died. Although they tried again the following year, their spirit was broken and the farm was finally sold to a group of Romanian immigrants, who later moved and established Rosh Pina.

Two other major farm settlements involved Safedean Jews. Both were on the eastern side of the Kinneret. One was called *Chobev Tziyon* and the other *Bnei Yehuda*. Both succeeded and were evacuated only sixty years later, during the Second World War.[10]

R' Heller's *Esrog* Plantation

R' Shemuel Heller devised a plan which would benefit Jewish farmers, as well as support Torah scholars studying in Safed. An *esrog* plantation would offer families an opportunity to farm land and support themselves. The *esrogim* would then be exported to Poland and sold as one of the four species for the festival of Succos. The profits would be shared by Kollel Warsaw, headed by R' Chaim Elazar Waxs, its counterpart in Safed, and the farmers.[11]

In 1873, land was bought in Kefar Chittim near Tiberias. The *esrog* trees already growing on the Kefar were known to be kosher according to a tradition dating back to the time of R' Yosef Karo and the Arizal. Hundreds of additional trees were planted by the new farmers.

Until now, most of Europe's supply of *esrogim* had come from the Greek island of Corfu. Although beautiful and free of blemishes, many halachic questions had arisen concerning possible grafting of *esrog* saplings with lemon trees. Now, for the first time, the Jewish communities of Europe would have the opportunity to choose a 100% pure *esrog* from *Eretz Yisrael*.

The first year's shipment brought bitter disappointment to all those involved. Most of the European buyers chose beautiful but halachically questionable esrogim over problem-free ones. R' Waxs initiated a vigorous campaign and succeeded in getting more than a hundred rabbis and *Admorim* to sign a declaration which said, "Wherever *esrogim* from *Eretz Yisrael* are sold, one is not allowed *l'chatchilah* to make a blessing on *esrogim* from Corfu."

This opened the door to the fulfillment of R' Heller's dream. Over the years, the farmers improved their cultivation and care of the fruit trees, and higher quality *esrogim* reached an ever more eager European market.

The Sephardi Influence

The Sephardi Rav of Safed at this time was R' Shemuel Abbu (1858-1880), assisted by his son R' Yaakov Chai Abbu (1888-1900). They bought land in Meron and unsuccessfully tried to establish a Jewish settlement. Some of the buildings still standing near the tomb of Rabbi Shimon bar Yochai were built by the Abbu family.

In the spring and summer of 1869, the Ben Ish Chai, R' Yosef Chaim of Baghdad, visited *Eretz Yisrael*. His sojourn in Safed changed his life. As was and still is customary, he went to the graves of the *tzaddikim*. Near the entrance to Safed was the grave of Beniyahu ben Yehoyoda, who had been the head of the Sanhedrin in the time of King David. While R' Yosef Chaim recited supplications at his graveside, a lofty spirit suddenly encloaked him, and gateways into the mysteries of the Torah were revealed to him. In honor of this heavenly gift, R' Yosef Chaim named most of his books after Beniyahu ben Yehoyoda.[12]

R' Yosef Chaim was a profound thinker, writer, *dayan*, and one of the greatest Kabbalist of his time.

Left: *R' Yosef Chaim (1835-1909), a great Sephardi Kabbalist.* Right: *R' Yaakov Abbu (1830-1900)*

Midrash Shemuel

R' Heller became a legend in his own time. For more than a jubilee cycle he had guided the city of Safed, patiently attending to its needs. Daily, people lined up at his door with an array of queries and requests.

He had weathered some of the hardest times in the city's history. With massacres, earthquakes, a lifetime of poverty, the death of his first wife and children, his cup of bitter waters was full. Yet his righteousness was proverbial; his smile genuine.

Once, in his later years, a certain known killer sought to murder him. Late one night the assailant found the venerable Rav studying alone in his upstairs library.[13]

R' Heller recognized him immediately. He stood up, smiled, and greeted him with the words, *"Baruch Habo!* Welcome!"

The would be assailant was stunned by such a salutation. His confusion quickly changed to awe.

"I came here," he told R' Heller, "with every intention to kill you. But this is the first time in my life that my hands shake and I can not go through with it."

They sat down and talked extensively. The assailant left a different person.

R' Shemuel Heller died at the age of eighty-eight on 22 Teves, 1884, and was buried near the Arizal. In his will, R' Heller asked that his home be converted into a House of Study, and his valuable library be open to all scholars to sit and study there. It was named *Midrash Shemuel*.

R' Heller's Successor

R' Shemuel Heller's successor was R' Raphael Zilberman, who served as Ashkenazi Rav of Safed from 1884 to 1918.

In 1887 an incident occurred which shocked and infuriated the entire Jewish community. A certain Dr. Balidan opened a secular school under the auspices of Baron Rothschild and managed to get a handful of parents to agree to send their children there. R' Zilberman was outspoken in attacking the school, and together with the other rabbis of Safed, succeeded in having Dr. Balidan ostracized and the school banned.[14]

Revival of Chassidus

In the last quarter of the nineteenth century Safed once again awakened to the sound and sight of a strong Chassidic community. Some old *shtibels*, like Chernobel, which had been destroyed by the earthquake, were rebuilt. Others shuls, like Sanz, Kosov, Radovitz, Vishnitz, Tochover, and Karlin, were built during this period. Hundreds of Chassidim and their families settled, bringing new enthusiasm to this city of noble ancestry.

Although no Chassidishe Rebbe set up his permanent court in Safed, several did visit their Chassidim there. The Sanz *shtibel* stands off of Meginim Square on Dovid St. It was built, together with a *mikve*, around 1870 under the guidance of the Shinever Rebbe, R' Yechezkel Shraga Halberstam. His father was R' Chaim of Sanz, known as the Divrei Chaim, and had been the motivating force behind the project. The Shinever Rebbe left his flock of thousands, first in 1868 and again in 1871, to come to *Eretz Yisrael*, touch her stones, pray at her holy sites, and build a tabernacle on her soil on the Galilean slopes in Safed.[15]

Close to a hundred Sanz Chassidim lived and studied there. When a Galician Jew, R' Naphtali Chaim Horowitz, moved to Safed sometime in the 1880's, word of his saintliness spread throughout the community. R' Naphtali was the son-in-law of R' Moshe Ungar, who was the son-in-law of R' Chaim of Sanz. R' Naphtali had lived an austere lifestyle in Europe, one of extreme solitude and meditation. His Torah wisdom shone about him. During the months prior to setting out for *Eretz* Yisrael, he locked himself in a darkened room, saying he didn't want to see the impurities of *chutz l'aretz*.

Known as *'hatzaddik hapelei,'* the amazing *tzaddik*, R' Naphtali hoped to settle quietly into Safed, and in the pure air of *Eretz Yisrael* to continue to serve God as his heart desired. After a short time, however, the Sanz Chassidim approached him with a request that he become the Rav of their community. His answer was straightforward and negative. He had always remained out of the public eye, and would continue to do so for the rest of his life. To ensure his privacy, he moved to Jerusalem, yet even there his fame followed him. His son, R' Eliezer Nisan Horowitz, remained in Safed and likewise refused the honorary post of Rav of Sanz. His daughter married the Vishnitzer Rebbe of Haifa, R' Baruch Hagar.[16]

The Kosover shtibel, located at the bottom of the central staircase on Alkabetz Street, was built around the same time. The Kosover dynasty began with R' Menachem Mendel Hagar and his son, R' Chaim. R' Chaim had three sons, and each grew up to become a rebbe in his own right. One continued as the Kosover Rebbe, one became the Rebbe of Radovitz, and one opened his court in Vishnitz. All three built their own shtibels in Safed. The Kosover *shtibel* hummed with the sound of Torah and prayer throughout the day.

Today, the Kosover *shtibel* is alive again as a center for American *baalei teshuva*.

SAFED: THE MYSTICAL CITY

A rare photograph of Meginim Square in 1890's, taken during the festival of Succos. Note the beduin boy with his camel and the chassidim wearing their festive garments.

The Radovitzer Rebbe, R' Yosef Alter Hagar, built his *shtibel* on a small lane near the Kosover Shul. He lived his last six years in Safed, the first rebbe to actually hold court in the city. R' Hagar passed away in 1879, while in Haifa for health reasons, and was buried there. His son, R' Moshe Hagar, moved to Israel in 1897 and lived in Haifa for several years. In 1900 he moved to Safed where he continued the Chassidishe dynasty of Radovitz until his death in 1902. He was buried near the Arizal.[17]

The third son, R' Menachem Mendel Hagar, became the first Vishnitzer Rebbe. After his father passed away in 1754, most of the Kosover Chassidim joined his court. He was a great Chassidic master and a deep lover of his fellow Jew. He was known to have as many as a hundred guests a day eat at his table. His love of *Eretz Yisrael* and her residents was just as strong. In his later years he wanted to settle in the Holy Land, but his Chassidim implored him to stay. The *shtibel* in Safed was his way of creating a bond between himself and *Eretz Yisrael*.[18]

The Chernobel shtibel is located on its original site just off the Meginim Square on Bar Yochai Street. It had been built before the terrible earthquake of 1837 with a downstairs *mikve*. R' Aharon of Chernobel had sent a Sefer Torah for the shul. R' Avraham Dov of Abritish, who had been very close to the Rebbe of Chernobel in his youth, surely had prayed in their *shtibel* when he first arrived in 1830.

The shul was rebuilt in 1865, a few years before most of the other Chassidic shuls. When the Shinever Rebbe came a few years later to guide the construction of the Sanz *shtibel*, he prayed at the Chernobel shul.

One Shabbos a small incident occurred which reflected the Rebbe's greatness. It is customary that when the Sabbath portion enumerating the curses and punishments which will be inflicted on the Jewish people if they disobey God's will is

The Chernobel Shtibel

read, that the reader himself should be called up to the Torah. That Shabbos, however, one of the congregants was called up by mistake. The poor man was distressed and refused to go up. He said it would be a bad omen for him, a sign that he would die prematurely. He turned to the Shinever Rebbe and asked him to bless him with long life. Once the Rebbe had blessed him, he immediately went up. He lived to be over a hundred years old, and always said that his longevity was due to the blessing he had received from the Shinever Rebbe.[19]

New life was breathed into Safed as the young, fiery Chassidic element integrated itself into the community. A warm and cordial relationship developed among the Chassidim, the Sephardim, and the Ashkenazim of the city. It was a period of physical growth and spiritual development. World War One, however, would put an end to this flourishing period.

The vicissitudes which befell the Jews of Safed during World War One shrunk the population to only a fraction of its pre-war census. The Chassidic community was no exception. When the Munkacher Rebbe visited in 1930, there was a small Sanz community. Rebbe Aharon of Belz arrived in Israel in 1946 and visited Safed. He prayed at the Chernobel shtibel. Only much later, in the 1970's, did the Chassidic community of Safed again experience a time of revival.

Midrash Shem v'Ever

Around the turn of the century, a long drought had parched the Galilean earth. The mayor of Safed turned to the Jews and beseeched them to pray for rain. In an unprecedented move, he gave them permission to enter the cave called *Midrash Shem v'Ever* and recite prayers there. Hopefully, God would harken to their prayer and rain would be forthcoming.[20]

The gigantic cave was located high up in the Moslem section of the city. The Arabs called it *Udal Yaakov*, meaning 'Cave of the Children of Jacob.' Tradition had it that Jacob secluded himself in the cave and mourned the mysterious

Left: *Entrance to the cave of Shem and Ever.* Right: *View of main cave with a small entrance to another cave. To the right is still another large cave*

death of his son Joseph. The Arizal said that the *Tanna*, Rabbi Dosa ben Harkinas, was buried there.[21] For hundreds of years the Arabs had refused Jews refused entry into the cave. This was a major exception.

(The only other exception occurred in 1839 when Sir Moses and Lady Judith Montefiore were granted permission to enter. "When we entered," wrote Lady Judith in her diary, "the area was so large and tall that it appeared more fitting as a lodging for the living than for the dead." Further in were entrance ways to more caves, large, dark ones full of cobwebs. Some had catacombs carved into the stone walls. "Dr. Loewe told us that these catacombs were similar to the catacombs used to bury the members of the Sanhedrin in Jerusalem."[22])

Several hundred Jews squeezed into the cave to pray for rain. It was so stuffy that there wasn't even enough air to light candles. Together the congregation recited Psalms and other supplications by heart. Although no rain was immediately forthcoming, the mayor thanked them for their efforts.

Doorway to the Future

As the nineteenth century came to a close, the outlook for the future of Safed appeared optimistic. And why not? The Jewish population was nearly seven thousand strong and growing. Although the citizens were not wealthy, produce was abundant and life was stable. There was a hope that the twentieth century would open new doorways in both physical and spiritual spheres, and an even brighter future would be the lot of the city of nobility.

NOTES
1. *Tivuos HaAretz,* p. 480
2. Author of *Sadei Yitzchak*
3. *Tivuos HaAretz,* p. 480 (footnote by Luntz publisher: "4950 Ashkenazim and 2190 Sephardim.")
4. The Komarna Rebbe, for instance, wrote very highly of him (see, Heichal *HaBracha, Yisro,*). Cf. *HaRav, HaManhig, v'HaRofeh,* a biography of him written by his grandson
5. *Derech Nesher* (1862), *Taharas HaKodesh* (1864), *Kavod Melachim* (1874), *Keser Chachma* (1880)
6. His responsa were published under the title, *Taharas HaKodesh.* For more details, see *HaRav, HaManhig, v'HaRofeh,* pp. 192-193
7. *HaRav, HaManhig, v'HaRofeh,* p. 187
8. *ibid.* pp. 216-217. When Montefiore returned a decade later, a petition was brought to him by a group of sixty families from Safed. They asked him to fund their new settlement. Naturally, he was interested, but the plan never materialized.
9. *ibid.* pp. 217-218
10. *ibid.* pp. 219-222
11. *ibid.* pp. 223-227
12. *Ben Ish Chai (halacha), Beniyahu ben Yehoyada (aggada).* R' Yosef Chaim was careful to have all his *seforim* published in *Eretz Yisrael.*
13. *HaRav, HaManhig, v'HaRofeh,* pp. 251-253
14. *Toldos Zefat,* pp. 227-228
15. *Masa'os Yerushalayim,* p.212
16. *Encyclopedia l'Chachmei Galiciya,* Vol. II, pp. 298-299
17. *ibid.* p. 42 and pp. 70-71
18. *ibid.* p. 56

19. Retold by Chassidim
20. *Eden Tziyon*, p. 27
21. *Chibas Yerushalayim*, p. 78
22. *Diary of Lady Montefiore*, cited in *Otzar Masaos*, p.310

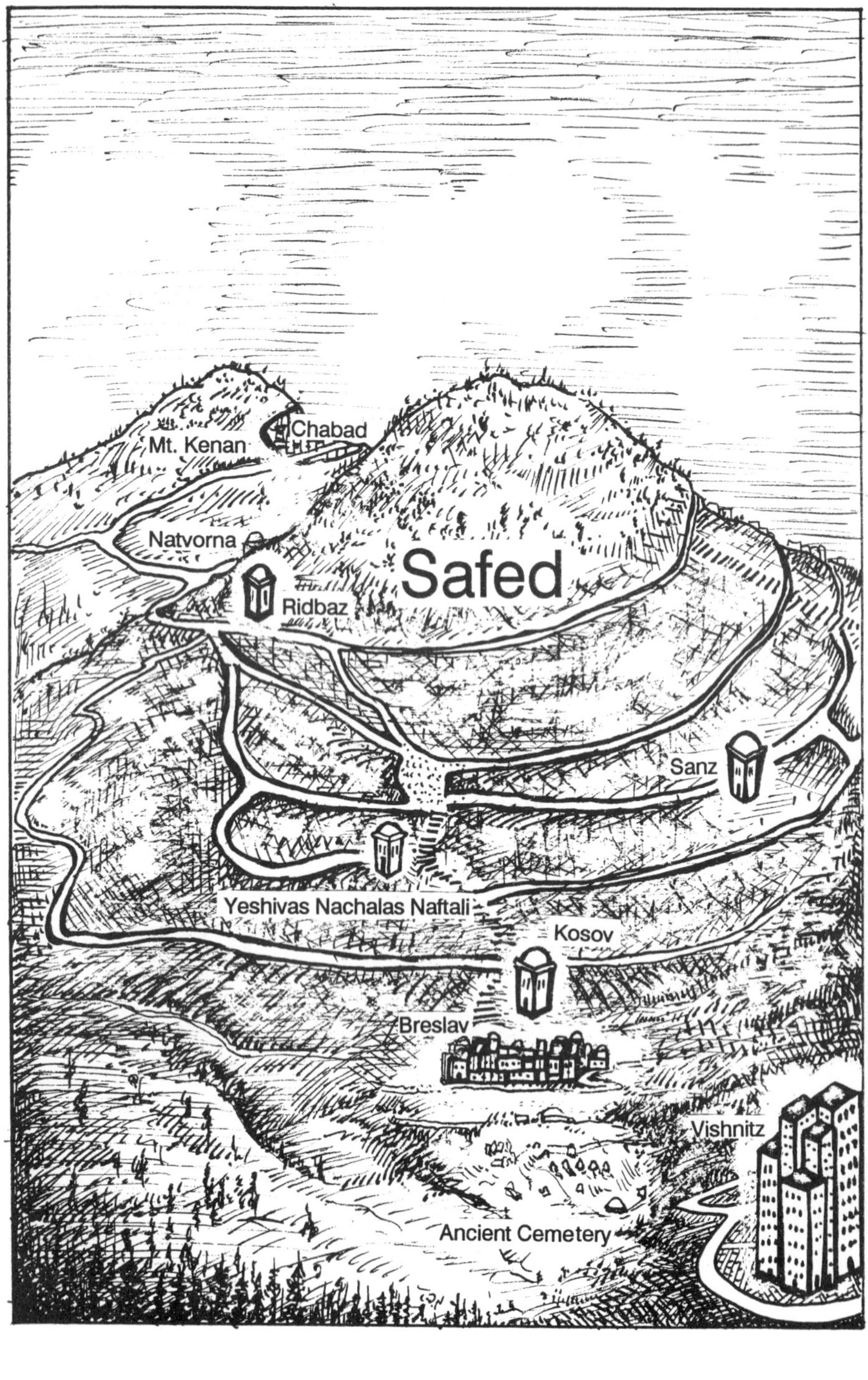

Chabad
Mt. Kenan
Natvorna
Safed
Ridbaz
Sanz
Yeshivas Nachalas Naftali
Kosov
Breslav
Vishnitz
Ancient Cemetery

11
20th Century Safed

As the twentieth century unfolded, the community of Safed had revived itself physically, yet there was a spiritual lack: Safed had no outstanding Torah leaders. This vacuum was partially filled by the appearance of two great Torah luminaries, one Ashkenazi and one Sephardi. R' Yaakov Dovid Villavsky of Russia came in 1905 and established Yeshiva Toras Eretz Yisrael. And R' Shlomo Eliezer Elfandari, the renowned sage of Constantinople, moved to Safed in 1910. Together, they would awaken Safed from her slumber.

Ridbaz

R' Villavsky, known by the acronym Ridbaz, had been a Rav in many cities throughout Russia before opening a yeshiva in Slozk to which many fine students were attracted, inspired by his genius. In 1904, the Ridbaz left the yeshiva in the hands of his *mashgiach*, R' Issar Zalman Meltzer, and accepted the position of president of Agudas HaRabbanim of America. He settled in Chicago and opened a yeshiva. After a year, however, he resigned, saying he could not establish there the type of yeshiva to which he was accustomed in Russia.[1]

Instead of returning to Russia, R' Villavsky decided to build a yeshiva in Safed. Yeshivas Toras Eretz Yisrael was opened in 1905, and within a short time the yeshiva was humming with the voices of several hundred students. It became one of the largest yeshivos in *Eretz Yisrael*, headed by his son-in-law, R' Kanavitz.

"Today," wrote a contemporary of the Ridbaz, "one of the great *tzaddikim* of our generation lives in Safed. He is the Ridbaz."[2] His greatness can be measured by his famous commentary to the entire Talmud *Yerushalmi*, which can be found printed in all editions of the Talmud.

R' Villavsky's total commitment to revitalizing the wellsprings of Torah met with immediate success. Safed began to blossom, once again redolent with the sweet scent of Torah. A number of rabbis and their families moved there, and a real yeshiva-based community sprang up. The Ridbaz personally attended to the spiritual and economic needs of the students, and maintained a close relationship with each one of them.

R' Yaakov Dovid Villavsky (1845-1914), known as the Ridbaz

During the Sabbatical year of 1910, R' Villavsky worked prodigiously to influence farmers to leave their fields fallow in accordance with Torah Law. He personally aided the farmers in every way he could. The deep importance which he placed on *shemitah* was reflected in the extensive commentary to these laws that he wrote, based on *Pe'as HaShulchan* by R' Yisrael of Shaklov.

In the wake of R' Villavsky's success, kollel Lemberg followed suit and opened Yeshivas Chasam Sofer. It, too, was a success. It's elementary school education system, in particular, was a vast improvement over the previously existing frameworks.

Years later, one of the Ridbaz's brilliant disciples, R' Yosef Shlomo Kahaneman, became head of Ponovitch Yeshiva. When he came to *Eretz Yisrael* in the early 1940's, he naturally went to investigate the possibility of building his yeshiva in the same city in which his mentor had established the Toras Eretz Yisrael Yeshiva. He hoped to arouse the interest of the Jewish community, and to work to-

Class picture from Yeshivas Chasam Sofer

gether with them to open the Ponovitch Yeshiva in Safed. For various reasons, the community did not respond with the excitement and readiness for which he had hoped, and so he temporarily abandoned the idea. Later, R' Kahaneman found more receptive ears in Bnei Brak, and thus came into being the Ponovitch yeshiva of today.[3]

On the first day of Rosh Hashanna, 1914, R' Yaakov Dovid Villavsky passed away. He was sixty-five years old. Among his writings was *Migdal Dovid,* a commentary to Talmud *Yerushalmi.* Without its mentor, the yeshiva slowly lost its momentum and finally dissolved. The hardships of the First World War reduced the size of the yeshiva until it shrank to only a fond memory. Even so, during the brief decade for which it stood, it succeeded in bringing back the romantic flavor of an ancient city, full of Torah life.

Chacham Elfandari

On a quiet summer day in Sivan, 1910, a very old man moved to Safed. He wore simple, traditional Sephardi garb, and lodged at the end of a narrow lane in the Jewish Quarter. Although his presence went unnoticed, the crates of books he brought with him did not.

Unpretentious in all his doings, the ninety-five year old man was completely self-sufficient, needing neither cane nor eyeglasses. He prayed with the sunrise *minyan* every morning, and spent most of his time by himself. Those who did come into contact with him, however, left vitalized by his wealth of Torah knowledge and his total commitment to the ideals of Torah excellence.

R' Shlomo Eliezer Elfandari, known as *Chacham* Elfandari until his last years in Jerusalem (1921-1930) when he was crowned the *Sabba Kedisha* (The Saintly Grandfather), was a 'lion coming up from *Bavel.*' Although he shunned rabbinical posts throughout his life, all the most delicate and complex halachic decisions were brought to him for consultation. His yeshiva in Istanbul produced a number of great rabbis, among them R' Chaim Chizkiyahu Medini, author of *S'dei Chemed*, and R' Yitzchak Alarish, the author of *Kiryat Arba*.[4]

Chacham Elfandari never wanted anything to stand in the way of genuine Torah life. Hypocrisy was a particularly grave sin in his eyes. Using the crown of Torah for any ulterior motives was, in his eyes, paramount to sabotaging the whole God-given Torah from Mount Sinai. He never let money, honor, or fear of repercussions affect any decision. His knowledge of Torah was phenomenal. He could recall the contents of hundreds of books as easily and thoroughly as if he had just read them. With a sharp mind and a strong heart, *Chacham* Elfandari was a towering paragon of Torah leadership, despite his external garb of simplicity.

Deeds of a *Tzaddik*

Safedean Jews were dazzled by the presence of such a venerated Torah personality in their midst. Every night he arose at midnight and studied until dawn. After reciting *tikun chatzos*, his voice could be heard resounding in the dark lanes as he studied Torah. People were amazed to see a pillar of fire ascend over his rooftop.[5]

His home soon became a frequent destination for people of all backgrounds. Some came to him for advice, others for blessings.

One middle-aged couple had been childless for years. The husband, a scholar in Safed, felt he had no alternative but to divorce his wife and, God willing, remarry and father children. Both the Sephardi and Ashkenazi rabbinic courts refused to comply to his request on the grounds that his wife was a God-fearing woman, and such a deed would be very detrimental for her. Someone told him that perhaps Chacham Elfandari could procure the divorce document.

R' Shlomo Eliezer listened to the man's story.

"Come next week on Purim," said the *tzaddik* curtly.

SAFED: THE MYSTICAL CITY

The man came on Purim day with *mishloach manos* for Chacham Elfandari, who in turn gave him the remainder of the open bottle of wine from which he had drunk, which was still standing on the table.

"Drink some of this and be sure your wife does the same. I'm sure, *b'ezras Hashem*," Chacham Elfandari added confidently, "that there will be no reason to separate. You will be blessed with a child!"

Within the year the man's wife bore a son.[6]

In Nisan, 1914, R' Shlomo Eliezer Elfandari blessed the new moon after the evening service. To the wonder of everyone present, he started to cry and beat one fist into the palm of his other hand. When asked what was wrong, he moaned, "There is going to be a world war soon." A few months later, the 'shot heard round the world' chilled the hearts of mankind, and the First World War was unleashed.

During the war, Turkish generals and infantry were stationed in *Eretz Yisrael*. One day, a high ranking general passed through Safed. All the dignitaries of the city, including the Jewish rabbis, went out to greet him. All, that is, except *Chacham* Elfandari. Later, he went alone.

"Why didn't you come with everyone else," asked the general with contempt.

"I don't go with robbers," he answered firmly. He was referring to the flattery the other rabbis had bestowed on the mounted warrior.

Stunned by the old sage's answer, the general asked him for a blessing.

"One must be humble in order to receive a blessing," answered the *tzaddik* politely. "Come down off your horse and I shall bless you."

The amazed general dismounted without a word.

"May the Almighty hearken to my words," ended *Chacham* Elfandari, "that the general will keep a good eye on the Jewish people to save them from 'the wolves of the forest'."[7]

R' Shlomo Eliezer Elfandari's seal when he was the Sephardi Chief Rabbi of Safed

Sabba Kedisha

Chacham Elfandari's health slowly deteriorated. From 1921 to 1923 he lived in Tiberias and Jerusalem in order to receive better medical attention. He returned to Safed for two more years until Elul, 1925, when he traveled to the hot springs in Tiberias. He left his library, manuscripts, and personal belongings in Safed. Suddenly his health deteriorated still further and he was forced to move to Jerusalem for intense medical treatment under the supervision of Dr. Wallach at Shaarei Tzeddik hospital. There, in the Holy City, he spent his last years inspiring a new generation of Torah leaders.

The Munkacher Rebbe, R' Chaim Elazar Shapiro, came on his sole visit to *Eretz Yisrael* in order to meet this unique sage. When the *Sabba Kedisha* heard that the Munkacher's party had arrived by train from Egypt and that a huge reception had greeted him there, he heaved a heavy sigh. When asked for an explanation, R' Elfandari answered evasively, "Oh, that his departure will be as joyful as is his welcoming."[8]

The day before the Munkacher Rebbe's departure, on 22 Iyar, 1930, the *Sabba Kedisha* passed away. He had lived nearly a hundred and twenty years.

In his last years, the *Sabba Kedisha* had compiled many of his responsa for publication. For no apparent reason, however, he stopped writing and the manuscripts disappeared. After his death they were discovered in the cemetery of Safed, buried in the cave of R' Dovid Shlomo Ivshitz, author of *Levishei S'rad*. Apparently, *Chacham* Elfandari had requested that they be put in *genizah* at that spot. The reason for this will forever remain a mystery.

First World War

At the onset of the First World War, the Jewish population of Safed numbered a hardy seven thousand men, women, and children. Four years later, at the war's end in 1918, less than one third that number remained.

During the war years, residents of Safed suffered from two predicaments, although direct military conflict between the Turks and the English-French forces was not one of them. First of all, the war caused food shortages, unemployment and severe lack of liquid capital. Inflation set in, along with the hunger. The *chaluka* system, the backbone source of income for many yeshiva families, was completely disrupted. It depended on a courier-post system linking scores of European cities with *Eretz Yisrael*. With postal service severed in many countries in war-torn Europe, and at best unpredictable in the others, the camel postal express from Tiberias usually arrived with near-empty saddle packs.

The result was a slow exodus from Safed. Some left to look for work in other areas. Those who remained lived on a near-starvation diet. Forced military induction by the Turks compelled many young men to dodge the draft and evade the law by going into hiding.

The second predicament was a typhus epidemic. Fully a fourth of the population died of typhus, as the epidemic continued for a whole year, beginning in the summer of 1916.

Safed's population shriveled. Hundred of homes were abandoned. Only 2,500 Jews were still living there when the

British signed a declaration of division of Palestine with France in the fall of 1919. In that agreement, the Galilee was incorporated into the British Mandate of Palestine, while France controlled Lebanon. The city's population remained small for the next thirty years.

Babba Sali Vanquishes Demons

The famous Ari Synagogue at the bottom of the Jewish Quarter had been kept barred and closed for years. Anyone who dared to enter had died within. Knowing this, the gatekeeper refused access to all comers because giving someone the key would be tantamount to signing his death warrant.

In 1921, a renowned member of the illustrious Abuchazera family of Morocco visited *Eretz Yisrael*. R' Yisrael Abuchazera, just thirty years old, was eager to reach the 'City of *Mekubalim*,' and stand by the graves and synagogues of the great *tzaddikim*. Of course, while there, he would speak with the venerable *Chacham* Elfandari.

The holy R' Yisrael, later known as the *Babba Sali*, was not dismayed by reports of strange deaths and of demons controlling the Ari synagogue. He sent his personal aide straight away to the gatekeeper's house to implore him to open the shul for him. In the meantime, R' Yisrael walked down to the Ari *mikve* and immersed in the spring water pool.

The old gatekeeper flatly refused to open the shul. "Don't you know," he told the aide, "how many corpses lie inside? It is impossible to remove them.

"I can not give the key to you or to anyone. I will not be party to certain death."

The aide explained that R' Yisrael Abuchazera was no ordinary sightseer, and that there were certainly special reasons that he was willing to endanger his life to enter the Ari shul.

In the end, the gatekeeper agreed on condition that a long cord be tied to the key of the inner door, so that it could be retrieved in case of tragedy.

SAFED: THE MYSTICAL CITY

A rare photograph of R' Yisrael Abuchazera (1890-1984) at the age of forty

The three of them met late that afternoon in the courtyard of the Ari shul. The *Babba Sali* unlocked the outer door and ordered his aide to hold on to his coat and enter with him. Breathlessly, they made their way to the inner door and unlocked it. The heavy old door creaked open. As they stepped inside, a strange sight lay before them. The shul was full of bright light, not at all what one would expect in the late afternoon.

Slowly, they tiptoed across the hall to the Holy Ark. R' Yisrael Abuchazera opened the Ark and read from a Torah scroll, before sitting down on a bench by the window.

20th Century Safed

The Ari Sephardi Synagogue

"You may release your hold of my garment, now," he whispered. "The danger is over."

After praying *mincha* in the shul, they walked outside. The old gatekeeper kissed the Babba Sali's hand. At last, in the merit of the *tzaddik*, the Ari shul was freed of the specter of death, and was once again open to all.[9]

Lean Years

Throughout the British Mandate period there was growing Arab unrest and tension as a new wave of Arab nationalism sparked violence in Palestine. The most violent anti-Jewish riots occurred in the summer of 1929. Three cities, Hebron, Jerusalem, and Safed were the major targets.

SAFED: THE MYSTICAL CITY

The British strove mightily to maintain order in Safed. The main stairway separating the Jewish and Arab Quarters was constantly patrolled. Even with these 'strong hand' tactics, they were powerless to halt a demonstration by six hundred Arabs who marched into the Jewish Quarter waving nationalistic flags, chanting anti-Jewish slogans, and throwing stones.

On 29 August, 1929, hundreds of Arabs suddenly launched a savage and frenzied pogrom against their Jewish neighbors. They stormed into the Jewish Quarter wielding guns, knives, and clubs. They beat and killed anyone they could get their hands on. Even old friends were shown no mercy. Hundreds of houses and shops were ransacked and looted. R' Yishmael Kohen, the eighty year old Sephardi Rav of the city, was ruthlessly murdered along with his wife. Even young children from the orphanage were killed and injured in the riot.

A Cheder in Safed during this period

The horror continued until the Arabs beat a hasty retreat when they realized that the wind had changed and a huge fire which they themselves had set was suddenly being blown towards their side of the city.

British troops, although dispatched before the outbreak, reached Safed two hours later. Their presence did, however, prevent further rioting.

The aftermath of the riots was heartbreaking. The British, in a 'retaliation' that was strikingly mild in relation to the havoc wrought, sentenced three Arab leaders from among all the disturbances in Palestine to death. One was from Safed.

Once again the Jewish population was reduced, as terrified survivors abandoned the city. Tension remained high throughout this period, and in 1936 there was yet another anti-Jewish riot.

A Change of State

In 1948 the Jews of Safed were outnumbered by Arabs ten to one. The security situation was touch-and-go throughout the early months of the year. Syria supported the Arabs, and the British attempted to foil Jewish military efforts. Yet, the Jews stood their ground, even in the face of severe food shortages.

On April 16, the British evacuated Safed, and the two opponents stood face to face in open war. First, the police station on Mount Kenan was captured by Jewish forces, and in early May the strategic stronghold of Matzuda at the top of the city fell to Jewish hands.

A few days later, on May 12th, Safed was completely freed when the Arabs lost their hold and fled from the city. A new era could now open without constant threat and tension from Arabs within the city.

A Dormant Seed Takes Root

The 1950's and early 1960's witnessed a slow but steady development in the establishment of a Torah community in Safed. Free from fear of Arab hostilities, a new group of immigrants ventured to settle in Safed. Among them were a number of Holocaust survivors and Chassidim. The old Chassidic shuls once again began to vibrate with life. Chernobel, Sanz and Tzemach Tzedek each had *minyanim* of their own.

The new Chief Rabbi of Safed was R' Simcha Kaplan. Educated in the traditional Lithuanian yeshivos of Mir and Slonim, he embodied the nobility of Torah greatness in his speech and actions. R' Kaplan opened Yeshivas Safed in a new building at the edge of the old city. When it came to declaring halachic judgments, R' Kaplan was known to be decisive, especially when handling divorce cases.

One of the first ordinances R' Kaplan enacted concerned the sanctity of the ancient cemetery. From the time of the terrible earthquake a hundred years earlier, bones from opened graves and overturned tombs had been scattered across the mountain slope, and tombstones had tumbled far from their original places. It was impossible to determine exactly where to place a new grave without the hazard of digging up bones, which would be a serious desecration of the dead. Therefore, R' Kaplan decreed that henceforth no one would be buried in the ancient cemetery. Instead, a new extension of the cemetery would be made available in the open plain at the bottom of the mountainside.[10]

For generations, the Ari *mikve* had been used for the last purification rites of the deceased. From there the bier had been taken to its final resting site. With the new ordinance, however, it became cumbersome to escort the bier down the winding dirt paths of the ancient cemetery in order to reach the plain below. In the early sixties, the burial society of Safed decided to build a direct route from the Ari *mikve* to the new cemetery via the steep ravine, a project which required building a bridge and a wide cement stairway. A few years later heavy rains destroyed part of the bridge, which was never repaired. Today, the Ari *mikve* is no longer used for the final purification rites.

The Ari *mikve*, although located west of the ancient cemetery, was ruled to have the same halachic status as the ancient cemetery. Bones had scattered across the entire side of the mountain slope and some had certainly been buried in the area of the mikve. Therefore, *kohanim* were forbidden entry into the Ari *mikve*.

R' Simcha Kaplan's sudden death in the winter of 1988 caught the community by surprise, and deeply saddened the hearts of all.

Growing... Through Loving-Kindness

Tucked away from the hustle and bustle of urban life, yet only minutes from the Old City, lives the Bannia-Natvorna Rebbe, R' Aharon Yechiel Leifer. A Holocaust survivor, he had married the daughter of R' Zeev Tirnoer, a scholar and author who had settled in Safed after the war. R' Tirnoer requested that the couple also settle in Safed, since his daughter was the only other member of his family who had survived the war. They agreed.

Left: *R' Simcha Kaplan, Rav of Safed (1948-1988)*. Right: *The Natvorna Rebbe, R' Aharon Yechiel Leifer*

SAFED: THE MYSTICAL CITY

Their first years in Safed were fraught with all the hardships that accompany poor housing, rationed food, and a large family to support. Slowly, the present-day *shtibel* came into being; rooms were added on one by one until a full-sized home and shul complex stood to serve the community.

Yet even this was not enough for Natvorner Rebbe. He had always prayed for the opportunity to give to others, to shower hospitality on his fellow Jew. Now he had the possibility to actualize his dream. His home has become a 'welcome house' for travelers to Safed. His genuine smile and warm personality make a deep impression on everyone who comes under his roof. Very rarely today does one have the opportunity to meet a Chassidishe Rebbe in the surroundings of his own home and lifestyle.

The Natvorner Rebbe's sense of joy reaches out to others. One Purim, the time that the Rebbe knows no bounds to his joyousness, he was waving a wand and very happy. The shul was filled with people. From the corner of his eye he noticed one of the young townsmen start to leave.

"Chaim!" exclaimed the Rebbe. "Where are you going?"

"I have to go home, now, Rebbe," he answered bashfully. "My wife is waiting for me."

"Chaim, do you want children?" questioned the Rebbe with a sincere smile on his face.

Chaim and his wife had been childless for many years. Obviously, it was a painful topic of discussion, especially in the public arena of a crowded shul.

"Yes, of course," he sighed.

"Well, then, stay here and be part of the festivities, and God willing you shall be blessed with a child soon."

With the blessings of the Rebbe, Chaim returned and enjoyed himself to the fullest. Within a year they had their first child.[11]

The Natvorner Rebbe's forty year residence in the city has brought back the unique flavor of an oldtime vintage to Safed. One feels confident that in the merit of openhearted loving kindness between Jews of all backgrounds, exemplified by the Rebbe, the continued growth of Safed is surely headed in the right direction.

Growing... Through Torah

The seeds of Torah growth, of organized yeshivos and kollels for married men, began to take root in the sixties. In 1967, R' Shemuel Avigdor Faivelsohn opened Yeshivas Nachalas Naftali right next to the historic Ari Ashkenazi Synagogue in the heart of the Jewish Quarter.

R' Faivelsohn's vision was to establish a strong foothold of young Torah scholars in Safed, who would be the future leaders of the Galilee. Capable students would deliver lectures in nearby kibbutzim and moshavim, as well as on the army posts. Later, as a Torah-oriented outlook would grow in the community, some disciples would open their own shuls in the surrounding areas.

A grandson of R' Naftali Tropp, R' Faivelsohn labored to achieve these goals. He spoke regularly to soldiers and lectured on moshavim. His kollel accepted candidates from diverse backgrounds. Chassidim studied with Sephardim, and *Baalei Teshuva* with *Bnei Torah*. In time, he expanded the kollel, and opened a low-priced store for the community. Furthermore, his fund-raising projects for the religious community became proverbial.

Chabad also became active during this period. Lubavitch Chassidim have been living in Safed since the end of the eighteenth century. Around 1820 the Lubavitcher Rebbe asked some of his chassidim in Safed to start a Chabad community in Hebron. In 1850, the Tzemach Tzedek shul was build in the upper section of the Jewish Quarter. That shul is still standing today.

Since the 1960's, Chabad has taken an active role in the revival of present-day Safed. Their large housing complex on the nearby Mount Kenaan has brought many religious families into the area. Over the years Chabad has grown, and today

SAFED: THE MYSTICAL CITY

The Lubavitch yeshiva on Jerusalem Street is located in the famous Ridbaz yeshiva, Toras Eretz Yisrael

over 200 families live there, praying and learning in a magnificent synagogue.

Although most Lubavitchers live a few minutes outside of Safed, their influence is strongly felt throughout the city. In the Old City one can find students learning at the Tzemach Tzedek kollel, and the Chabad House down the street hums with an array of programs. On Jerusalem Street is the large young women's seminary for *Baalas Teshuva*, Machon Alta, and nearby stands a men's yeshiva in the renovated building that housed the Ridbaz's yeshiva less than a century ago. All together some 1500 students study in one of the Chabad schools of Safed. The Ascent program, located nearby, is a unique type of outreach effort run by local Lubavitchers.

The revival of Sanz institutions in Safed really began in 1955 when the Klausenberger Rebbe, R' Yekutiel Yehuda Halberstam, came on his first trip to *Eretz Yisrael*. He was already fifty years old, a survivor of the Holocaust, a builder of

Torah and Chassidus in post-war America, and aspiring to continue to help his people in the Land of the Patriarchs. His visit was crucial to the transplanting of Sanz institutions in *Eretz Yisrael*. At first, he had mixed impressions. But once he came to Safed, he resolved to make the move, saying that he had become enamored of the special holiness of the mountaintop city. Naturally, the Klausenberger Rebbe's first choice was to re-establish the Sanzer institutions in Safed. Did not R' Chaim of Sanz build a shul there less than a hundreds years ago? But, alas, it was not yet an auspicious time. An array of bureaucratic complications melted his dream into thin air and he was forced to look for another site which, with the Almighty's helping hand, he found at the seashore town of Netanya, north of Tel Aviv.

The Rebbe did, however, leave a *cheder* which would serve the needs of the young religious community of Safed. Even in his new location, the Klausenberger Rebbe always nurtured a warm affinity for Safed. In 1971, he sent thirty families there as a nucleus kollel, rebuilt the *mikve*, and acquired land to build a Sanz community.

The history of Breslav Chassidim in Safed is quite a different story. During the nineteenth century, they had no shul or Chassidic community of their own in the city. Their relationship with Safed is more closely associated with today's rebuilding of the city.

In 1968 R' Gedaliya Kenig set the wheels in motion which would one day bring Breslav Chassidim to Safed. Because an integral part of his vision was a Breslav complex in the Jewish Quarter itself, land was purchased at that time near the Ari Sephardi Synagogue. Over a decade later twenty homes were built as the first stage of a carefully planned complex of homes, shuls, and *mikve*.

Much of the municipality's initiative to modernize the Old City while maintaining the nostalgic flavor of its glorious past comes from Breslav's assertion that the future of Safed lays just there. Slowly, new cobblestone lanes have replaced poorly paved streets, and old-fashioned lamp posts are lighting previously dark alleyways. More and more art galleries are opening on Alkabetz Street, once the main shopping center of the old Jewish Quarter.

Although R' Kenig passed away before his dream became a reality, his sons continued to inspire the Chassidic community. Besides a large Talmud Torah and kollel, the old Trisk shul was completely renovated by Breslav in 1990 as an evening learning center.

The newest community in Safed is Vishnitz, located in a long series of modern apartment buildings southwest of the ancient cemetery. Vibrant with a character all its own, the Vishnitz neighborhood is a fragrant blend of Chassidic, Sephardic, and Ashkenazic Jews living together and sharing their rich heritages.

Vision of the Future

When all is said and done, we must admit that Safed is no ordinary town. She has a timeless secret all her own. And, as with any legacy, she can pass it on to whomever she pleases.

Below the ancient cemetery lies the new Vishnitz community

Her choice of heirs depends on their approach. Is it external, with merely superficial trimmings? Or does it represent something deeper, more refined – something mystical?

Those who have settled in Safed and live there, are indeed fortunate. They are creating her future today. We have seen with our own eyes what can develop and grow in only a few decades.

Those who visit her holy and historical sites and walk her lanes are also fortunate, for they help to ignite the sparks of holiness tucked away under every stone, and to keep her flame aglow.

And those who quench their thirst for the wonder of Safed, the 'City of *Mekubalim*,' by studying her history, and thus relive, as it were, her glorious past, also endear themselves to God.

There is a future for Safed, a living, dynamic future, a future built on the foundation stones of Torah. And as the time approaches for the blast of the ram's horn on the Galilee mountaintop, it is certain that much will unfold before our eyes, more than we can begin to imagine.

NOTES
1. *Melitzei Aish*, vol. III, p. 85, no. 449
2. *Admas Kodesh*, p. 246
3. Retold by R' Y. M. Zacharish, a disciple of the Chazon Ish
4. Cf. biography in *Massaos Yerushalayim*, called *Maamar Chaiyos Aish*, pp. 267-320
5. *ibid*. p. 293
6. *ibid*. p. 296
7. *ibid*. p. 294
8. *ibid*. p. 315
9. *Babba Sali*, pp. 42-43
10. Retold by his son, R' Mordechai Dov Kaplan
11. Retold by Chaim, and others

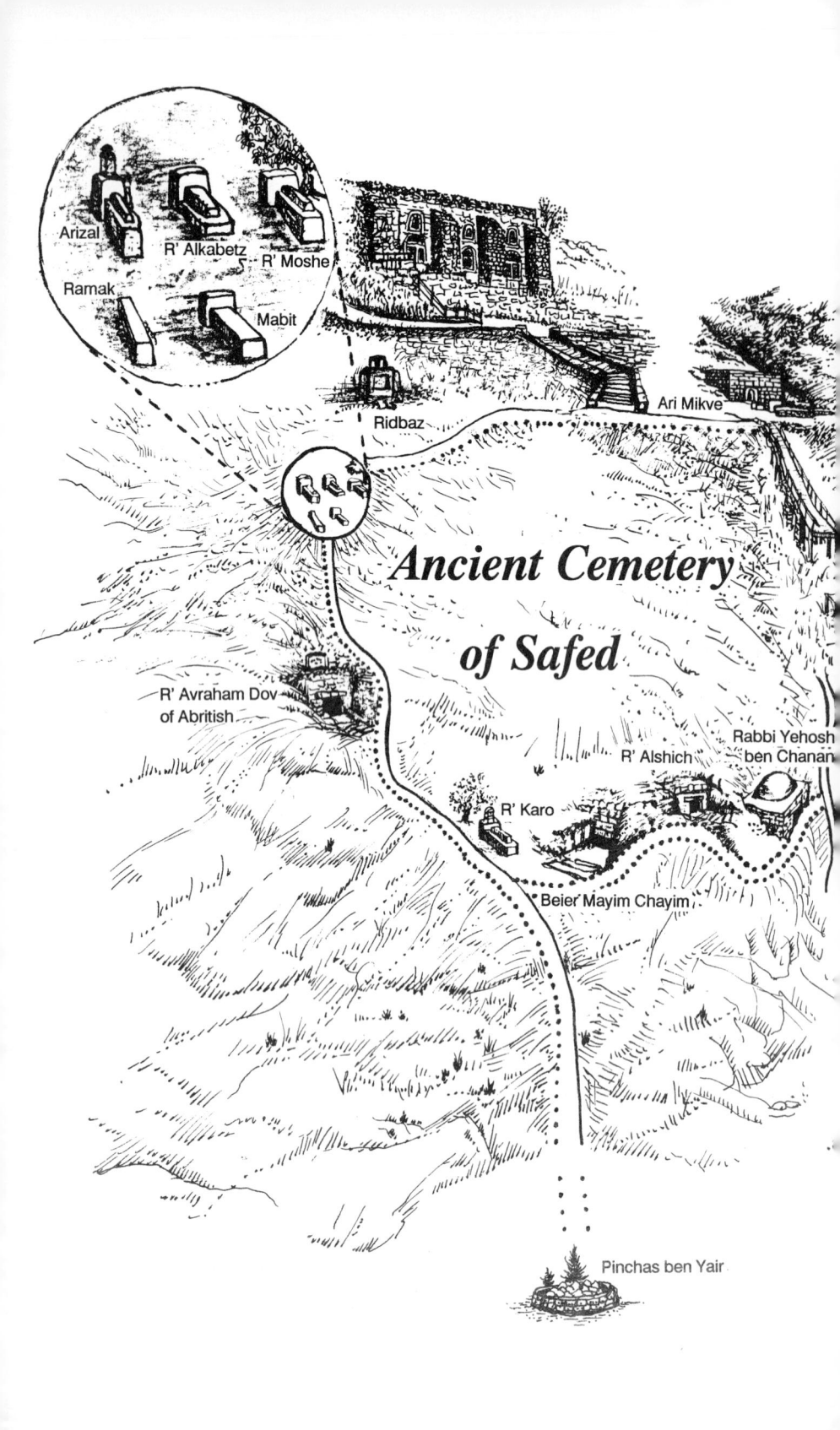

Ancient Cemetery of Safed

- Arizal
- R' Alkabetz
- R' Moshe
- Ramak
- Mabit
- Ridbaz
- Ari Mikve
- R' Avraham Dov of Abritish
- R' Karo
- R' Alshich
- Rabbi Yehosh ben Chanan
- Beier Mayim Chayim
- Pinchas ben Yair

12

Abode of the Living
A Guide to the Tombs of the Tzaddikim

One of the Hebrew expressions for 'cemetery' is 'abode of the living.' Why? "*Tzaddikim* after death are called living" (*Berachos* 18a). Many observant visitors to Safed place a high priority on going to the ancient cemetery and praying at the grave sites of the great *tzaddikim* buried there. There are many sound reasons for this investment of time and energy. The Arizal himself said, "It is beneficial to go to the graves of the *tzaddikim* and pray there."

The *Zohar* (2:16a) explains the benefit that one receives. "R' Abba said, 'How do we know that the prayers of the dead protect the living?' And he answered, 'From the verse, "They traveled from the Negev and (Caleb) came to Hebron" (Num. 13:22)." There, Caleb prayed at the burial place of the Patriarchs for protection from the scheme of the spies.

Halacha permits us to ask that our supplications be heard in the merit of the departed soul. We are also allowed to request that the *tzaddik* plead our case before the heavenly court, since we may feel inadequate and full of spiritual blemishes which might prevent our prayers from ascending heavenward. Direct requests of the *tzaddik*, however, are strictly forbidden.

Laws and Customs

The following is a summary of the laws and customs which should be observed when visiting the graves of *tzaddikim*:

1. One should not visit the same grave more than once a day.

2. When entering a cemetery for the first time in thirty days, the following blessing should be recited: "Blessed are You, O Lord our God, King of the Universe, who has created you (the deceased) in justice, and sustained you in justice, provided for you in justice, and brought death upon you in justice, knowing your number; who in the future shall revive and restore you to life in justice. Blessed are You, O God, who restores life to the dead."

3. It is forbidden to eat, drink, or act in a lightheaded manner.

4. It is forbidden to study Torah, unless it is in honor of the deceased.

5. It is forbidden to sit on grave stones, or to tread on them.

6. *Kohanim* are forbidden to enter – even to the grave of a great *tzaddik*. Also, men who are impure *(k'ri)*, pregnant women, and women in *nidah* should refrain from going into the cemetery.

7. It is forbidden to enter a cemetery on Shabbos and Yom Tov.

8. After leaving, one should wash his hands without drying them. This is to impress on us that we are not consciously diverting our attention away from the 'day of death.'

Auspicious Times to Visit the Cemetery:

The 15th of the lunar month, the eve of *Rosh Chodesh*, Friday morning, a *yartzeit*, the eve of Rosh Hashanna, and the eve of Yom Kippur are all considered auspicious.

The reason that Friday mornings and the *Rosh Chodesh* eves are auspicious, says the *Zohar* (1:81a, 1:234a), is that on the following day (*Shabbos* and *Rosh Chodesh*) the soul of the *niftar* is elevated and can carry the prayers with him up to heaven.

Charity:

It is customary to give charity when first arriving. If there is not charity box, one may verbally vow to give a certain sum later. "Repentance, prayer, and charity dispel an evil decree."

Placing a Stone on the Tomb:

There are two different customs in this regard:

1. To place a stone on the tomb upon arrival, and to leave it there. The stone is placed in honor of the *niftar*, and is not removed when leaving.

2. To place a stone on the tomb upon arrival, and remove it upon leaving. The stone represents a resting place upon which the spark of the *tzaddik's* soul can descend and dwell while you are praying there. Therefore, upon leaving the stone should be removed.

Circling the Grave:

It is customary to circle the grave counterclockwise seven times. One who physically goes around a grave enacts below what God does in *Gan Eden* when He inscribes each *tzaddik*. In addition, the act of circling the grave silences the negative powers.

Placing a Hand on the Grave:

The left hand may be placed on the tombstone while studying and praying. Some have the custom of first saying the verse in Isa. 58:11, which has fifteen Hebrew words, corresponding to the fifteen joints in the hand. The Chida, after reciting the verse, would add this prayer: "May you dwell in peace, and rest in peace until the redeemer shall come and proclaim *shalom*."

Studying the Torah of the Tzaddik:

It is praiseworthy to quote the words and deeds of the *tzaddik* buried there. This should be done before saying one's personal supplications. Thus, one arouses the *tzaddik's* soul ("the lips of the *tzaddik* murmur in the grave"), and he will then be willing to plead for your heartfelt requests before the heavenly court.

Casting Grass over your Shoulder:

After leaving the cemetery, it is customary to pull out some grass and toss it over your shoulder as an allusion to the resurrection. Recite: "May they flourish in the city like the grass of the earth" (Psalms: 72:16).

In the Shadow of the Tzaddik: A Guide to the Grave Sites

The following table lists a few grave sites, their location, and some appropriate prayers.

In the City

****Nachum Ish Gamzu** (*yartzeit*, unknown):

Location: In south Safed, on Ish Gamzu St.

Deeds: A *Tanna*, he was Rabbi Akiva's mentor for twenty-two years. According to one tradition, *'Ish Gamzu'* refers to how he related to everything that befell him. He would always say, "This, too, *(gam zu)* is for the good." According to another tradition, his hometown was Gamzu. Thus, he was Nachum, the man *(ish)* from the town of Gamzu.

****Benyomin HaTzaddik** (*yartzeit*, unknown):

Location: In south Safed, at the bottom of HaNassi St., to the left.

Deeds: A *Tanna* and disciple of Rabbi Akiva. Because of his love of the *mitzva* of charity, he became a *gabbai tzeddaka*. Once, when there was no money in the charity fund, he supported a widow and her seven sons from his own re-

Left: *Tomb of Rabbi Benyomin HaTzaddik.* Right: *Tomb of Rabbi Nachum Ish Gamzu*

sources. Later, when he became critically ill, the heavenly court recalled his deed of kindness and added twenty-two years to his life. (*Babba Basra* 11a)

****Rabbi Dosa Ben Horkinas** (*yartzeit*, unknown):
Location: In Cave of Shem and Ever, above the bridge on Yerushalayim St., off HaPalmach St. See photos, page 187.
Deeds: He lived for over 400 years, from the time of the prophet Hagai, until the time of Rabbi Akiva. He said, "A morning nap, or drinking wine in the afternoon, or indulging in childish talk, or idling the time away with ignorant people, takes a person out of this world." (*Avos* 3:10)

****Rabbi Yossi Bannai** (*yartzeit*, unknown):
Location: His tomb, located in the women's gallery of the synagogue which bears his name, is in the lower section of the Old City, on Mekubalim St.

Deeds: A *Tanna*, he lived in the time of Rabbi Meir. The *Midrash* brings a dialogue between him and a gentile philosopher concerning the creation of the world. (*Shemos Rabba* 13:1)

In the Ancient Cemetery

**Arizal, R' Yitzchak Ben Shlomo Luria (*yartzeit*, 5 Av):
Location: Enter the cemetery from the staircase below the Ari Sephardi Synagogue. At the bottom of the stairs bear to the right and continue along the clearly marked path for several minutes until you reach the blue-painted tombstone.

Prayer: Master of the Universe! We stand here ready to mention the praises of Your servant, the *tzaddik*, R' Yitzchak ben Shlomo, *zecher livracha*. We know how You cherish the praises of the *tzaddikim* – for their praise is Your glory. May we merit thereby to have some of the aura of Your servant, R' Yitzchak ben Shlomo, dwell upon us. Purify us by removing all the impure thoughts and blemished images in our mind, and let us be privileged to higher states of consciousness. Assist us to always think lofty thoughts when engaging in the study of Your Torah and when doing Your *avoda*. May we merit to bind ourselves to You, and to pray to You with pure-minded intentions. "May the words of my mouth and the meditation of my heart be pleasing before Your countenance, O God, my Rock and my Redeemer" (Psalms 19:5).

**Ramak, R' Moshe ben Yaakov Cordovero (*yartzeit*, 23 Tammuz): Location: Just below Arizal's grave.

**R' Shlomo Alkaketz (*yartzeit*, unknown):
Location: To the side of Arizal's grave.

**Radbaz, R'Dovid ben Zimra (*yartzeit*, unknown):
Location: To the side of the Arizal's grave.

**Mabit, R' Moshe ben Yosef Terani (*yartzeit*, 23 Nisan):
Location: To the side of Arizal's grave.

Abode of the Living

Within a few feet of each other lies some of the great tzaddikim from the time of the Arizal. Clockwise from the left foreground: Mabit, Ramak, Arizal, R' Shlomo Alkabetz, and (to the left of the tree) R' Moshe, the Arizal's son who passed away in Safed.

**R' Avraham Dov of Abritish *(yartzeit,* 12 Kislev):
**R' Dovid Shlomo Ivshitz *(yartzeit,* 22 Cheshvan):
Location: Both are in the same cave. From the Arizal's grave continue along the path down the mountain to the left. Not far away to the right is the cave. Photograph on page 220.

**R' Yosef ben Ephraim Karo *(yartzeit,* 13 Nisan):
Location: Continue down the mountain slope along the same path until reaching a single tree on the left side. The tombstone is under the tree. Photograph on next page.

**R' Chaim of Chernovitz *(Beier Mayim Chayim) (yartzeit,* 27 Kislev):
Location: Close to R' Karo's grave, on the left, is the cave of R' Chaim. See photograph, page 139.

SAFED: THE MYSTICAL CITY

Above: *R' Yosef Karo.* Below: *(left) the domed tomb of R' Yehoshua ben Chananya, (right) the cave of R' Avraham Dov of Abritish and R' Dovid Shlomo Ivshitz*

**R' Moshe Alshich (*yartzeit*, 13 Nisan):
**R' Yaakov Berav (*yartzeit*, 30 Nisan):
Location: Both are buried in the same cave, slightly further to the south. See photograph, page 34.

**Rabbi Yehoshua ben Chananya (*yartzeit,* unknown):
Location: Slightly further to the south stands a prominent cave within a domed-top structure, the only one in the ancient cemetery. An additional tradition says that the prophet Hoshea is buried there.

Deeds: A disciple of Rabbi Yochanan ben Zakkai, and mentor of Onkelos and Shimon ben Azai. He was *Av Beis Din* in the time of Rabban Gamliel. "Rabbi Yochanan ben Zakkai enumerated the merits of his chief disciples: '...Rabbi Yehoshua, Happy is the she who bore him.' " (*Avos,* 2:11)

**Rabbi Pinchas ben Yair (*yartzeit,* unknown):
Location: At the bottom of the mountain, past the new cemetery, inside a large circular stone wall, under a pile of stones, and without any tombstone.

Deeds: A *Tanna*, he was the father-in-law of Rabbi Shimon bar Yochai. The Arizal pinpointed the exact spot of the unmarked grave. According to tradition the fact that no tombstone was ever erected alludes to the altruism of the *tzaddik*, who never accepted benefits from others. Thus even after death the *tzaddik* refused, as it were, to allow people to construct a tombstone over his grave. Attempts were made, but they all ended in failure.

It is customary to circle the monument seven times while reciting the prayer *Ana b'Koach* and Psalm 91 seven times.

In the early 19th century, an Arab farmer forbade Jews from crossing through his field to reach the grave site. That year, to the farmer's dismay, his wheat crop failed. When he mended his ways and permitted passage through field, the crop was again productive.

SAFED: THE MYSTICAL CITY

Rabbi Pinchas ben Yair

There is a tradition of an underground tunnel connecting the burial site of Rabbi Pinchas ben Yair and Rabbi Shimon bar Yochai. The two caves, one in Safed and the other in Meron, about three miles away as the bird flies, alludes to the words of the Sages, "Even after death, the *tzaddikim* are called living" (*Berachos* 18a). The cemetery of Safed, like other cemeteries with graves of *tzaddikim* buried there, is the abode of the living.

* * *

The following prayer is appropriate to recite at the grave of any *tzaddik:*
"Let the righteous rejoice in honor, let them exult upon their beds" (Psalms 149:5). *Shalom Alechem!* (When by the grave of one *tzaddik*, say in the singular, *Shalom Alecha!* our teacher and master, so-and-so...) May your soul(s) and the souls of your companions and disciples be bound up in everlasting life with God beneath the Throne of Glory. How for-

tunate are you *tzaddikim*. How fortunate are you, O pious and pure ones, who toiled in Torah. You are the mighty ones, the foundation stones of the world. The Merciful One, may He be blessed, eagerly awaits the time when He shall restore you to life. May I merit to gaze on your face which shines like the luminous skies. I have come to prostrate myself on the tombs of the *tzaddikim* buried here. I request from my Creator, the King of Kings, that He should recall these *tzaddikim*. May their merits and righteousness stand by me, protect me, and save me from the evil inclination which constantly seeks to ensnare me by interfering with my Torah and *avoda*. Strengthen my good inclination as You aided these *tzaddikim* buried here. Help me to repent wholeheartedly. Open my heart to understand Your Torah, and let it be a place where I can unite Your Name. Let me be among the *tzaddikim* who inherit the World to Come. Furthermore, as I have been privileged to see the tombstones of these *tzaddikim*, if it be the will of the Creator, may I be privileged to see them alive along with all the rest of our people. May the merits of the *tzaddikim* and their prayers guard us at times of trouble, and save each one of us wherever he may be. Send a complete and healthy recovery to the sick ones of Your people (especially to ....). Let us be privileged to see *Mashiach* soon. "May the words of my mouth and the meditation of my heart be pleasing before Your countenance, O God, my Rock and my Redeemer" (Psalms 19:15). (from *Shaarei Dima*, pp. 25-27)

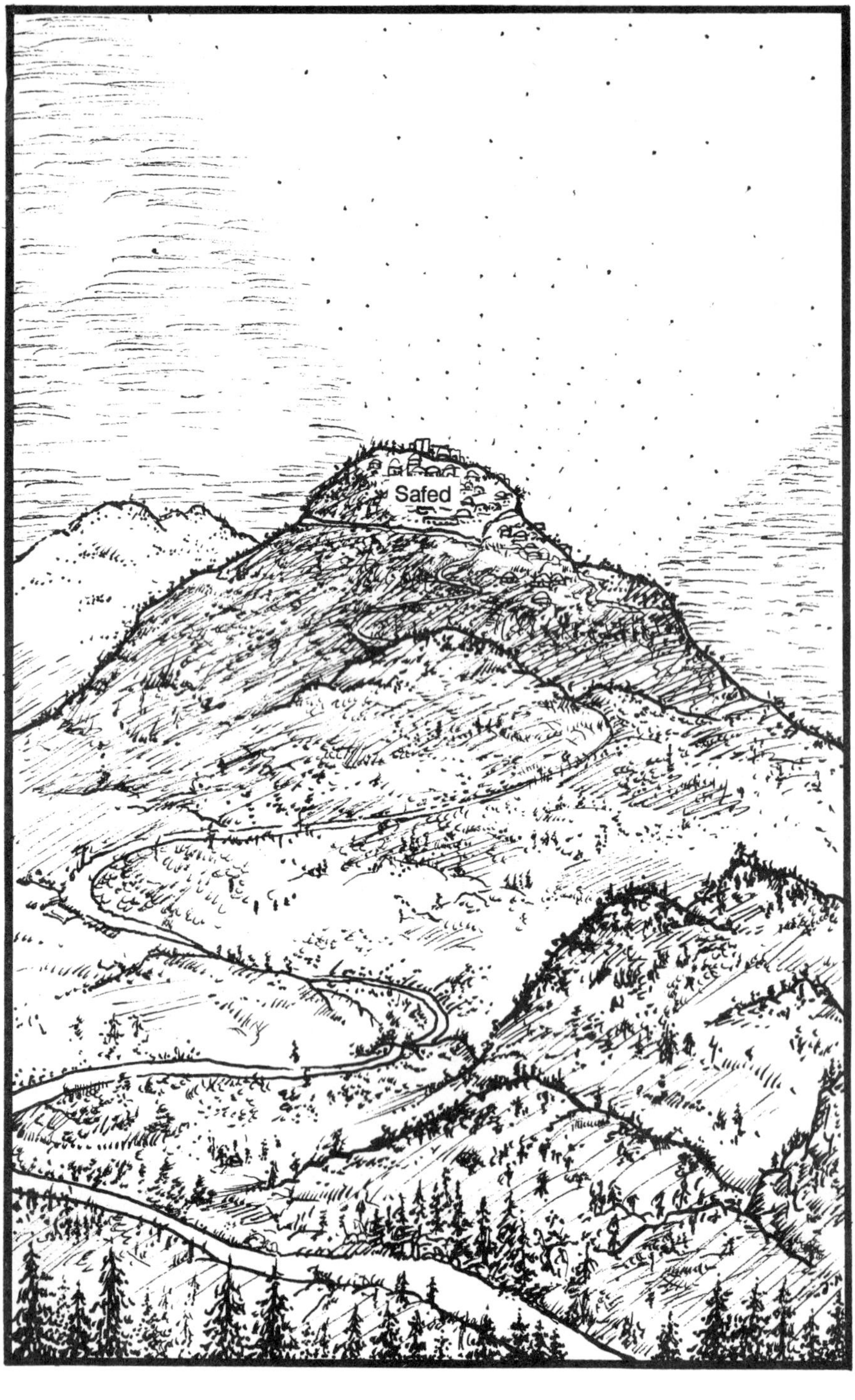
Safed

13
Farewell, Oh Safed

Once Upon a Time

As you are about to bid farewell to Safed, your mind reels. The charming little city has been transformed into a majestic royal city of Torah sages and their mission to further noble goals far beyond the ken of mortal man. Their superhuman efforts almost touch on the legendary. Yet their history is the genuine history of Safed.

Safed beckons you not to leave. Just one more day, one more hour, one more farewell embrace. Somehow the magic of Safed is tied to the *tzaddikim* who were privileged to have the Divine Presence descend and enlighten them. The shuls still hum with the vibrations of their Torah studies. We feel enamored by the beauty of the synagogues. Yet, it is not the old stone floors or arched ceilings which really captivate our imagination. They are merely a vehicle to enhance our appreciation of the sanctity of these places. Over the generations, the Torah, prayers, and deeds of the Jews of Safed have imbued these stones and arches with the sparks of the Divine. That is what stirs us.

Until Next Time

The time has come. You must leave. Your mission is somewhere else. But you want to leave something behind, something from you which will acknowledge your sense of graditute to Safed, the mystical city.

You turn this way and that, lost for a moment in thought how to express your farewell. Then, almost unconsciously, you whisper a prayer, "Until next time... Oh, Safed, until next time."

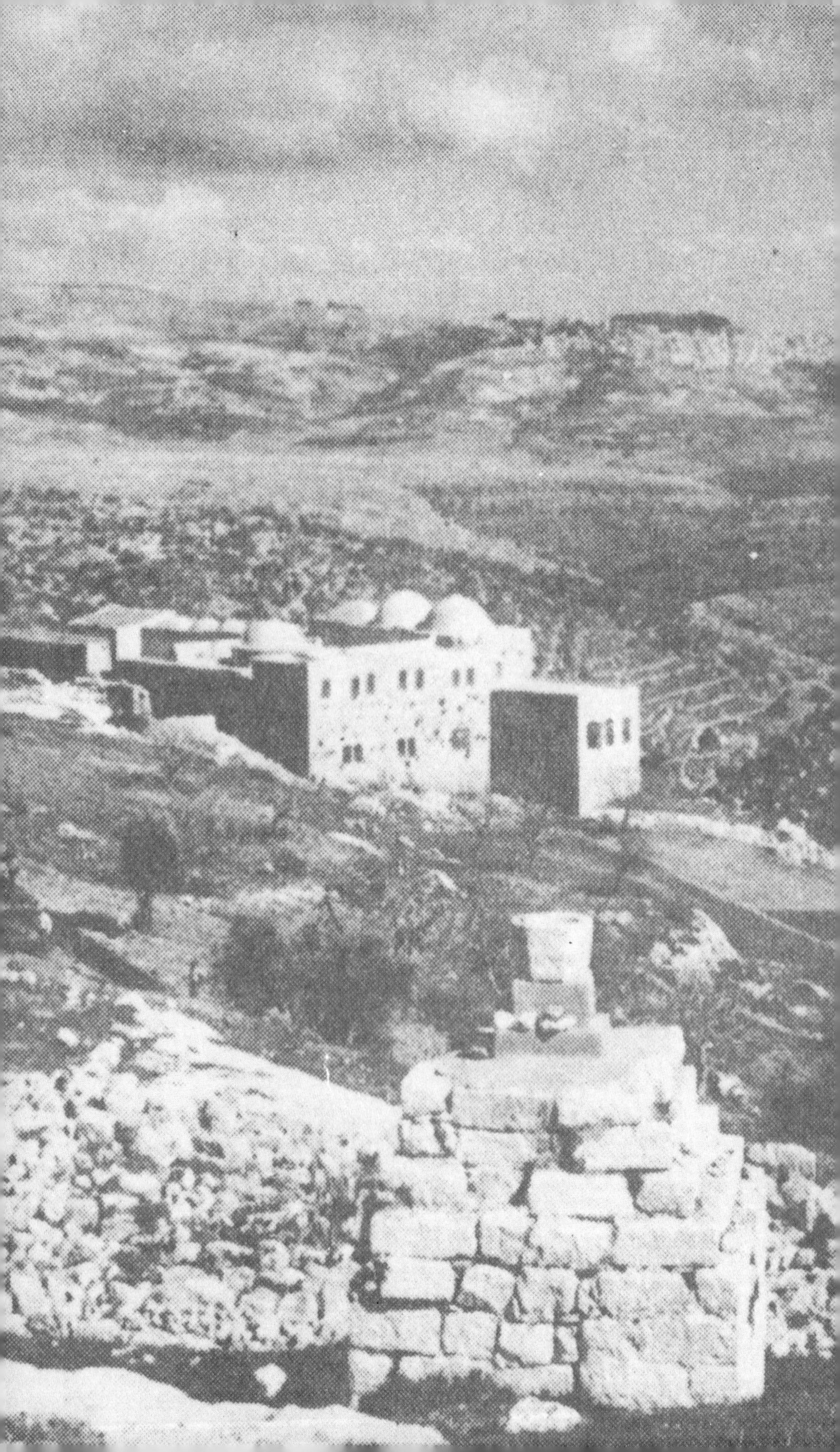

14
Meron

We can hardly bid farewell to Safed without gazing across the valley to the mountain range of Meron. There, near the foot of the mountain, is the cave of Rabbi Shimon bar Yochai and his son.

The same things that draw us to Safed, beckon us to go also to Meron, the source of the wellsprings of holiness which have watered Safed over the generations, the teachings and life of the *Tanna*, Rabbi Shimon Bar Yochai. He was the author of the *Zohar*, the *Book of Splendor*, which reveals vast mysteries of creation to the initiated, and succeeded in bringing into the world aspects of the Torah never divulged to man.

Before we cross the valley and visit his cave, let us begin by sketching a portrait of this singularly profound man.

Rabbi Shimon bar Yochai

Born some fifty years after the destruction of the second Temple, Rabbi Shimon bar Yochai studied in the Academy of Rabbi Akiva, where he excelled in his studies to the highest possible degree, and drew very close to his mentor. Their relationship was so close, in fact, that he even endangered his life to visit Rabbi Akiva after he had been imprisoned by the Romans for disseminating Torah to the masses. "More than a calf wants to suck from his mother," Rabbi Akiva responded to his disciple's pleas, "the mother cow desires to nurse her offspring."[1] Yet, Rabbi Akiva refused to teach him under such dangerous circumstances for fear that his disciple, too, would be apprehended.

One of the five principal disciples of Rabbi Akiva, Rabbi Shimon received rabbinical ordination both from his mentor and from Rabbi Yehuda ben Babba.[2]

In time, Rabbi Shimon began to teach publicly. When his life was threatened by the Romans, he was compelled to escape with his son Elazar to Peikin in the upper Galilee. They studied together in Peikin for thirteen years, and perfected themselves in both the revealed and the esoteric aspects of the Torah.[3]

Rabbi Shimon, a master of Jewish law, participated in many Talmudic debates, and his opinions are quoted over three hundred times in the *Mishna*. However, it was his accomplishments in the world of Kabbalah which so far exceeded those of his contemporaries that he was compared to Moses. Just as Moses was the greatest of all prophets, Rabbi Shimon was the greatest of all mystics.[4]

Rashbi and His Companions

Rabbi Shimon bar Yochai, known by the acronym Rashbi, had a yeshiva in Meron which attracted a number of students. From these, the Rashbi chose those disciples whom he knew were worthy of initiation into Kabbalah. His 'companions,'[5] as he called them, together with their mentor, transcended the world of everyday matters and ascended to the celestial spheres where they conversed with the departed souls of great Sages and with heavenly angels who revealed to them mysteries of Creation.[6]

Mysteries of the Torah had been passed from generation to generation by men of great caliber since the time of the giving of the Torah on Mount Sinai. Due to the exalted nature of these secrets, they were hidden from the realm of common men. Even among mystics the secrets were merely alluded to and not spelled out in detail. Now, for the first time, Rabbi Shimon was granted permission to teach Kabbalah openly to his disciples.[7] He received permission from Above to disclose these mysteries, as well as others that had never before been revealed to man.[8] Among the natural beauties of the Galilean hills, in the yeshiva or on one of their many excursions, the Divine Presence hovered over the Rashbi and his 'companions' and illuminated their way.

The Book of Splendor

The *Zohar* is the legacy which Rabbi Shimon bar Yochai and his companions left for the Jewish people. It was written down by Rabbi Abba, the Rashbi's scribe, and second among his disciples. Rabbi Elazar, his son, was nearly on par with his father. The teachings are cloaked in homilies, stories, and parables, which may be understood on various levels. Only the initiated can fathom the true depth of the mysteries which lie beneath the surface.

Once Rabbi Shimon bar Yochai was traveling away from home. When he came to the town of Lud he was informed of a great tragedy which had befallen the town. An epidemic had ravaged the area and many Jews had lost their lives. The townmen turned to the *tzaddik* for help.

The Rashbi entered Lud and was aghast at the sight he saw before him. Bodies were lying on the roadside, unable to be buried because of the intensity of the plague.

"All of this is happening while I'm in this town!?" cried Rabbi Shimon. "I demand that the plague stop immediately!"

A heavenly voice broke through the skies and said to the angels of destruction, "Depart from this town! Don't you know that Rabbi Shimon is here! Although the Holy One blessed be He decreed that there should be this epidemic, the *tzaddik* has come and annulled that decree."

Later, this episode was told over to Rabbi Meir. He rejoiced at the story and added this interpretation. "Truly, who can appreciate the greatness of Rabbi Shimon! It even surpassed that of Moses! When Korach and his companions died for their insurrection, the Jewish people complained and threatened Moses and Aaron, and a plague resulted that ravaged the camp in the wilderness. Moses said to Aaron, 'Take this firepan and, with burning incense in it, race into the camp and make atonement for the people.' Afterwards, Scripture says, 'He stood between the dead and the living, and the plague ended' (Num. ch.17).

"Moses had to go through so many steps in order to stay the plague, while Rabbi Shimon just uttered a single sentence and annulled what the Lord had decreed!"[9]

Between Safed and Meron

At the very bottom of the ancient cemetery of Safed is the grave of Rabbi Pinchas ben Yair, the Rashbi's father-in-law. These two *tzaddikim* had been very close companions in their lifetime, and deserved to be near one another after their deaths. However, the deep valley between Safed and Meron separates them.

There is a tradition that an underground tunnel connects Rabbi Pinchas ben Yair's grave to the cave of the Rashbi in Meron. Rabbi Pinchas travels, as it were, to Meron via this tunnel, and together with his son-in-law studies the esoteric aspects of the Torah.[10]

The Rashbi's Departure

Rabbi Shimon bar Yochai's time to depart from the world came on the thirty-third day of the counting of the *Omer*, around the year 200 C.E. He was eighty years old.

All of his closest disciples were present at his bedside, as were many townsmen, but close to the time of his passing an

Mount Meron rises high above the Galilean countryside. The tomb of Rabbi Shimon bar Yochai lies near the bottom.

intense spiritual flame surrounded his house, causing everyone to withdraw except his son, Rabbi Elazar, and Rabbi Abba.

Rabbi Shimon sat up and smiled. "Where are my companions?" Rabbi Elazar went outside and called them in. The Rashbi turned to Rabbi Yitzchak and said, "How nice a place has been set aside for you in heaven! Today you shall depart from the world along with me." Some twenty years earlier the Rashbi had sworn that his disciple, then cognizant of his imminent death, would live as long he would live.[11]

"Now is a most auspicious time," announced their mentor. "Before I depart, completely unashamed, for the future world, I want to reveal to you mysteries that I have never before divulged. But first, I want to arrange your seating. Rabbi Abba, my scribe, should come closer and write down everything I am about to say. My son Rabbi Elazar should repeat my words, and my other companions should meditate on what I have said."

Then, Rabbi Shimon wrapped himself in a *tallis* and prefaced his discourse with a homily on the verse in Psalms 115:17, 'The dead shall not praise God....' "Behold," he said, "the glory of the Almighty has descended along with the souls of the *tzaddikim* in *Gan Eden* to listen to my final discourse."

The Rashbi commenced the main part of his discourse by explaining the esoteric meaning of the verse in Song of Songs 7:11, "I am my Beloved's, and He longs for me."

Rabbi Shimon smiled. "Throughout my lifetime I thought about the verse, 'My soul shall praise the Lord, hearken you humble ones and rejoice.' Today my soul shall indeed unite with the Lord and go to its eternal abode. Therefore, rejoice you humble *tzaddikim* who await me in *Gan Eden*."

The Rashbi continued expounding secrets of the Torah while Rabbi Abba wrote them down. Rabbi Shimon was quoting the verse in Psalms 133:3, "Like the dew of Hermon descending upon the mountains of Zion, for there the Lord has commanded the blessing..." when he passed away. Rabbi Abba, not realizing that his mentor had died, continued to write the end of the verse, "...life for evermore."

The ethereal fire which surrounded the Rashbi's house in Meron remained there throughout the day. At first, the disciples were uncertain as to whether or not their mentor was dead. Once the fire departed and they saw him lying on his right side smiling, they knew he had passed away.

Rabbi Elazar kissed his father's hands, and Rabbi Abba cried out, "I shall lick the dust under his feet." Tears streaming down their cheeks, they were speechless for some time.

Outside, the townsmen began to discuss where the *tzaddik* should be buried. Villagers from the nearby town of Zippori demanded that Rabbi Shimon be buried near them, while the citizens of Meron claimed he should be buried in Meron. Soon a quarrel broke out between them.

Just then the door of the house opened and the disciples came out carrying the body of the *tzaddik* on a bed.

Suddenly, the bed rose above the heads of the townsmen and flew into the air. Stunned, everyone gazed at the miracle in awe and wonder. The Rashbi, as it were, would choose his own resting place.

And so it was. The body of the *tzaddik* flew into the cave of Meron and there the Rashbi came to his final resting place. The townsmen heard a voice call out from the cave, "This man, who shakes the earth and enrages the Roman empire, has today silenced all heavenly prosecution against Jewish wrongdoers."[12]

The Cave of Rashbi

The Rashbi's cave is located on a hill at the foot of the mountain range of Meron. The cave is completely sealed and no one has entered it since Talmudic times.

There are two recorded instances of people pinpointing the exact entrance to the cave. The first was at the end of the 16th century when R' Avraham Galante, built the first structure over the cave. One of the workers, while digging part of the foundations, accidentally uncovered the opening, and immediately his soul left him. R' Galante ordered the entrance resealed. Later, when the author of *Ahavas Tziyon* lived in Safed in the 1760's, he was informed that there was an entrance to the cave on the west side of the courtyard. "Once," he was told, "someone removed some of the stone floor and testified that there was a cave underneath."[13]

An ancient drawing of the tombs of the Rashbi and Rabbi Elazar when they stood under the open skies.

SAFED: THE MYSTICAL CITY

Rabbi Shimon bar Yochai is not the only *tzaddik* buried in this cave. His son, Rabbi Elazar, is also buried there. When Rabbi Elazar was about to die, he told his wife not to inform anyone of his passing and, for certain reasons, to place his body on a bed in the attic. For over twenty years he lay there as if asleep, until one day the rabbis discovered the truth.

The Rashbi came to them in a dream and said, "My only fledgling lies with you. If you so desire, you may bring him to me."

It was the eve of Yom Kippur when the rabbis brought Rabbi Elazar to Meron for burial. At the cave's entrance they found a large snake with his tail in his mouth.

"Oh snake! Oh snake!" they called out. "Open your mouth and make way for Rabbi Shimon's son to enter and lie at his father's side."

The snake immediately took its tail out of its mouth and moved away. The rabbis were then able to enter the cave and at last bury Rabbi Elazar next to his exalted father.[14]

The last person buried in the huge cave is Rabbi Yitzchak, the close disciple of the Rashbi who died on the same day as his mentor. His tombstone is on the right side of the entrance of the inner courtyard.

There was one other person whom the rabbis sought to bury in this cave, but they were unsuccessful, and that was Rabbi Elazar's only son, Rabbi Yossi. In his youth, Rabbi Yossi, for one reason or another, had fallen away from studying Torah and fulfilling the commandments. When Rabbi Yehuda the Prince had found the young man so detached from a Torah life, he immediately ordained him rabbi, and asked a relative to teach him Torah. With time Rabbi Yossi became a great Talmudic Sage, and after he died the rabbis brought him to the cave of Meron for burial. To their surprise they found a large snake blocking the entrance, coiled up with his tail in his mouth.

"Oh snake! Oh snake!" they called out. "Open your mouth and let Rabbi Elazar's son enter and be buried next to his father."

The snake refused to budge. The rabbis reasoned that the reason Rabbi Yossi was denied entry was that he was not as great in Torah as his father.

"No!" rang out a heavenly voice. "The reason is not that the father was greater than the son. The reason is that the father suffered exceedingly for thirteen years in Peikin while the son did not."[15]

The Courtyards of Meron

The first structure known to be built over the cave was commissioned by the wealthy Kabbalist, R' Avraham Galante, a disciple of R' Moshe Cordovero. It was small, and surrounded only the spot where the Rashbi was buried. His tombstone, located along the northern wall, was very low. R' Galante built a smaller room next to it which had a staircase

The inner courtyard

leading up to the tomb of Rabbi Elazar. Outside, he built a stone courtyard which extended to the grave of Rabbi Yitzchak.[16]

During the next hundred and fifty years, more and more rooms and chambers were built. The main hall had a domed ceiling, but even it did not reach to the tomb of Rabbi Elazar. Outside, rooms for wayfarers lined the courtyard.

In 1825, more rooms and courtyards were built, including a row of rooms on the second floor. Later in the century, under the auspices of R' Shemuel Abbu and the Jews of Safed, further renovations were completed. The main hall was enlarged, incorporating one of the courtyards, and the gravestones of the Rashbi and Rabbi Elazar were raised and metal fences erected around them.[17]

The way the it appeared a hundred years ago is essentially what we see today.

Rashbi's Yeshiva

Rabbi Shimon bar Yochai's yeshiva is located further up the hill to the north, off to one side of a dirt road. It is called *Midrash Rashbi,* and records show that by the early sixteenth century it already lay in ruins. The only remnant is the western wall with its huge doorway.

In the mid-eighteenth century, a local Arab organized the construction of a low wall around the area so that animals would not be able to wander inside and desecrate the spot. "This area," he explained, "like the shrine of Rabbi Shimon, is on holy ground."[18]

Approaching Meron

There are stories in the *Zohar* of some of the Rashbi's disciples coming to pray at his cave, and studying his discourses there.[19]

Rabbi Yehoshua ben Levi, a great Talmudic Sage, merited studying Torah with Elijah the Prophet. Once Rabbi Yehoshua found Elijah standing at the entrance to the cave of

Ruins of Midrash Rashbi

Rabbi Shimon bar Yochai, and there they discussed sublime matters.[20]

The *Midrash* tells the story of one of the Rashbi's students who forgot his learning. In those times, when all learning was done orally, there was no way for the student to open a book of *Mishna* or Talmud and review what he had forgotten. So he went to Meron, to the cave of his mentor, and cried out all that was in his heart, begging God to have mercy on him. Afterwards, he slept and dreamed that the Rashbi stood before him saying, "When you rise up with three voices, I shall come."

He awoke, bewildered by his dream, and sought an interpretation. He was told, "Repeat every chapter you study three times, and then Rabbi Shimon will come to you and help you retain your learning." The student followed these instructions and rapidly advanced in his studies.[21]

From these stories we learn that it was a common practice for the Rashbi's disciples to pray by his cave in a time of need.

Thus developed the custom to pray and study the *Zohar* there.[22]

In the sixteenth century, R' Yosef Karo traveled with some of his disciples to Meron during Succos. There were no buildings or courtyards over the cave in those days, so they slept in the nearby village of Meron. Each day, they walked to the cave where they studied the *Zohar*, prayed, and shook the four species. *Lulavs* in hand, they circled the tombs of the Rashbi and his son.

One day, as they were circling the tomb of Rabbi Elazar, clouds suddenly appeared and a heavy downpour stopped them from continuing. Because the *Mishna* states that rain during Succos is not a good sign, they worried that the cloudburst boded ill.

That night the *Maggid*, the angel who came to R' Karo to speak with him and teach him, revealed the meaning of the sudden downpour. "Don't fear that the rain which fell today forecasts drought in the coming season. In fact, the heavenly court rejoiced at your Torah studies at the cave of the Rashbi and his son. But, when you circled Rabbi Elazar's tomb with the four species, which represent man's spiritual ability to elicit a year of good rainfall, your act generated a downpour of bountiful rain. Had you circled the tomb one more time, the downpour would have lasted much longer, as it did in the time of *Choni HaMagel*, resulting in major flooding throughout the country. Thus, the rainfall came just at that time to interrupt your prayers.

"Furthermore," continued the *Maggid*, "whenever the Land is threatened by drought, go to Meron and pray for rain while circling the graves of the *tzaddikim* buried there, and you will be answered. The same is true for any dangerous predicament in which Jews find themselves."[23]

On another occasion R' Yosef Karo went to Meron with R' Moshe Cordovero and his disciples. It was the Shabbos before Purim, and both these *tzaddikim* delivered homiletic interpretations of the Torah before a captivated audience.[24]

The inner chamber. To the left is the tomb of Rabbi Shimon bar Yochai, and to the right is the tomb of Rabbi Elazar

One of the most intriguing stories of someone coming to Meron occurred in the early 1740's, when R' Chaim Attar, a great mystic, visited the cave with a group of his disciples. At the very foot of the mountain, R' Chaim descended from his mule and started going up the hill on foot. As he got closer, he started to climb the path with his hands and feet, uttering strange sounds. Upon arriving at the cave, R' Chaim ordered his disciples to study the *Zohar* with him. After some hours of spirited learning, a wonderful aroma filled the building. As the days passed, the intensity of their *Zohar* study elevated everyone present and filled them with joy.[25]

Studying the Zohar at Meron

As we have learned, Meron is a propitious spot at which to study the writings of Rabbi Shimon bar Yochai, and to this day we find Kabbalists and men of great stature journeying to Meron to study his words next to his grave.

SAFED: THE MYSTICAL CITY

Scholars studying beside the tomb of the Rashbi

In earlier generations, before the halls and courtyards were built, the sages would stretch a canopy from the grave of the Rashbi to the grave of Rabbi Elazar to shield them from the sun, and sit and learn day and night. Food was prepared for them, and Arab guards were hired to insure their safety from marauders.

There are two times in the year that traditionally have been set aside for those who love the *Zohar* to go to Meron and study together. These are the ten days before Shavuos and the ten days before Rosh Hashanna.[26] Today, however, we find people studying these sacred writings in Meron throughout the year.

Miracles at Meron

In the merit of this great *tzaddik*, many miracles have occurred in Meron. A number of stories have been recorded, but one from the recent past exemplifies them all.

In 1923, Meron was filled with visitors for *Lag b'Omer*. Since the festival that year came out on a Friday, many of the two thousand pilgrims remained for Shabbos. That morning, while the men were praying the morning service inside the main hall, a young Sephardi mother began to wail outside in the courtyard. Her three year old son had suddenly collapsed and lay unconscious. Within minutes a doctor arrived and pronounced the child dead. The British police announced that everyone inside the courtyard and rooms would be quarantined there for several days until a full investigation of the incident could be made. This news threw a number of people into panic and they dashed out of the courtyard and into the hills, leaving their children screaming as the British soldiers locked the gates of the courtyard. Yet, the sobbing of the bereaved mother was heard above them all.

The child's body was placed in one of the upstairs rooms. His mother had brought him to Meron to have his first haircut, even though her husband was unable to attend, because she felt that the journey there was very important for the child's future. Now completely heartbroken, she was hysterical, and in a state of shock.

Suddenly, she stopped crying and solemnly lifted this, her firstborn son, in her arms, carried him downstairs into the main hall and laid him by the tombstone of Rabbi Shimon.

"*Tzaddik! Tzaddik!* Rabbi Shimon!" she cried. "Your maidservant came here to honor you with the traditional first haircut of my only child. I fulfilled my vow to bring him on *Lag b'Omer*, and yesterday, among the singing and dancing, his countenance shone, framed by his new earlocks. "But now," she wailed, "how can I return home without my son?

"*Tzaddik! Tzaddik!* Here is my son. Don't let me leave here ashamed and brokenhearted. Return him to life, and let him be as healthy as he was yesterday. Sanctify the name of God, and your name by letting the world know that there is a living God, and that the *tzaddikim* rule over the earth."

It was decided to leave the child alone in the chamber, and even his mother went out into the courtyard. Everyone waited as the main door was locked.

Within seconds the child cried, "Mother! Mother!" and as soon as the door was opened he ran out into his mother's arms. "Give my some water to drink," he asked, "I'm so very thirsty."

When the doctor came to re-examine the child, he said, "What has happened is not within the realm of science. It is clearly miraculous! Rabbi Shimon bar Yochai has resurrected the dead!"

The gates were unlocked and the quarantine lifted, as the exuberant crowd wished the child a long life, and pronounced the blessing, "...who resurrects the dead."[27]

Lag b'Omer in *Halacha*

During the fifty days between Passover and Shavuos, we have an obligation to 'count the *Omer*' every day in remembrance of the *Omer* offering of flour brought on the altar of the Temple on the day following the Passover Seder. This act permitted Jews everywhere to eat of the new grain. Fifty days later, on the festival of Shavuos, another flour offering was brought on the altar. [28]

In the time of Rabbi Akiva, most of his thousands of disciples died during this period. In commemoration of this tragedy, various signs of mourning were halachically instituted. We have no weddings, do not cut our hair, and do not play music. Just as the tragedy continued over thirty-three days, so does the mourning period. The thirty-third day of the *Omer* was the day on which Rabbi Akiva's disciples stopped dying, and in *halacha* it is a day of rejoicing, a day for weddings and haircuts, and a day of festive meals. The thirty-third day, in Hebrew, may be referred to as *'lag,'* which is the pronuncia-

Meron

Walking from Safed to Meron around the turn of the century

tion of the acronym of 'thirty-three' according to the numerical value of the letters in the Hebrew alphabet. Hence, this day is traditionally called *Lag b'Omer,* the thirty-third day of the counting of the *Omer*.[29]

Hilulah d'Rashbi

Lag b'Omer is also the *yartzeit* of Rabbi Shimon bar Yochai, and is called *Hilulah d'Rashbi*, the festival of Rabbi Shimon bar Yochai. On this day Jews from all walks of life come to Meron to rejoice, pray, and study by his tomb.

Back in the fifteenth century, a visitor found over a thousand pilgrims at Meron. The road from Safed to Meron was full of people traveling on horses and mules and by foot. Families came from as far away as Damascus and Baghdad. Bonfires were lit in honor of the Rashbi, and the men danced to rhythmic drumming. Beside the tomb, men and women prayed fervently, and off to the side sat scholars studying the holy *Zohar*.[30]

Today, the picture is much the same, except that the numbers are much greater. Where once stood a thousand pilgrims, stand fifty thousand, and instead of traveling a few hundred miles to Meron, people come from all around the world. Today, *Lag b'Omer* takes on the appearance of a national holiday.

What is the source of all this excitement and rejoicing, the likes of which we find associated with no other *tzaddik*, not even with Moses?

The *Tzaddik's Yartzeit*

There are several reasons that the *yartzeit* of the Rashbi is in a category of its own. For example, with no other *tzaddik* do we find that his son was as great as he. Rabbi Elazar, however, was his father's equal, as Rabbi Shimon said, "If there are only two *tzaddikim* in the world, then they are me and my son."[31]

It is not uncommon that with the passing of a great *tzaddik* people forget some of their learning, due to the great psychological loss. This is precisely what happened at the death of Moses. However, on the day of his passing, Rabbi Shimon bar Yochai revealed a treasure trove of secrets, and even more of the light of Torah was brought into the world.

As we know, the festivals are not merely a commemoration of some historical event in Jewish history. Rather, some of the original divine light which sparked that holiday returns every year at that same time. Hence, the light of redemption which marks Passover returns every year to open our awareness and lift us spiritually. On this day of *Lag b'Omer* a very unique light was brought into the world. Rabbi Shimon bar Yochai transformed the higher, celestial worlds while revealing mysteries of the universe in a way that had never been done before. That light of rectification of the spiritual spheres is emitted every year on this day, and this is what is unique to the Rashbi and not found with any other *tzaddik*.[32]

A Day of Joy

Lag b'Omer is a day for rejoicing. We are not permitted to fast on this day, or to eulogize. One of the best expressions of joy is through song and dance. All day long the courtyard is filled with men's singing and dancing.

One *Lag b'Omer* the Arizal came to Meron with his disciples. While they were dancing, another group of pilgrims danced nearby led by a tall, well-statured old man dressed in white. Suddenly, the Arizal joined the other group and began to dance alone with the old man. They danced together for a long time, ecstatically, while his disciples looked on with joy in their hearts.

R' Asher Zelig Margoliyos, a great Kabbalist of the last generation, dances before an enthralled audience on Lag b'Omer

When the Arizal returned, he immediately took the hand of a simple Jew of Safed and began to dance alone with him before his disciples. They danced together for a long time, the Arizal's face full of joy.

Later, his disciples politely asked their mentor for an explanation of why he had danced with such a simple Jew, not in keeping with his stature as the greatest mystic since the Rashbi.

The Arizal laughed. "If that old man dressed in white, who was none other than the Rashbi, chose to dance with that 'simple Jew,' then who am I to say that it is not dignified to dance with him!"

That 'simple Jew' was R' Elazar Ezkari, the author of *Sefer Charedim*. At that time his greatness was hidden from the masses, and he was thought to be a simple Jew, the beadle of one the synagogues of Safed.[33]

Initiation into Boyhood

There is an ancient tradition not to cut a male child's hair until he is three years old. This first haircut then fulfills the commandment of leaving the locks of hair around his ears *(peyos)*, and is like an initiation rite from babyhood into boyhood. This is the time when he begins to learn the Hebrew alphabet, and dons his first set of fringes. Obviously, this is a very significant event for the child.[34]

The *Midrash* finds a metaphoric reference to this custom in the verse in Lev. 19:23, "Three years your fruit trees shall remain unpicked (i.e., we are forbidden to benefit from it), and in the fourth year their fruit is holy (and may be eaten in Jerusalem)." This verse, says the *Midrash*, refers to a child during his first three years. He still belongs to God, like the unpicked fruit from which may not benefit. Once he has had his third birthday and begins his fourth year, he enters the realm in which we are to participate in his development as a Jew. Now, the father actively sanctifies his son with Torah and commandments.[35]

Although most children are not born on *Lag b'Omer*, it is still customary to give the first haircut, called *chalaka*, at this time whenever possible. Many bring their children to Meron for this joyous event.[36] The father first dances in the courtyard, his son on his shoulders, accompanied by the men singing the traditional song, *Bar Yochai*. He then accords various people the honor of snipping off a lock of the boy's hair. With a drink of *"l'chaim"* and hearty cries of *"mazel tov,"* the boy's appearance is slowly transformed, and by the end of the day his initiation is complete.

The custom in earlier generations differed from today's only slightly. To the accompaniment of drum music and dancing, they used to escort the child first to the tomb of Rabbi Yochanan HaSandler, and then return with him to the courtyard.[37] Thus the Arizal fulfilled the custom in Meron with his son. He took his whole family, and stayed there for three days.[38]

Rabbi Yochanan HaSandler

Rabbi Yochanan HaSandler, a disciple of Rabbi Akiva, had been a close associate and friend of Rabbi Shimon bar Yochai. His tomb is located several hundred yards northeast of the Rashbi's tomb, further up the mountain side.

The name Sandler probably refers to his profession as a shoemaker, and the cave next to his tomb is believed to be the place where he softened the leather after receiving it from the tanner.[39] On *Lag b'Omer* bonfires are lit at his tomb, as visitors go back and forth between the courtyards at Meron and Rabbi Yochanan's tomb.

In earlier times, the fields around his tomb were owned by an Arab who grazed his sheep in the area. At night he would shelter them in the adjacent cave, and hired a Arab youth to watch over them.

One morning the Arab found his flock by the cave, unattended. When his young employee appeared, the farmer slapped and scolded him for such negligence. As his anger in-

People praying by the tomb of Rabbi Yochanan HaSandler. The Rashbi's tomb and surrounding courtyards are in the background.

creased and he continued to hit and curse the shepherd, the boy defended himself, saying, "Why are you yelling at me? I was careful to leave the sheep in the cave where the holy man buried here would surely watch over them."

This only infuriated the man more, and he continued hitting the lad and also cursed the *tzaddik* buried there. Suddenly, he gagged and fell to the ground in a spasm.

The youth raced to the village to bring help. When he told everyone what had happened, they realized that their neighbor had stirred God's wrath against himself by speaking against a holy man with such disparaging language. In order to appease God, they sacrificed the sheep, and prayed by Rabbi Yochanan's tomb that he forgive their friend.

The Arab farmer's health was restored, although he suffered a speech defect the rest of his life. As a token of appreciation for his cure, he promised to light a candle in the cave from then on.[40]

A Day of Soul Searching

On this festive day, we might think that personal prayers and supplications are inappropriate. Far from it! *Lag b'Omer* is a particularly auspicious time for soul searching, for pouring out our hearts to God, and for aspiring to greater meaning in our life.

The anniversary of the passing of a *tzaddik* is known to be an opportune time to make personal requests, whether for health, livelihood, career, spouse, or children. The soul of the *tzaddik* returns to his tomb on this day, and may be a vehicle to elevate one's prayers to heaven because the *tzaddik* is no longer cloaked in a physical body and has direct access to the heavenly abode, while we are full of human imperfections and sin that prevent our prayers from ascending to heaven.

Some people choose to read from one of two books of prayers and sayings from the *Zohar* written especially for this day, one by the Ben Ish Chai, *Hilulah Rabba*, and the other by R' Asher Zelig Magoliyos, *Shevachin d'Rashbi*. Others, however, prefer a direct heart-to-heart relationship, and recite Psalms or whisper spontaneous prayer.

For couples who have not yet been blessed with children, a journey to Meron sometimes elicits divine intervention. Many have come and prayed in the merit of the Rashbi for a child, offering to name their son Shimon after Rabbi Shimon bar Yochai. A greater number have been answered than random chance would suggest.

The *Midrash* tells of a childless couple who came to Rabbi Shimon bar Yochai. The husband told the Rashbi about their problem, and said that he felt that since ten years of marriage had passed that it would be best for them to separate. The Rashbi answered, "I agree with you. But I make one request

The tomb of Rabbi Elazar as it appeared at the turn of the century

of you. Mark your separation with a festive meal, as you did your wedding."

They followed his advice, and ate and drank together for one last meal. They became intoxicated, and at one point the husband told his wife, "When you return to your father's house tomorrow, you may take with you any precious object from here that you desire." He then fell into a heavy slumber.

She ordered the servants to carry him on the bed to her father's house. In the middle of the night he awoke and asked where he was. She explained that she had followed his wish and had taken the most precious object home with her.

The next day they returned to the Rashbi's house. Rabbi Shimon realized that the couple was genuinely fond of each other, and prayed that they should have offspring. Nine months later, a child was born to them.[41]

Meron

Beware of the Rashbi's Honor

Although we may pour out our hearts to God on *Lag b'Omer*, we still must take care not to become depressed. The Rashbi himself asks us only to rejoice with him on this day.

One year around 1570, the Arizal went to Meron on *Lag b'Omer*. One of his disciples, R' Avraham HaLevi, led the prayer service. His custom was to add a prayer over the destruction of the Temple every day, a prayer usually reserved for Tisha b'Av, and today he made no exception.

After he concluded the service, the Arizal reproached him. "I just saw Rabbi Shimon standing by his tomb and he told me, 'Ask R' Avraham HaLevi why he is mourning over the destruction of the Temple on this day of rejoicing? Tell him that he shall surely be in need of consolation in the near future.'"

A few weeks later one of R' Avraham's children died and he had to sit in mourning.[42]

There are several incidents of rabbis attempting to stop the festivities of *Lag b'Omer*. Their motives were pure, as they felt that the inevitable mixing of men and women during the celebrations might lead to improper conduct.

On the night of *Lag b'Omer* in 1911, a wall collapsed, killing ten people. The Rav of Sanz in Safed interpreted the tragedy as a divine punishment for allowing mixed company, and decreed that women were forbidden to attend the festivities on *Lag b'Omer*.

Other rabbis warned him that such a decree was dangerous, especially to the one who initiated it. R' Rabin, however, was adamant and succeeded in getting the other Ashkenazi rabbis to support his ruling. A couple of years later he became seriously ill, and after returning from Europe for treatment, he died.[43]

One of the greatest rabbinic leaders of the 19th century, R' Moshe Sofer, had also spoken out against the festivities. He based his opinion on the fact that no miracle on *Lag b'Omer* was mentioned in the Talmud that should elevate the festivities in Meron to the level of a national holiday. Yet he prefaced his opinion by praising the motives of the people who traveled to Meron as "devote and sincere, and whose reward is great."[44]

After World War One the Arabs threatened violent dispersion of the crowds of Jewish pilgrims on *Lag b'Omer*. Many, therefore, were afraid to travel to Meron and endanger their lives. The whole night long R' Shlomo Eliezer Elfandari, the revered Sephardi mystic, prayed to God. In the morning he announced that he had annulled the decree, and would personally accept any divine repercussions. To the everyone's delight, the festivities were free of any interference.[45]

Hillel and Shammai

The area around Meron has a sanctity of its own. Among the grave sites known to us, two tower above the others. Hillel is buried in a huge cave fifty yards east of the Rashbi's buildings. Inside are catacombs where a number of his disciples were once buried. On the mountaintop to the west, is the tomb of Shammai and his wife. Nearby are the graves of some of his disciples.

The cave of Hillel the Elder and some of his disciples

Shammai and Hillel lived in the era before the destruction of the Second Temple. Shammai was the *Av Beis Din*, the Head of the Rabbinic Council, and Hillel was the Prince. Generally speaking, Shammai adopted a stringent opinion while Hillel held a more lenient one.

Their graves are separated by the valley of Meggido, yet are relatively close. Since every controversy between them was surely for the sake of heaven, without any personal feelings attached, then it is very fitting that their tombs should be close by each other.

In the 12th century, the Rambam's grandson, R' Dovid HaNaggid, prayed in Rabbi Hillel's cave. He had been severely persecuted by blasphemers in Egypt. Suddenly, a stream of fresh water issued out of the cave, and seeing it, he condemned his persecutors. Immediately, five hundred blasphemers died in Egypt, and not long afterwards their wives and children followed.[46]

The Light which Never Wanes

Across the wide valley lies Safed. Her light has waxed and waned over the generations. That noble city captivates us in her own special way. Both Safed and Meron have their own appeal, and cannot be measured one against the other. Both beckon us to return to them, to replenish our spiritual reservoirs and delight in their eternal glow.

The intensity of the spiritual light which emanates from Meron has gotten only brighter, even after 1800 years. The *Zohar* says that the *Mashiach* will reveal himself in the Galilee, and surely this light of Meron is a preview of great things to come, may they be soon and in our own time.

NOTES
1. *Pesachim* 112a, *Ketuvos* (marriage) 62b, Lev. *Rabba* 21:8
2. *Sanhedrin* 14a, Jer. *Sanhedrin* 1:2
3. *Shabbos* 33b. During this period he excelled at both the revealed and mystical aspects of the Torah. For instance, prior to his sojourn in Peikin his father-in-law, Rabbi Pinchas ben Yair, was sharper in

SAFED: THE MYSTICAL CITY

learning than him. Afterwards, however, Rabbi Shimon was able to answer all the questions his father-in-law asked (*ibid.*). In Kabbalah, too, the Rashbi achieved unbelievable heights. Elijah came twice a day to study with him, and his perception of Godliness superceded that of everyone in his generation. (*Kocho d'Rashbi*, pp. 6b-7b).

4. *Zohar*, Deut. 298a. The Rashbi was a *gilgul* of Moses. (Cf. *Kocho d'Rashbi*, pp. 26a-33a, and *Hilulah d'Rashbi*, pp. 11-33)
5. Cf. *Kocho d'Rashbi*, pp.34a-38a, 45a-b. There were nine disciples in the Rashbi's inner circle: Rabbi Elazar his son, Rabbi Abba his scribe, Rabbi Yehuda, Rabbi Yossi bar Yaakov, Rabbi Yitzchak, Rabbi Chizkiya bar Rav, Rabbi Chiya, Rabbi Yossi, and Rabbi Yiso. Together with their mentor they numbered ten, corresponding to the ten *sefiros*. Cf. ibid. 57a-b
6. *ibid*. p. 41b
7. Cf. *Kocho d'Rashbi*. p. 42b, 66a
8. See *Tikkunim*, p. 17a, where Elijah tells Rabbi Shimon to stand and reveal secrets of the Torah, "for you have been granted permission to divulge mysteries of the Torah which no other human being has been granted." Cf. *Kocho d'Rashbi*, pp. 43b-44a, for another reason. Also, the Rashbi admitted that mysteries were revealed because of the love and peace which enveloped him and his companions all the time. (*ibid*. 56b)
9. *Zohar Chadash*, Ruth 5:3
10. *Chibas Yerushalayim*, p. 95 fn
11. *Zohar* 1:217b
12. *Idra Zutta, parshas Azinu*. Cf. *Kocho d'Rashbi*, pp. 74a-76b, where he concludes that every year on his day of passing, the Rashbi compels the heavenly court to forgive the sins of Jews.
13. *Eden Tziyon*, 253; *Ahavas Tziyon*, (cited in *Chibas Yerushalayim*, p. 154)
14. *Babba Metzia* 84b. Cf. *Maamrei Rabbi Elazar b'Rashbi*, pp. 14b-19b for a full discussion of the story based on variations of the Midrashic version of the episode.
15. *ibid*. 85a; he was probably buried nearby, although the location is unknown
16. *Shem HaGedolim*, Part I, no. 36; *Hilulah d'Rashbi*, pp. 56-58, fn. 31
17. *Chibas Yerushalayim*, pp. 154-155, *Eden Tziyon*, p. 253
18. *ibid*. 163
19. *Zohar* 1:126a, 1:4a, 2:14b
20. *Sanhedrin* 98a
21. Eccl. *Rabba* 10:10
22. *Hilulah Rabba*, pp.34, 37
23. *Maggid Mesharim, parshas Emor*
24. *Sefer Gerushin*, p.5

Meron

25. *Kavod Malachim*, in the name of R' Shemuel Heller who heard it from elderly Sephardim who heard it from eye-witnesses; Letter of one of the Ohr HaChayim's disciples.
26. *Emek HaMelech*, ch.7
27. *Hilulah d'Rashbi*, pp.63-65. R' Asher Zelig Magoliyos, the great Ashkenazi Kabbalist of that generation, witnessed the whole incident. He adds that the Rashbi's name, Shimon bar Yochai, has the same numerical value as the Hebrew words, "resurrects the dead." Other miraculous stories are cited in *Chibas Yerushalayim*, pp.159-160
28. Lev. 23:9-22
29. *Orech Chayim*, 493
30. *Chibas Yerushalayim*, p.158
31. *Succah* 45b
32. Cf. *Hilulah d'Rashbi*, pp.92-96
33. *Masaaot Yerushalayim*, pp.212-213
34. *Shaarei Teshuva, Orech Chayim* 531:6 fn.7, who cites the custom of coming to Meron for the first haircut; *Yoreh Deah* 245:8; *Eliyahu Rabba, Orech Chayim* 17:2
35. *Tanchuma, Kedoshim* 14
36. In Jerusalem, the custom was once for those who do not travel to Meron to go to the tomb of Shemuel the Prophet. Today, the custom is to go the cave of Shimon *HaTzaddik*.
37. *Chibas Yerushalayim*, p.159
38. *Shaar HaKavannos, Sefiras HaOmer*, drash 12
39. Cf. *Eden Tziyon*, pp.66-67 for full discussion
40. *Chibas Yerushalayim*, pp.160-162
41. Song of Songs *Rabba*, on the verse, "I shall be happy and glad with you." The *Midrash* learns from this story: If a couple who find there is nothing more precious to each of them than each other are redeemed with a child, than surely the Jewish people who daily await their redemption, and admit their eternal love of God, shall be redeemed.
42. *Shaar HaKavannos, Sefiras HaOmer*, drash 12
43. *Eden Tziyon*, p.252; Cf. *Chibas Yerushalayim*, p.156
44. Responsa, *Yoreh Deah* 233; Cf. *S'dei Chemed, Maarechet Eretz Yisrael*, no. 6
45. *Masaos Yerushalayim*, p.293
46. *Seder HaDoros*, p.215 (4954)

Acknowledgements

A book of this scope can not have come to fruition by itself. There were many people who helped made the pieces fit together into a whole, some economically, others with words of encouragement, and others with professional expertise. I feel indebted to them all, yet not all allow me to mention them by name.

First, several rabbis reviewed parts of the manuscript, and continually encouraged me. Rabbi Yaakov Hillel and Rabbi Shlomo Eliezer Margoliyos were among them. Reb Shlomo Fox, a master book designer and editor, helped revamp the inner structure of the book. Reb Daniel Eidensohn applied both his literary talents and his production know-how to help see this work reach its final destination. His patience and perseverance were key factors in the inner dimensions of the book. And Rav Baruch Kaplan said, "Call it 'The Mystical City'."

A number of behind-the-scene people gave freely of their time, energy, and wealth to encourage me to see this project through during some difficult hurdles. May God bless them.

There were some 'chance' meetings with very special *tzaddikim*, espeically in Safed, that helped deepen my awareness of the living sparks of this noble city. The only one which I am at liberty to mention is the Natvorna Rebbe, Rebbe Leifer, under whose roof I stayed during my various sojourns to Safed.

And, of course, no man can acommplish anything without his helpmate by his side. Her support and devotion gave me the momentum see a dream come true. May we be worthy to see our children firmly planted in the Garden of *Hashem*.

Glossary

A
Aggada: Talmudic legends and homiletic passages
aliyah: immigration to Israel
Amora (Amoraim): Talmudic Sages of the 3rd, 4th, and 5th centuries C.E.
avodas Hashem: divine work
B
baal teshuva: one who returns to God's Torah
Baruch Hashem: Bless the Lord
Beis Din: rabbinical court
Beis Midrash: House of Study
Bezras Hashem: with the help of God
C
chacham: wise man
chalaka: the first haircut a boy receives at the age of three
chaluka: allocation of funds to needy families
chaverim: companions, comrades
Chazal: The Talmudic Sages
Chumash: the Five Books of Moses
Churbah: The Destroyed Place
chutz l'aretz: any place outside of Israel
D
dayan: judge
drash: homily, discourse
E
Eretz Yisrael: Land of Israel
esrog (esrogim): a citrus fruit, citron
G
gabbai: guardian of a synagogue
Gan Eden: Garden of Eden

genizah: storing away of disused sacred books and articles, usually by burial
gerushin: separation, to be sent away
gilgul (gilgulim): reincarnation
H
halacha: Jewish law
hisnagdos: opposition to the Chassidic movements
K
Kabbalos Shabbos: prayers inaugarating the Sabbath
kares: excommunication
kavanna: intention, concentration, metitation
kelipos: the negative side, the opposite of holiness
Kiddush HaChodesh: sanctification of a new month
kohen (kohenim): priest
kollel: yeshiva for married men
M
maggid: a teller, speaker
malkos: lashes
mashgiach: spiritual leader of a yeshiva
Mashiach: Messiah
mekubalim: mystics, Kabbablists
Midrash (Midrashim): Talmudic interpretations of Scripture
mikve: immersion pool, ritual bath
mincha: the afternoon prayer service
minyan (minyanim): ten men or more gathered together for prayer
Mishna (Mishnayos): six orders of the Oral Law
Misnagad: opposition to the Chassidic movements
mitzva (mitzvos): commandment(s)
moshavim: modern-day cooperative settlement
N
niftar: deseased person
P
parshas: the weekly portion of the Torah
Perushim: lit. separated apart, disciples of the Vilna Gaon
R
Rabbeinu: Our Master
Rosh Chodesh: first day of a lunar month
Rosh Yeshiva: Dean of the Talmudical Academy
S
Sefer Torah: Torah scroll
sefiros: Divine emanations
selichos: special prayers of supplication
semicha: rabinical ordination
Shabbos: Sabbath
shacharis: the morning prayer service

Glossary

Shavuos: Festival of Weeks
Shechina: Divine Presence
sofer: a scribe
Succos: Festival of Booths
T
tallis: a special four-cornered garment, with fringes attached, worn when praying
Tanna (Tannaim): Talmudic Sages of the 1st and 2nd centuries C.E.
tefillin: phylactery
teshuva: repentance
tikun chatzos: midnight prayers recited over the destruction of the Temple
tikun: rectification
tzaddik (tzaddikim): righteous person
Y
yartzeit: day of death
Yerushalayim: Jerusalem
yeshiva: Talmudic academy
yishuv: settlement in Israel
Yom Tov: one of the three festivals

Bibliography

Abritish, Rabbi Avraham Dov of, *Bas Aiyn,* Jerusalem, 1968.
Alfasi, Rabbi Eliyahu, *Babba Sali,* Jerusalem, 1984.
Alshich, Rabbi Moshe, *Toras Moshe,* Jerusalem, 1968.
Amsel, Rabbi Yitzchak, *Toldos Yitzchak,* Jerusalem, 1982.
Azulai, Rabbi Avraham, *Chesed l'Avraham,* Lvov, 1863.
Azulai, Rabbi Chayim Yosef Dovid, *Shem HaGedolim,* Warsaw, 1876.
Bachbot, Rabbi Aharon, *Rabbeinu Chayim Abulafia,* Jerusalem, 1987
Baruch, Rabbi Aharon Moshe, *Toldos Aharon v'Moshe,* Jerusalem, 1979.
Ben Ish Chai, *Daas v'Tevuna,* Jerusalem, 1965.
Ben Ish Chai, *Hilula Rabba,* Jerusalem, 1973.
Chen, Yaakov, *Aliyos Eliyahu,* Tel Aviv, 1980.
Cordovero, Rabbi Moshe, *Pardes Rimonim,* Munkatsh, 1922.
Cordovero, Rabbi Moshe, *Sefer Gerushin,* Jerusalem, 1962.
Cordovero, Rabbi Moshe, *Shiur Koma,* Jerusalem, 1966.
Cordovero, Rabbi Moshe, *Tomer Devora,* Jerusalem, 1928.
Dayan, Rabbi Shaul, *Shvichei HaAri,* Aram Zova, 1872.
Eisenstein, Rabbi Yehuda Dovid, *Otzar Massaos,* Tel Aviv, 1969.
Ezkari, Rabbi Elazar, *Sefer Charedim,* Jerusalem, 1986.
Forgas, Rabbi Yom Tov, *Introduction to Responsa of Rabbi Moshe Alshich,* Safed, 1975.
Gafner, Rabbi Yaakov Shalom, *Ohr HaGalil,* Jerusalem, 1976.
Gagin, Rabbi Shem Tov, *Keser Shem Tov,* London, 1954.
Galis, Rabbi Yaakov, *M'Gedolei Yerushalayim,* Jerusalem, 1967.
Garnetstein, Yechiel, *Eretz Yisrael Shel Maala,* Tel Aviv, 1985.
Goldhar, Rabbi Yitzchak, *Admaas Kodesh,* Jerusalem, 1913.
Goldstein, Rabbi Chayim, *Anaf Etz Avos,* Jerusalem, Yeshivas Kodesh Hilulim, 1972.
Goldstein, Rabbi Moshe, *Massaos Yerushalayim,* Munkatsch, 1931.
Helprin, Rabbi Yechiel, *Seder HaDoros,* Warsaw, 1867.

Bibliography

Hillel, Rabbi Yaakov, *Shanos Chayim,* Jerusalem, Ahavas Shalom, 1982.
Horowitz, Rabbi Chayim HaLevi, *Chibas Yerushalayim,* Jerusalem, 1964.
Horowitz, Rabbi Yeshaya HaLevi, *Eden Tziyon,* Jerusalem, Mesorah, 1956.
Horowitz, Rabbi Yeshaya, *Shnei Luchos HaBris,* Jerusalem, 1965.
Kadmonenu, Jerusalem, 1987.
Karo, Rabbi Yosef, *Beis Yosef,* Jerusalem, Meoros, 1960.
Karo, Rabbi Yosef, *Maggid Mesharim,* Vilna, 1875.
Karo, Rabbi Yosef, *Shulchan Aruch,* Jerusalem.
Kednavor, Rabbi Tzvi Hirsh, *Kav HaYashar,* Warsaw, 1879.
Kohen, Rabbi Chayim, *Tur Berekas,* Petrakov, 1878.
Lachmi, Rabbi Dovid, *Chachmei Yisrael,* Bnei Brak, 1980.
Makir, Rabbi Moshe, *Seder HaYom,* Jerusalem, 1980.
Margoliyos, Rabbi Asher Zelig, *Biur HaShir 'Bar Yochai,'* Jerusalem, 1967.
Margoliyos, Rabbi Asher Zelig, *Hilula d'Rashbi,* Jerusalem, 1974.
Margoliyos, Rabbi Asher Zelig, *Kocho d'Rashbi,* Jerusalem, 1964.
Margoliyos, Rabbi Asher Zelig, *Midos Rashbi,* Jerusalem, 1979.
Margoliyos, Rabbi Asher Zelig, *Shevchin d'Rashbi,* Jerusalem, 1966.
Margoliyos, Rabbi Asher Zelig, *Shimush Chachamim,* Jerusalem, 1983.
Menachem Azariya, Rabbi of Pino, *Pelach HaRimon,* Munkatsh, 1922.
Minz, Rabbi Benyomin, *Toldos R' Yisrael of Shaklov,* Jerusalem, 1968.
Sathon, Rabbi Chayim, *Eretz Chayim,* Jerusalem, 1908.
Shabtai, Rabbi, *Siddur Arizal,* New York, 1961.
Shaklov, Rabbi Yisrael of, *Pe'as HaShulchan,* Jerusalem, Luntz, 1911.
Shapiro, Rabbi Natan, *Tuv HaAretz,* Jerusalem, 1891.
Shemuel HaKatan, *Shaarei Dima,* Jerusalem, Eshkol, 1968.
Shwartz, Rabbi Yosef, *Tivuos HaAretz,* Jerusalem, Luntz, 1900.
Sofer, Rabbi Moshe, *Responsa,* Vein, 1895.
Sofer, Rabbi Moshe, *Toras Moshe,* Jerusalem, Machon Chasam Sofer, 1972.
Sorasky, Rabbi Aharon, *Dimoyos Hod,* Bnei Brak, 1967.
Sorksy, Rabbi Aharon, *Oros m'Mizrach,* Bnei Brak, 1974.
Stern, Rabbi Avraham, *Melitzei Aish,* Jerusalem, 1975.
Sternbuch, Rabbi Moshe, *Moadim v'Zemanim,* Jerusalem, 1964.
Ta'amei HaMinhagim, Jerusalem, Eshkol, 1960.
Tennenbaum, Rabbi Moshe, *Massaos Moshe,* Tarna, 1925.
Tukatzinsky, Rabbi Nisan, *HaAretz l'Givuloseya,* Jerusalem, 1980.
Tukatzinsky, Rabbi Yechiel Michal, *Eretz Yisrael,* Jerusalem, Lewin-Epstein, 1956.
Tukatzinsky, Rabbi Yechiel Michal, *Gesher HaChayim,* Jerusalem, 1960.
Tukatzinsky, Rabbi Yechiel Michal, *Iyr HaKodesh v'HaMikdosh,* Jerusalem, 1970.
Vital, Rabbi Chayim, *Etz HaDaas Tov,* I & II, Jerusalem, 1982.

Vital, Rabbi Chayim, *Kitavim Chadashim,* Jerusalem, Ahavos Shalom, 1988.
Vital, Rabbi Chayim, *Shaar HaGilgulim,* Jerusalem, 1903.
Vital, Rabbi Chayim, *Shaarei Kedusha,* Jerusalem, 1928.
Vital, Rabbi Chayim, *Shivchei Rabbi Chayim Vital,* Jerusalem, 1966.
Vitebst, Rabbi Menachem Mendel of, *Miktavei Kodesh,* Jerusalem, Mesora, 1989.
Vitebst, Rabbi Menachem Mendel of, *Pri HaAretz,* Jerusalem, Mesora, 1989.
Weinstock, Rabbi M. Y., *Introduction to Ohr Yakar by Rabbi Moshe Cordovero,* Jerusalem.
Wunder, Rabbi Meir, *Encyclopedia l' Chachmei Galitziya,* Jerusalem, 1982.
Zohar, Vilna, 1895.

Index

(**Note:** *Rabbi* indicates a Talmudic Sage, *R'* indicates a later rabbi)

Abba, Rabbi, 96, 213, 231, 233-234
Abbu, R' Shemuel, 180, 238
Abbu, R' Yaakov Chai, 180, 181 (photo)
Abuchazera, R' Yisrael, 199-201, 200 (photo)
Abuhav, R' Yitzchak, 125
Abulafia, R' Chaim, 121
Acco, 37, 117, 124, 127, 133, 143, 146, 167
Acco, 40
Adrianople, 55
Aharon, R' (Belzer Rebbe), 186
Aharon, R' (Chernobel Rebbe), 185
Ain Ziton, 45, 151, 166
Akiva, Rabbi, 111 fn, 216, 217, 229-230, 244, 249
Alarish, R' Yitzchak *(Kiryat Arba)*, 195
Alkabetz, R' Shlomo *(Lecho Dodi)*, 51, 74, 79-80, 218
Alshich, R' Moshe *(Toras Moshe)*, 35, 36 fn, 44, 45, 56-58, 85, 89, 91, 105, 111 fn, 141, 221
Ana b'Koach, 221
Arazin, R' Yaakov, 97
Arizal, *see* Luria
Ascent, 208
Ashi, Rabbi, 50
Ashkenazi, R' Bezalel *(Shita Mekubetzes)*, 63, 73, 85, 87
Attar, R' Chaim *(Ohr HaChaim)*, 121, 241
Avraham Dov, R' of Abritish *(Bas Aiyn)*, 150, 157-171, 173-174, 185, 219, 220 (photo)
Azariya, R' Menachem of Pino *(Pelach HaRimon)*, 74, 88-89

Azida, R' Shemuel *(Midrash Shemuel)*, 111 fn
Azulai, R' Avraham *(Chesed l'Avraham)*, 22-23
Baal Shem Tov, 123, 126, 128-129
baal teshuva, 63, 207
Babba Sali, *see* Abuchazera
Bak, R' Yisrael, 151-152
Bar Yochai (song), 249
Beis Midrash Ari, 159, 176-178
Beis Midrash HaG'ra, 140
Beis Midrash shel Yankel Doktor, 178
Beniyahu ben Yehoyoda, 180
Benyomin *HaTzaddik*, 216, 217 (photo)
Berav, R' Yaakov, 29-35, 43, 55, 62, 221
Bnei Brak, 194
Boruch, R' of Pinsk, 148-149
Breslav, 112 fn
Breslav, *see* shtibel
British Mandate, 199, 201
Cairo, 30
Candia, Crete, 63
Chabad, 207-208
Chaim, R' of Chernovitz *(Beier Mayim Chaim)*, 141 (photo), 219
Chaim, R' of Volozhin *(Nefesh HaChaim)*, 142
chalaka, 251
chaluka, 142, 162, 178, 198
Chaviv, R' Levi ben, 32-34
Chaviv, R' Moshe, 118
Chazon, R' Raphael Yosef, 140
Chernobel, *see* shtibel
Chicago, 191
Chida *(Shem HaGedolim)*, 121, 215
Choni HaMagel, 240

265

SAFED: THE MYSTICAL CITY

Churbah, 120-121, 153
chutz l'aretz, 52, 131
Citadel of Yorafas, 39
Cities of Refuge, 46 fn
Constantinople, 60-62, 127, 128, 132, 191
Cordovero, R' Moshe *(Pardes Rimonim)*, 21, 29, 32, 44, 58-59, 70-80, 83, 88-90, 91, 115, 218, 237, 240
Corfu, Greece, 179-180
Damascus, 34, 37, 43, 116-117, 119, 130, 146, 245
David, King of Israel, 117, 180
Dosa ben Harkinas, Rabbi, 187, 217
Earthquake, 25, (of 1759) 124-126, (of 1837) 157-161
Elazar bar Rabbi Shimon, Rabbi, 96, 231-240
Elfandari, R' Shlomo Eliezer, 191, 194-198, 197 (photo), 199, 254
Elijah the Prophet, 107, 110 fn, 125, 238, 256 fn
Esrog Plantation, 179-180
Ezkari, R' Elazar, 45, 248
Faivelsohn, R' Shemuel Avigdor, 207
Fez, Morocco, 30
Fortress of Safed, 60-62
G'ra, *see* Vilna Gaon
Galante, R' Avraham the Second, 119
Galante, R' Avraham, 79, 235,237
Galante, R' Moshe the Second *(Rav HaMagen)*, 118, 134 fn
Galante, R' Moshe, 30, 32, 58, 105, 111 fn
Gershon, Rabbeinu, 63
gerushin, 79
gilgulim, 86, 101, 111 fn
Gliko, R' Elisha, 59
Golan Heights, 159
Goyatos, R' Yitzchak, 174
Goydon, 39
HaChassid, R' Yehuda, 120
Hagar, R' Baruch (Vishnitzer Rebbe of Haifa), 183
Hagar, R' Chaim (Kosover Rebbe), 183
Hagar, R' Menachem Mendel (Kosover Rebbe), 183
Hagar, R' Menachem Mendel (Vishnitzer Rebbe), 184

Hagar, R' Moshe (Radovitzer Rebbe), 184
Hagar, R' Yosef Alter (Radovitzer Rebbe), 184
Haifa, 167
Halberstam, R' Chaim of Sanz *(Divrei Chaim)*, 182-183, 209
Halberstam, R' Yechezkel Shraga (Shinever Rebbe), 182, 185-186
Halberstam, R' Yekutiel Yehuda (Klausenberger Rebbe), 208-209
Halevi, R' Avraham, 89, 94, 253
HaNaggid, R' Dovid, 255
Haparchi, R' Ishtori, 17
Hebron, 40, 121, 123, 201, 207, 213
Heller, R' Shemuel *(Kavod Melachim)*, 158-159, 162-163, 170-171, 176, 178-182
Hillel, Rabbi, 28, 254 (photo)
Hilulah d'Rashbi, 245-246
Horowitz, R' Chaim *(Chibas Yerushalayim)*, 147
Horowitz, R' Elierzer Nisan, 183
Horowitz, R' Naphtali Chaim, 183
Horowitz, R' Yeshaya *(Shnei Luchos HaBris)*, 19-22, 116-117
Hoshea the Prophet, 221
Idra Rabba, 96-97
Isralosh, R' Moshe (Rama), 60
Ivshitz, R' Dovid Shlomo *(Levushei S'rad)*, 141, 171, 198, 219, 220 (photo)
Jacob, 24, 57
Jaffa, 127
Jerusalem, 22
Jordan River, 146
Joshua, 27
Kabbalos Shabbos, 80, 102
Kahaneman, R' Yosef Shlomo, 193-194
Kanavitz, R', 192
Kaplan, R' Simcha, 204-205
kares, 29
Karlin, *see* shtibel
Karo, R' Yehuda, 64
Karo, R' Yosef *(Shulchan Aruch)*, 21, 29, 32, 44, 45, 49-66, 70-71, 90, 91, 141 (photo), 179, 219, 220 (photo), 240
Katz, R' Avraham of Kalish, 133
Katz, R' Chaim, 143
Kefar Chittim, 179
Kenig, R' Gedaliya, 209-210

Index

Kiddush HaChodesh, 29
Kinneret (Sea of Galilee), 37,92
Kisvei Ari, 103-104
Kitover, R' Gershon, 123-124
Kohen, R' Yishmael, 202
Kohen,R' Yitzchak, 102-103
Kollel Lemberg, 193
Kollel Warsaw, 179
Korach, 232
Koriel, R' Yisrael di, 63
Kornel, R' Nachman Natan *(Teshuvos HaGaonim),* 160 (photo)
Kosov, *see shtibel*
Laban, 57-58
Lag b'Omer, 243-254
Lecho Dodi, 80
Leifer, R' Aharon Yechiel (Natvorna Rebbe), 205-207 (photo)
Levi Yitzchak, R' (Berdechiver Rebbe) *(Kedushas Levi),* 162
Loewe, Dr. Eliezer, 165-167
Lost Tribes, 148-149
Lud, 231
Luria, R' Yitzchak, 15-16, 21, 35, 45, 49, 57-58, 64-66, 72-74, 78, 83-112, 141, 179, 187, 218, 221, 247-249
Mabit, *see,* Metrani
Maggid of Mezeritch, 128
maggid, 52-53, 59, 66, 91, 240
Maimonides, R' Moses *(Mishna Torah),* 31, 33, 50, 74
malkos, 29
Mamluk, 32, 42
Margoliyos, R' Asher Zelig, 247 (photo), 251
Margoliyos, R' Gershon, 150
Marranos, 30, 63-64
Mashiach ben Yosef, 111 fn
Mashiach, 23, 31, 35, 98, 109-110, 137, 148, 163-164, 223, 255
Massacre of, (1834) 149-150, (of 1838) 164-166
Matzuda, 203
Medini, R' Chaim Chizkiyahu *(S'dei Chemed),* 195
Meggido, 255
Meginim Square, 182, 184 (photo), 185
Meir Baal HaNess, Rabbi, 92, 232
Meltzer, R' Issar Zalman, 191

Menachem Mendel, R' of Shaklov, 134 fn, 138, 152
Menachem Mendel, R' of Vitebst *(Pri HaAretz),* 128-133
Meron, 37, 41, 96, 180, 222, 229-255
Metrani, R' Moshe, 29, 32, 44, 62-63, 218
Midrash Rashbi, 238
Midrash Shem v'Ever, 186-188, 187 (photos)
Midrash Shemuel, 181-182
mikve, 15, 108-109 (photos), 125, 182, 185, 204-205, 209
Mizrachi, *chacham,* 169
Montefiore, Sir Moses, 152, 165, 167-170, 178, 187
Mordechai, R' (Chernobel Rebbe), 162
Moses, 27
Mount Kenan, 203, 207
Mount Meron, 233 (photo)
Mount Tabor, 37
Nachman, R' of Breslav, 122
Nachman, R' of Horodnak, 122, 126
Nachmanides, R' Moses, 40
Nachum *Ish Gamzu,* 216, 217 (photo)
Nachum, R' (Chernobel Rebbe), 162
Naphtali, Tribe of, 37
Napoleon, 133, 142
Netanya, 209
Omer, 232-233
Onkelos, 221
Parchi, Chaim, 130, 144-146
Paruch, Even, 116-117
Pasha, Ibrahim, 147-148, 149
Passover, 244
Pe'as Hashulchan, 150-152
Peikin, 124, 230, 237
Petach Tikva, 179
peyos, 248
Pinchas ben Yair, Rabbi, 95-96, 221, 222 (photo), 232
plague, of (1555) 59, (1572) 99, (1814) 143, (1916) 198
Pri Chadash, 118
Purim, 195-196, 206, 240
Rabin, R', 253
Radbaz, *see,* Zimra
Radovitz, *see shtibel*
Rama, *see,* Isralosh
Ramak, *see,* Cordovero

267

SAFED: THE MYSTICAL CITY

Rambam, *see,* Maimonides
Ramban, *see,* Nachmanides
Rashbi, *see,* Shimon bar Yochai
Ravina, 50
Ridbaz, *see,* Villavsky
Rivlin, R' Hillel, 152
Rokeach, R' Eliezer, 122-123, 130, 134 fn
Rosh Chodesh, 28, 39, 214-215
Rosh Hashanna, 125, 130, 214, 242
Rothchild, Baron, 182
Sabba Kedisha, see Elfandari
Sadiya, R' of Vilna, 140, 144
Saladan, 39-40
Salonika, 64
Sambtiyon River, 148
Sanhedrin, 22, 180
Sanz, *see shtibel*
Saragossi, R' Yosef, 40-42
semicha, 27-35, 55, 59
Shammai, Rabbi, 254-255
Shapiro, R' Chaim Elazar (Munkacher Rebbe), 135 fn, 186, 197
Sharabi, R' Shalom *(Nahar Shalom),* 121, 124
Shavuos, 50, 92, 125, 242, 244
Shechina, 24, 52, 79, 101
Shem v'Ever, cave of, *see, Midrash Shem v'Ever*
Shimon bar Yochai, Rabbi, 79, 96, 182, 221, 229-255
Shimon ben Azai, 221
Shneur Zalman, R' (Lubavitcher Rebbe) *(Tanya),* 128
Shomiel, R' Shlomo *(Shivchei Ari),* 105
shtibel, Breslav, 207-208
shtibel, Chernobel, 182, 185 (photo), 204
shtibel, Karlin, 182
shtibel, Kosov, 182-183
shtibel, Radovitz, 182
shtibel, Sanz, 182-183, 204, 208-209
shtibel, Tochover, 182
shtibel, Trisk, 210
shtibel, Vishnitz, 182, 210
Shuk Elijama, 140
Sidon, 124
Sidon, 40
Simcha ben Yehushua, R' *(Ahavas Tziyon),* 127-128, 235
Slozk, 191

Sofer, R' Moshe *(Chasam Sofer),* 23-27, 253
Spanish Inquisition, 30, 63
Succos, 240
Sufim, 38, 39
Sultan Selim I, 43
Synagogue, Abuhav, 57, 125, 173, 174-175 (photos)
Synagogue, Abulafia (Tiberias), 122 (photo)
Synagogue, Alshich, 57, 174
Synagogue, Ari Ashkenazi, 176 (photo), 177-178, 207
Synagogue, Ari Sephardi, 42, 106, 107-108 (photo), 199, 201 (photo), 209
Synagogue, Bas Aiyn, 161 (photo), 169, 173
Synagogue, Beis Yosef, 174
Synagogue, Eliyahu, 42
Synagogue, Morisko, 42
Synagogue, Pressburg, 25
Synagogue, Succos Shalom, 153
Synagogue, Tzemach Tzedek, 206, 209
Synagogue, Yossi Bannai, 32, 125, 126 (photo), 127, 173
Tiberias, 25, 117, 121, 127, 133, 154, 198
tikun chatzos, 195
Tirnoer, R' Zeev, 205
Tochover, *see shtibel*
Toledo, R' Benyomin of *(Travels),* 40
Trisk, *see shtibel*
Tropp, R' Naphtali, 207
Ture, 40
Tzemach, R' Yaakov, 120
Ungar, R' Moshe, 183
Vidas, R' Eliyahu di *(Reshis Chachma),* 77-78, 89, 105
Villavsky, R' Yaakov Dovid, 191-194, 192 (photo)
Vilna Gaon, 128, 134, 137-138, 150
Vishnitz, *see shtibel*
Vital, R' Chaim, 35, 45, 56-57, 79, 83-112, 119-120
Vital, R' Shemuel, 120
Wallach, Dr., 197
Waxs, R' Chaim Elazar, 179-180
Well of Miriam, 91-93
Yaakov ben Asher, R' *(Tur),* 50
Yehoshua ben Chananya, Rabbi, 220 (photo), 221

Index

Yehoshua ben Levi, Rabbi, 238
Yehuda bar Iloy, Rabbi, 96, 98, 111 fn
Yehuda ben Babba, Rabbi, 230
Yehuda the Prince, Rabbi, 28, 50
Yeshivas Beis El, 124, 144
Yeshivas Chasam Sofer, 195 (photo)
Yeshivas Mir, 204
Yeshivas Nachalas Naftali, 205
Yeshivas Ponovitch, 193
Yeshivas Safed, 204
Yeshivas Slonim, 204
Yeshivas Toras Eretz Yisrael, 192, 193
yishuv, 142, 167
Yisrael, R' of Shaklov *(Pe'as HaShulchan)*, 138-154, 157, 160, 162, 193
Yitzchak, Rabbi, 233, 236, 238
Yochanan ben Zakkai, Rabbi, 221
Yochanan HaSandler, Rabbi, 249-251
Yom Kippur, 125, 236
Yosef Chaim, R' of Baghdad *(Ben Ish Chai)*, 180, 181 (photo), 251
Yossi Bannai, Rabbi, 125-126, 126 (photo), 217
Yossi ben Elazar, Rabbi, 236-237
Zilberman, R' Raphael, 182
Zimra, R' Dovid ben, 40, 62-63, 87, 218
Zippori, 234

ואלו יעמדו על הברכה

IN LOVING MEMORY
OF OUR BELOVED PARENTS

Reuven ben Melech (ר' ראובן בן מלך ע״ה)
July 1910 - Sept. 7, 1974 (כ׳ אלול תשל״ד)

Hannah Mindle bas Benjamin (חנה מנדל בת בנימין ע״ה)
Jan. 1915 - Aug. 3, 1190 (י״ב אב תשי״ן)

AND OUR BROTHER

Berl Benjamin ben Reuven ע״ה
Jan. 1944 - Dec. 3, 1977 (כ״ג כסלו תשל״ח)

May their souls be bound up in the bonds of eternal life.
May their memories continue to inspire and guide us.
May we be worthy of the sacrifices they made for us.
"In peace, in harmony, I lie down and sleep, for you Hashem,
will make me dwell safe and secure"   *(Tehillim 4:9)*

Ezra and Edward Berg

Rabbi Meir Sachs
in memory of

יצחק בו יוסף זסס ע״ה
נלב״ע י״ז תמוז תשל״ח

ר' עזרא ציוו בו מאיר רחמים נחמד ע״ה
נלב״ע י״ז טבת תשמ״ט

ר' שלום עובדיי חיים ע״ה

ת.נ.צ.ב.ה.

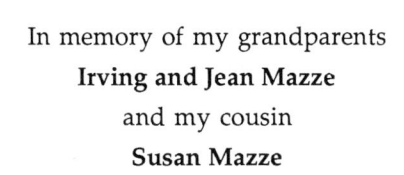

In memory of my grandparents
Irving and Jean Mazze
and my cousin
Susan Mazze
Dr. Rand Pellegrino
"to Safed and my friends there where my heart still dwells"

In memory of
Yisrael Ben R' Dovid Weiss ע״ה
Yartzeit, 25 Tishre, 5749

ת.נ.צ.ב.ה.

By his children
Dr. Dovid Weiss and Mrs. Judy Leichtberg

Sherman Shapiro
In memory of his sisters
Anna Burg and **Esther Green** ע״ה

ת.נ.צ.ב.ה.

Rav Shemuel Buchwald
in memory of his father
לז"נ אביו ר' דוד שמואל לייב   David Buchwald
נלב"ע ח"י טבת תשמ"א
ת.נ.צ.ב.ה.

Rav Yosef Chaim Lester
in loving memory of his parents
R' Yisrael Leib ben R' Shemuel Leib Lester
נלב"ע ט"ז אייר תשמ"ז
Miriam bas R' Yaakov
נלב"ע כ' שבט תשכ"ט
ת.נ.צ.ב.ה.

Rabbi Gershon Ginsburg
לז"נ האשה הצדקת
פריידא בת ר' שלום ע"ה
ת.נ.צ.ב.ה.

Rav Ezra Harris
in memory of his father
R' Yaakov Tzvi ben R' Nachum ע"ה
ת.נ.צ.ב.ה.

Moshe Meer
in memory of
ר' פנחס נתן בן ר' אלעזר מיר ע"ה
נלב"ע ב' סיון תש"ן
ת.נ.צ.ב.ה.

IN LOVING MEMORY OF OUR
BELOVED WIFE, MOTHER, GRANDMOTHER

Libby Black   ליבי בת ר' יצחק מאיר ז"ל

Love of Torah and Eretz Yisrael burnt within her heart,
and the Mitzvos of her Creator she performed with *Mesiras Nefesh*

She accepted her suffering with love - עוז והדר לבושה

March 20, 1939 - February 25, 1991 (י"א אדר תשנ"א)

ת.נ.צ.ב.ה.

Avraham, Yehudit, Shevach, Rafael, Elisheva & Yosaif Leib

IN MEMORY OF

Rabbi Shlomo Freifeld ז"ל

ת.נ.צ.ב.ה.

Yosef and Elizabeth Kaufman

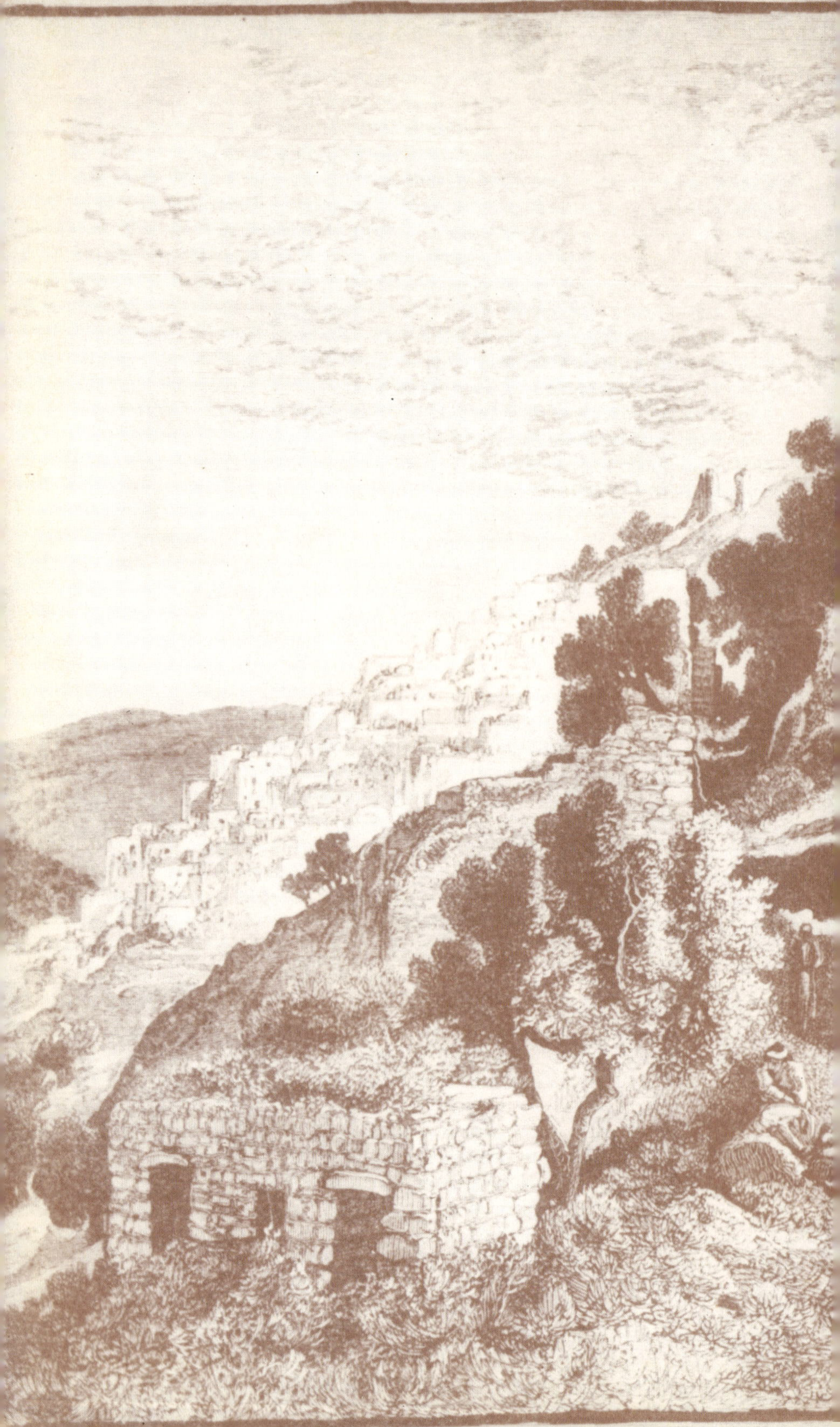